Studien zur Theorie und Empirie der Demokratie

edited by

Prof. (apl.) Dr. Markus Linden
Prof. Dr. Winfried Thaa

Christine Chwaszcza

Migration, Citizenship, and Democracy

 Nomos

The Deutsche Nationalbibliothek lists this publication in the
Deutsche Nationalbibliografie; detailed bibliographic data
are available on the Internet at http://dnb.d-nb.de

ISBN   978-3-8487-8367-0 (Print)
        978-3-7489-2759-4 (ePDF)

British Library Cataloguing-in-Publication Data
A catalogue record for this book is available from the British Library.

ISBN   978-3-8487-8367-0 (Print)
        978-3-7489-2759-4 (ePDF)

Library of Congress Cataloging-in-Publication Data
Chwaszcza, Christine
Migration, Citizenship, and Democracy
Christine Chwaszcza
224 pp.
Includes bibliographic references and index.

ISBN   978-3-8487-8367-0 (Print)
        978-3-7489-2759-4 (ePDF)

Onlineversion
Nomos eLibrary

1st Edition 2021
© Nomos Verlagsgesellschaft, Baden-Baden, Germany 2021. Overall responsibility
for manufacturing (printing and production) lies with Nomos Verlagsgesellschaft mbH
& Co. KG.

Table of Contents

Introduction   11

The Topic of the Book   11

Overview   14

A Preemptory Remark   18

Acknowledgments   19

Chapter 1.   The Main Theoretical Building Blocks   20

1.1.   Citizenship: The General Idea of a Rule-based Account   20

1.2.   Ordinary Language Philosophy and Conceptual Analysis   22
    1.2.1.   The Concept of a Social Practice   23
    1.2.2.   "Rules" and Normativity in Human Agency   25
    1.2.3.   Two Problems of Rule-following   26
    1.2.4.   The Normative Justification of Social Institutions   30
    1.2.5.   A Few Caveats   32

1.3.   Voluntary Migration as a Transnational Phenomenon   32

1.4.   The Normative Framework: Philosophical Liberalism   35

Chapter 2.   State Citizenship and Transnational Justice   40

2.1.   Why Birthright Citizenship is Not a Fact: The First Objection
to Carens   41
    2.1.1.   Birthright Citizenship as State Citizenship   43
    2.1.2.   State Citizenship and the Universal Right to
        Citizenship   44
    2.1.3.   Involuntary Citizenship: A Normative Justification   45
        (1) Consent-based Accounts of Political Association   47
        (2) Voluntary-exchange-based Accounts of Political
            Association   49
        (3) Justice-based Accounts of Political Association   50
    2.1.4.   The Procedural Element in a Rule-based Account of
        Citizenship   51

2.2.   Political Agency and the Limits of Cosmopolitan
        Consequentialism: The Second Objection to Carens   52
        2.2.1.   The Theoretical Relevance of Political Agency   54
        2.2.2.   The Normative Relevance of Political Agency   56
        2.2.3.   Non-ideal Theory: Why Consequences are Not All that
                 Matters   57

Chapter 3.   Migration as a Problem of Transnational Justice: The
             Moral Status of Individuals and Societies   60

3.1.   Is There an Individual (Human) Right to Free Movement
        Across Borders?   62

3.2.   Beyond Claim Rights: Freedom of Migration as a Requirement
        of Transnational Justice   64

3.3.   The Competitive Nature of Current Migration Dynamics   66

3.4.   A Criticism of Normative Reductionism I: Ethical
        Individualism and the Moral Standing of Persons in
        Institutional Contexts   69
        3.4.1.   Methodological Individualism in Contractarian
                 Theories of Global Justice   70
        3.4.2.   Ethical Individualism and the Holistic Nature of Social
                 Institutions   75
        3.4.3.   The Idea of Government by Authorization: A Non-
                 voluntaristic Interpretation   77
        3.4.4.   A First Interim Conclusion   78

3.5.   A Criticism of Normative Reductionism II: How to Reconcile
        Universalistic and Particularistic Conceptions of Justice   78
        3.5.1.   Goodin's Argument against Moral Particularism   79
        3.5.2.   Political Philosophy without Politics? – A Criticism of
                 Goodin   80
        3.5.3.   Political Agency as a *sui generis* Source of Sociopolitical
                 Justice: A Defense   82
        3.5.4.   A Second Interim Conclusion   84

3.6.   The Moral Standing of Societies   84
        3.6.1.   Societies as Spaces of Political Agency   84
        3.6.2.   Societies as Bearers of a Right to Collective Self-
                 determination   86
        3.6.3.   Societies as Addressees of Collective Responsibility 87
        3.6.4.   A Third Interim Conclusion   89

3.7. Summing up: Transnational Justice and Normative
Assessments of Rules of Inclusion and Exclusion   89

3.8. Beyond the Model of the Nation State: Internationalism or
Transnationalism?   91

Chapter 4. Normative Particularism Without Nationalism or
Statism: A Liberal-democratic Account   94

4.1. Miller's Liberal Nationalism: A Constructive Criticism   95
  4.1.1. A Brief Outline of Miller's Argument for Liberal
         Nationalism   95
  4.1.2. National Integration and the Development of the
         Model of the Social State   97
  4.1.3. A Counter-thesis: Democratic Legitimacy vs. Liberal
         Nationalism   98

4.2. State Sovereignty and Normative Particularism: A Criticism of
Blake's Argument from Coercion   100
  4.2.1. Blake on Citizenship and Coercion   100
  4.2.2. Beyond Coercion: Political Sovereignty Bottom-up
         rather than Top-down   101

Chapter 5. Pure Procedural Justice and Democratic Legitimacy   103

5.1. Democratic Legitimacy and the "All Affected Persons"
Principle   105

5.2. Democracy as a Mechanism of Pure Procedural Justice: An
Outline   106

5.3. The Moral Point of Democracy   107

5.4. Democratic Legitimacy as a Social Practice   111

5.5. The Idea of Transnational Democracy in Light of the Practical
Pre-conditions of Democratic Legitimacy   112

5.6. The Limits of Metaethical Proceduralism: A Criticism of
Discourse Ethics   113

Chapter 6. Citizenship and Immigration from a Transnational
Moral Point of View   116

6.1. Impartiality as a Standard of Moral Justification   119
  6.1.1. Practical Reasons   120
  6.1.2. Moral Reasons   121

6.1.3.	Impartiality and the Construction of a Moral Point of View	123
6.1.4.	Normative Reasoning	124
6.2.	Requirements of Fairness concerning Different Groups of Migrants	125
6.2.1.	Equal Respect: Why the Least Well Off Should Not Always Have Priority	125
6.2.2.	The Moral Status of Voluntary Migrants: A Justice-based Criticism of Miller	128
6.2.3.	The Deficiency of Arguments from Emergency	129
6.3.	Three Standards for the Settlement of Conflicts of Morally Substantive Claims and Justified Interests	132
6.4.	Fairness of Access: A Preliminary Conclusion	135
Chapter 7.	Migration and Selective Exclusion from Democratic Citizenship	136
7.1.	The Case Against Discrimination	137
7.2.	Democratic Citizenship and Justified Discrimination	138
7.2.1.	Discrimination on the Basis of Religious Belief	139
(1)	Three Caveats	139
(2)	What is at Stake? The Moral Weight of Freedom of Religion in Arguments for Democratic Inclusion	141
(3)	The Moral Difference between Citizens and Non-citizen Residents	146
7.2.2.	Discrimination on the Basis of Political Beliefs	147
7.3.	Discrimination from the Perspective of Different Groups of Potential Migrants	148
7.4.	Citizenship Tests	149
7.5.	A Short Remark on Group-discrimination on the Basis of Special Historical Relations	152
Chapter 8.	Residence and Democratic Inclusion	154
8.1.	Do Immigrants Have a Duty to Naturalize?	155
8.2.	Walzer on Social Integration, Community, and Citizenship	159
8.3.	Rubio-Marín on Immigration and Democratic Inclusion	162

8.4. Partial and Multiple-layered Citizenship: Bauböck's Stakeholder Argument for Democratic Inclusion   163

8.5. Beyond Residence: Challenges to Transnational Citizenship   165

    8.5.1. Dual or Multiple Citizenship   165

    8.5.2. Illegal Immigration and the Normative Weight of *de facto* Social Integration   167

Chapter 9. Family Migration: A Transnational Perspective   171

9.1. Exposition of Two Problems   172

    9.1.1. The Family as a Social Institution   172

    9.1.2. The Protection of the Family in International Human Rights Documents   173

    9.1.3. Transnational Social Pluralism and Transnational Legal Pluralism   175

9.2. Who is Authorized to Define the Institution of the Family?   176

9.3. Polygamy in Practice   178

9.4. Polygamy in Normative Debates concerning Immigration and Women's Rights   182

9.5. Immigration and Transnational Legal Pluralism: Some Principled Objections   183

9.6. A Brief Remark concerning the Normative Weight of Personal Preferences   186

9.7. Beyond Access: Liberal Limits of Transnational Legal Pluralism with Respect to Foreign Residents   187

9.8. Family-based Immigration and Requirements of Fairness among Different Groups of Immigrants   189

    9.8.1. Access   190

    9.8.2. Naturalization and Democratic Inclusion   191

9.9. A (Very) Preliminary Conclusion   191

Chapter 10. Society and Culture: A Plea for Pluriculturalism   193

10.1. "Multiculturalism": Conceptual Sense and Nonsense   194

10.2. Culturalism as a Normative Social Ideal   197

10.3. Culturalism as a Descriptive Analysis of Individual and Social Identity   198

    10.3.1. A Criticism of Cultural Identity Concepts   198

10.3.2. The Difference between Culturalism and a Practice
Account   200

10.3.3. The Methodological Background of Early Culturalism
Debates   202

10.3.4. The Practice Account as a Methodological Alternative
to Culturalism   203

10.4. A Reassessment of the Value of Cultural Belonging   204

10.5. Pluriculturalism: A Liberal-democratic Proposal   206

10.6. A Final Thought   210

Bibliography   212

Name Index   223

Introduction

The Topic of the Book

Society no longer is what it used to be. Economic globalization and mass migration are transforming traditional images of social community and political affiliation. Although the majority of people worldwide live, work, and die in the society into which they were born, an increasing number of persons practice a transnational lifestyle – as guest workers, cross-border commuters, seasonal workers, or temporary migrants who seek work abroad in order to build up a capital stock for starting a business at home. The social relations of those persons are not post-national. They are transnational. And it appears fully justified to assume that the entire number of persons who aspire to a transnational lifestyle by far exceeds the number of those, who currently practice it.

Transnational migration in many respects differs from what Catherine Dauvergne calls the traditional paradigm of "settler migration".[1] Transnational migrants do not leave one society in order to join another, but rather move back and forth and synchronically uphold socioeconomic and political relations in multiple societies. What normative stance should liberal societies take towards those new forms of migration?

The nature of transnational migration does not fit well with traditional ideals of citizenship and democratic inclusion which still dominate normative debates concerning citizenship and migration in political philosophy. Traditional normative ideals revolve around the assumption that society of origin, country of residence, and political affiliation coincide. Since this assumption is exactly what is challenged by transnational migration, two normative tendencies ought to be avoided: a tendency to over-exclusion motivated by an emphasis on the particularistic quality of citizenship, and a tendency to over-inclusion motivated by appeal to the ideal of universal citizenship. This book tries to steer a middle course by exploring how traditional concepts and arguments have to be rethought, revised and adjusted to recent transformations of social reality.

This is easier said than done, because the normative logic of traditional citizenship debates implicitly assumes that all societies resemble liberal

---

1 See Dauvergne (2016).

societies, in the traditional sense of liberalism, and that all citizens share liberal ideals of democracy, the rule of law, and social pluralism. Hardly surprisingly, most contributions to citizenship debates are not merely normative, in the sense that they present *ideal* conceptions of citizenship, but endorse specifically liberal ideals of democratic citizenship. A normative assessment of the practical challenges of transnational migration, however, cannot take it for granted that everybody shares those liberal premises, for the obvious reason that the world is currently divided in a multiplicity of societies that endorse a heterogeneous plurality of normative ideals of social life and of political association.

To be sure, every normative assessment of issues concerning citizenship and migration has to start from some normative premises. This book explicitly starts from liberal premises and addresses immigration as concerns liberal societies. At the transnational level, however, it cannot be assumed that everybody shares those ideals. For that reason, we cannot simply apply traditional theories of citizenship to a normatively different context, but we have to rethink their normative logic.

As I will argue, liberal societies – like any other type of society – have a right to collective political self-determination. If liberalism is committed to social pluralism at the intra-societal level, then it also should be committed to inter-societal pluralism. If liberal societies choose to preserve liberal pluralism, they should be permitted to do so as far as that is compatible with due respect for normative claims of potential migrants. Normative assessments of the practical challenges of transnational migration, accordingly, have to combine an intra-societal perspective with a transnational perspective on the moral status of individual migrants.

Pending details below, I will argue that current debates on citizenship and migration are prone to draw a false contrast, i.e., an opposition of open versus closed borders. Not only are there a lot of possible options between the two extremes, but the basic assumptions of the open border argument tend to undervalue the normative essence of citizenship as *political* membership, whereas nationalist arguments for closed borders tend to undervalue the liberal commitment to the protection of individual liberties.

Thus, cosmopolitan arguments for open borders, such as Joseph Carens', tend to ignore the particularistic implications that the current organization of political associations in distinct states (*statism*) has for conceptions of political justice. By contrast, justice-based arguments for a right to control immigration, such as David Miller's, tend to downplay the normative implications that derive from the fact that statism is itself a normative order, whose present organization is justified from a liberal point of view only to the extent that we can think of it as justifiable to all affected persons – conceived of as citizens as well as potential migrants.

From a normative point of view, the real challenge consists in integrating requirements of domestic, international and transnational political justice. Disentangling and re-aligning the different spheres of justice requires us to revisit some of the implicit analytic assumptions and normative premises of traditional political philosophy.

As concerns transnational migration, I will argue that it requires us to balance a liberty right of individual persons to migration – i.e., *individual* self-determination – with a right of societies, considered as collective entities, to *collective* self-determination, which in the case of liberal societies includes a normative commitment to democratic self-government. The overview of the chapters of the book below will give a short preview of the main points.

Before that, however, I would like to address an obvious objection to the focus on transnational migration. In the light of current dynamics of mass migration by refugees, it might be argued that transnational migration is a marginal phenomenon, or at least ethically marginal. I doubt it. Given the fact that a huge percentage of current migrants do not qualify as refugees or asylum seekers, it must be conceded that many migrants are motivated by economic and cultural interests.[2] In addition, the humanitarian framework of support for refugees is supposed to provide temporary relief rather than work permits, options of permanent residence, or naturalization, because humanitarian relief works on the assumption that most refugees will return to their country of origin once the crisis ended. It seems that this assumption is no longer adequate. More and more refugees come from failed states or are victims of ethnic cleansing or worse, and do not need temporary shelter, or subsistence and care, but rather the option of starting a new life and the prospect of a better future. An adequate response to their situation then raises questions similar to those of transnational migrants.

The sheer demand for options of permanent or temporary migration requires an adequate normative response besides support of refugees. Tra-

---

2 Unfortunately, it is hard to get estimates about the real number of transnational migrants because official migration statistics register only persons who spent at least 12 consecutive months abroad. That leaves out commuters, seasonal workers, and probably also other groups of migrants.

ditional settler migration, of course, remains an option, but it should not be the only one.

I take it to be obvious that from a liberal point of view, all persons should be free to pursue justified interests to the extent that all persons can be granted equal freedom, and that the exercise of those freedoms can be arranged in ways that are compatible with the rights and freedoms of all relevant parties. In my view, justified interests include economic interests. In a globalized economy, the arena for the pursuit of those interests stretches across borders. Respect for justified interests is as good a basis as any for the recognition of a *prima facie* liberty right. The crucial question is how a *prima facie* liberty right to migration can be balanced with equally valuable freedoms of all affected individuals and the rights of societies to collective self-determination.

As I will argue, acknowledgment of a *prima facie* liberty right to migration does not demand open borders. But it sets serious constraints on reasons for socio-economic and political exclusion, and thus demands a more open concept of society and more differentiated concepts of social and political membership.

Overview

The first chapter introduces the methodological building blocks. The first is what I will call the "practice account". The practice account is a style of conceptual analysis that draws on insights and methods of so-called ordinary language philosophy, as developed by J.L. Austin, Ludwig Wittgenstein and others. The chapter provides a brief sketch of the general ideas, and its implementation in legal philosophy by H.L.A. Hart, political philosophy by John Rawls, and moral philosophy by Kurt Baier. The main point of the first chapter is to indicate how the practice account presented here differs from homonymous accounts in postmodern thinking. Readers who are well acquainted with the Oxford style of ordinary language philosophy can skip the section. The second building block defines the type of migration phenomena in which I am interested. And the third building block specifies the normative premises of the liberal position that I am defending.

Chapters 2 to chapter 5 construct the main analytical elements of a transnational moral point of view by exploring the normative and systematic relations between citizenship concepts and their relevant background rules. Since there is no need to start repeatedly from scratch, each chapter addresses a syndrome of contested issues concerning the analysis and normative logic of the concepts of citizenship, political association, and democracy.

In chapter 2, I will address two flaws in Carens' criticism of birthright citizenship. First, I will argue – *pace* Carens – that citizenship assignments are not arbitrary facts, but are based on rules which are embedded in broader background systems of rules. As concerns citizenship we obviously face a plurality of concepts, at least a concept state citizenship (*nationalité*) on the one hand, and a concept of democratic citizenship on the other hand. The difference between the two concepts has been widely noted. But it has rarely been explained.

Employing a practice account, I argue that the difference between the two concepts derives from the fact that the meaning of those concepts is tied to their normative role in different background institutions. The background rules relevant for the concept of state citizenship are those that constitute the international system of statehood, whereas the background rules relevant for democratic citizenship are the principles of popular sovereignty and democratic government. Once the distinction is noted, it is obvious that the two concepts follow a different normative logic, serve different purposes, and should be distinguished.

Secondly, I point to a crucial deficit of the purely consequentialist structure of Carens' cosmopolitan ideal of justice. Carens conceives of migration as a measure for the realization of justice, i.e., equal access to social opportunities for all persons regardless of their country of origin. An unfortunate implication of Carens' end-state-oriented focus on a cosmopolitan ideal of justice is his disregard of the fact that social opportunities have to be produced, and that the usual form of their production is political agency. As I will argue, political agency is a *sui generis* source of requirements of sociopolitical justice, different from requirements that concern the basic structure of society. Although political agency is not restricted to the level of domestic societies – or, as I will also say, political associations –, nevertheless, societies continue to be important spaces of political agency. The normative challenge raised by phenomena such as migration is that assessments of moral duties and responsibilities *vis-à-vis* potential migrants must distinguish those normative requirements that arise at the domestic level from those that arise at an inter- or transnational level, and must find a way of coherently combining them.

As I will argue, such a combination requires that we conceive of the normative status of migrants not merely as their status as individual persons, but as individual persons who are current and potentially future members of societies.

This requires that we conceive of their normative status as that of individual persons *vis-à-vis* societies conceived of as collective entities, whether societies of origin or potential host societies. Citizenship, after all, is an inherently relational status. It concerns the standing of individuals *vis-à-vis* co-citizens within the institutional framework of political associations, conceived of as collective entities.

Political philosophers are deeply divided about the analysis of societies conceived of as collective entities. Chapter 3 reinvestigates systematic and normative arguments concerning the moral standing of individual persons as citizens, and the moral standing of societies in the international system of statehood. Pending details below, the main conclusion of chapter 3 says that as long as societies function as spaces of collective political agency, they generate particularistic requirements of justice, besides and beyond universal moral requirements and duties of inter- or transnational justice.

Bringing the various strands of discussion together, I will argue that liberals ought to acknowledge a *prima facie* individual liberty right to migration as a requirement of transnational justice. This right has to be weighed against equal liberty rights of relevant parties, i.e., citizens of host societies, co-citizens in societies of origin, other migrants, and the right of societies to collective political self-determination.

Chapter 4 will defend the acknowledgment of such a *prima facie* liberty right against particularistic accounts of political justice, as presented by Miller's liberal nationalism, and also against state-sovereignty-based objections as presented by Michael Blake. More importantly, the chapter will also defend the claim that from a liberal point of view, societies' right to collective self-determination is restricted to issues related to their political constitution.

Chapter 5, then, examines the social and institutional conditions of democratic forms of collective self-determination, more precisely the normative function of procedural legitimacy in democratic decision making. Although procedural legitimacy is essential for collective decisions in pluralistic societies, democracy cannot be reduced to those procedures, nor can those procedures be detached from non-procedural elements of democratic government or the institutional frameworks of statehood. Democratic standards of legitimacy, accordingly, are confined to domestic institutions, and neither provide universally applicable procedures of justification (as claimed by proponents of discourse ethics), nor can they be transferred to a transnational level (as proponents of transnational democracy suggest).

The chapter concludes that the maintenance and preservation of the social and normative preconditions of democratic government qualify as major elements of the right to collective political self-determination of liberal societies. Considerations concerning the preservation and maintenance of those conditions accordingly articulate valid moral claims that (potential) democratic host societies can make *vis-à-vis* individual immigrants as concerns democratic inclusion.

Having identified the morally relevant parties and their morally justifiable claims, chapter 6 shows how the considerations so far developed can be integrated into the construction of a transnational moral point of view for normative assessments of phenomena of transnational migration. The chapter will situate the normative approach presented here within the broader field of theories of normative justification currently employed in political philosophy. Finally, I will propose three general standards for the weighing and balancing of competing and conflicting normative claims of the morally relevant parties with regard to questions concerning the legitimacy of immigration quotas and the prioritization of preferred groups of immigrants by host societies.

Chapters 7 and 8 will focus on prominent arguments from debates concerning the *democratic* inclusion of immigrants. Since the defense of a *prima facie* right to migration imposes special burdens of justification on arguments for the exclusion of immigrants, I will explore the permissibility of democratic exclusion (as distinct from questions concerning access to host societies or temporary residence).

Since a major strand of arguments that favor democratic inclusion of immigrants invokes principles that have been influential for intra-societal democratic inclusion (most prominently, the principle of non-discrimination), chapter 7 will explore to what extent those arguments are valid in the context of migration, if we pay attention to the normative distinction between the concepts of state citizenship and of democratic citizenship, and to the transnational quality of new forms of migration.

Another major strand of argument in favor of democratic inclusion ties inclusion either to residence within the territory of political associations, or to socioeconomic integration. Chapter 8 will critically discuss those arguments in light of the fact that migration is increasingly of a *transnational* quality, i.e., non-permanent and combined with dual or multiple citizenship.

Chapter 9 explores a rather special issue of family-related immigration. Recently, some theorists argued that legal recognition of polygamy in immigration law should be used as a tool for the promotion of rights of immigrant women and children. A closer review of the arguments casts serious doubts about whether those expectations are warranted. The main reasons why the chapter has been included, however, are more abstract. First, the institution of the family is constitutive for societies conceived of as intergenerational entities. Accordingly, determinations of the institution of the family address core issues of collective self-determination. Second, depending on empirical and legal circumstances, rules of family-(re-)unification tend to prioritize immigrants with family ties over those without them. This raises issues of fairness among different groups of potential migrants. Third, some states practice transnational legal pluralism in family law. That raises the question as to what extent liberal societies ought to tolerate non-liberal conceptions of the status of women, of children, and of the relations between spouses.

Chapter 10, finally, will address normative ideals of social self-organization. Current debates are largely divided into nationalist ideals of society on the one hand, and multiculturalist ideals on the other. Chapter 10 will criticize both accounts, and outline a genuinely liberal ideal of social and civic life, which I will call *pluriculturalism*. Pluriculturalism is characterized by the acceptance of social pluralism and a commitment to democratic forms of government.

A Preemptory Remark

In writing this book, I have frequently felt overwhelmed by the sheer number of publications in various disciplines that are relevant for the construction of a *transnational* perspective on migration. In order to advance my own approach, I have had to be selective and to focus on general lines of argument rather than details. Given the challenge that philosophical explorations of transnational justice hardly exist so far, and the fact that most normative conclusion have to be made in light of case-sensitive empirically contingent conditions, many arguments in the book still have a preliminary character.

Given the current state of politicization of migration debates, the pressures of political correctness in academia, and the magnitude of current real-world migration crises, it is probably unavoidable that many arguments and considerations will be contested. My position concerning the matter is simply this: if arguments are deficient, they have to be revised; and if empirical evidence does not support descriptive assumptions, then those assumptions have to be corrected. Political philosophy is not an exercise in virtue-signaling, but in rational reasoning. It is better served by the exchange of controversial arguments than by moral conformism.

Acknowledgments

I want to thank Friedrich Kratochwil, Dorothea Schulz and Nicholas White for critical comments and repeated discussions of various arguments. Without their encouragement, I would have lacked the stamina to rewrite the manuscript as many times as I did. All controversial claims and deficiencies, of course, are my personal responsibility. I also want to thank Bodo Bützler and Lukas Franzen for critical comments on earlier versions of the manuscript. The University of Cologne supported the book project by granting me a sabbatical semester of uninterrupted research. That time was spent partly in the city of Nice in Southern France, an excellent place for experiencing the many heterogeneous phenomena of modern migration at first hand. I want to thank Sylvie P. for her hospitality, and Sylvie from the brasserie for good humor and generous aperitifs in the evenings.

Chapter 1. The Main Theoretical Building Blocks

Let me start with a few preliminary clarifications concerning the method of conceptual analysis, the specification of the practical problem, and the normative premises employed in what follows.

1.1. Citizenship: The General Idea of a Rule-based Account

Citizenship is best conceived of as a status concept.[3] The term oscillates between state citizenship (*nationalité*, *Staatsbürgerschaft*) and democratic citizenship, but in both cases it is meant to stand for the normative status of individuals as members of a sociopolitical collective entity, i.e., of a particular society in the case of state citizenship, and of the *demos* in the case of democratic citizenship.

It is easy to see that state citizenship and democratic citizenship do not necessarily coincide. Members of non-liberal societies hold state citizenship but not democratic citizenship, and even in liberal societies not all members of the society qualify as members of the *demos*, the most obvious example being children. The difference can be easily marked by distinguishing state citizenship from democratic citizenship, but it is important that the difference be explicitly noted, because the normative background rules that define the respective status differ significantly.

In what follows, I will propose a rule-based account of concepts of citizenship and the unity of society. According to a rule-based account, citizenship assignments are determined by rules of inclusion and exclusion, where rules are understood (i) to be normative and conventional, and (ii) to apply generally to all relevant cases alike. In practice, most societies endorse a heterogeneous plurality of rules for the assignment of state citizenship – most importantly, *ius sanguinis*-rules,[4] *ius soli*-rules, immigration policies, and regulations concerning family-(re-)unification.

---

3 See, e.g., La Torre (2012).
4 *Prima facie*, rules based on *ius sanguinis* appear to articulate naturalistic criteria. I therefore want to emphasize that, while descendance might be considered a natural fact, the assignment of citizenship to descendants of citizens is not natural fact but a social convention.

The rule-based account is not meant to define or determine the substantive contents of those rules – which vary from society to society –, but to disclose the normative function and purpose of different citizenship concepts against the background of the broader system of the relevant background rules. This requires a reconstruction of the normative function, logic, and purpose of those background systems, which provide what Frederick Will calls the "latent content" of a concept.[5] Roughly – and in my own words –, the latent content of citizenship concepts consists in the knowledge or understanding of the background norms and practices with which one has to be acquainted in order to understand the manifest normative point of rules of citizenship assignments. As I will argue in more detail in chapter 2, the latent content of the concept of state citizenship is the international order of statehood, whereas the latent content of the concept of democratic citizenship is the principle of popular sovereignty and the constitutive rules of democratic government.

My phrase the "unity of society" is supposed to indicate what makes societies distinct and particular political associations. The unity of society, accordingly, is determined by conceptions of state citizenship rather than democratic citizenship. The concept of the unity of society in this sense is different from concepts of the unity of society in terms of social cohesion, shared historical traditions, or shared cultural community. Conceiving of the unity of society in terms of state citizenship responds to the specific interest of the present investigation, because a transnational perspective on migration has to work with concepts of citizenship and the unity of society which also apply (i) to citizens of non-democratically organized political associations, and (ii) to societies as they are rather than to normative ideals of what they ought to be. Conceptual analysis aims at an understanding of the meaning of different citizenship concepts. It is not *per se* a normative analysis, but it provides us with a starting point for normative criticism.

As a method of conceptual analysis, a rule-based account proceeds by contextualization, in contrast to abstraction or definition. It provides an alternative to traditional accounts of citizenship and the unity of society, such as communitarian, republican, culturalist and nationalist accounts, which focus on normative (liberal) ideals of citizenship. The problem with normative accounts is that they fail to mark the difference between state citizenship and democratic citizenship, and that they tend to start from the assumption that the *demos* roughly coincides with the people who reside

---

5 See Will (1997).

in the territory of the relevant political association. These background assumptions are unwarranted when we explore transnational migration.

The general methodological idea of a rule-based account of conceptual analysis is far from new. It is best called a practice-account, because it conceives of conceptual analysis primarily as an elucidation of the function and the normative structure of the social practices in which those concepts are used. The approach is inspired by so-called ordinary language philosophy, as one attributes it to Ludwig Wittgenstein, J.L. Austin, and others, and has been most famously employed by H.L.A. Hart in legal theory, by John Rawls in political philosophy, and by Kurt Baier in moral philosophy.[6] I think it would be fair to say that it underlies most accounts of political and legal philosophy in the analytic tradition, even though its methodological roots are rarely discussed explicitly in current contributions.[7]

In what follows, I will use the terms practice account and ordinary language approach interchangeably. Unfortunately, practice accounts do not follow a well-defined method. The idea is employed in different ways by different theorists within and beyond philosophy, including the social sciences[8] and international relations theory[9]. The term has also been adopted by theorists committed to postmodernist approaches, which use it quite differently from ordinary language philosophers.[10] I therefore would like to indicate the main characteristics of an ordinary language understanding of a practice account.

1.2. *Ordinary Language Philosophy and Conceptual Analysis*

For obvious reasons, Wittgenstein's remark concerning the "meaning of meaning"[11] is of special relevance for the analysis of non-referential terms. Normative terms and mental terms are paradigm examples of non-refer-

---

6   See Hart (1961/1997), Rawls (1971), Baier (1965).
7   A notable exception is Beitz (2009b).
8   See, e.g., Schatzki et.al. (2001), and Grimmel/Hellmann (2019).
9   See, e.g., Kratochwil (2018).
10 See, e.g., Bourdieu (1998).
11 See Wittgenstein (1958), § 43: "For a *large* class of cases – though not for all – in which we employ the word 'meaning' it can be defined thus: the meaning of a word is its use in the language" (emphasis in the original).

ential terms.[12] Unsurprisingly, ordinary language philosophy has been frequently endorsed for the analysis of legal terms and status terms.[13]

Less obviously, quite a few terms that frequently appear in widespread accounts of normative justification, such as "consent", "reasons", "social contract", or "authorization", are also best understood as non-referential. They do not refer to *de facto* acts or events, or psychological states, but to standards of normative justification which are socially shared by participants in a social practice.[14] Whereas standards of *justification* in moral contexts are not *per se* different from standards of justification in non-moral contexts, *moral* justification appeals to additional standards besides consistency, coherence, etc., such as requirements of impartiality or universalizability, which are not relevant in most non-moral contexts. In order to indicate why it makes sense to conceive of normative justification in terms of a practice account too, let me recall three philosophical motivations of ordinary language philosophy.

1.2.1. The Concept of a Social Practice

Ordinary language philosophy is in part a philosophical response to some notorious problems in early modern philosophy, as represented by, e.g., René Descartes, John Locke, or David Hume.[15] Most relevant for the present context is the criticism of mentalistic explications of meaning, agency, reasoning, and normativity – to borrow a phrase of Willard Van Orman Quine's: the "idea idea".[16]

In the present context of inquiry, it might be best to start with human agency. Whereas early modern accounts of human agency conceive of actions primarily in Cartesian style analysis as "bodily movements caused by a mental state" and investigate what are thought to be the relevant mental states, ordinary language philosophy starts from the observation that human agency is overwhelmingly constituted and regulated by socially shared practices.[17]

---

12 See, e.g., Goldberg (1971), Anscombe (1957/2000), Hanfling (2000).
13 See, e.g., Hart's and Feinberg's seminal analyses of the concept "individual claim right" in (Hart 1955) and (Feinberg 1970).
14 See Baier (1978).
15 See Descartes (1647), Locke (1689), Hume (1739/1740), bk.I.
16 See Quine (1973).
17 This characterization includes speech-acts; see, e.g., Austin (1979a).

Social practices can be simple, but are usually constituted by complex sets or systems of rules, which are interlinked with background rules and further practices. A full-fledged analysis of human agency would have to elucidate all of the relevant rules and background-rules. Thus, an analysis of what is involved when we identify an intentional activity as "purchasing of a pair of shoes" would include the whole range of rules that constitute the economic practice of market exchange, the relevant aspects of the system of property rights, of contract laws, of the use of money, etc. A full-fledged analysis, fortunately, is rarely required – not even for the explication of the latent content of a particular rule. It usually suffices to identify some background rules of a particular practice, and to indicate how that practice is related to other practices.

The focus on social practices for the analysis of agency resembles the way in which modern philosophy of language conceives of the analysis of meaning.[18] The method of analysis responds to the observation that agency – no less than language – has a communicative dimension: agents usually "understand" what other agents are doing, and whether they are engaged in activities that are intentional or not – without having direct access to the agent's mental states.[19] The understanding of agency, similar to the mastering of a first language, is understood to be acquired through participation in the relevant practices. The understanding, thus, qualifies as a form of genuinely practical knowledge, i.e., knowledge acquired by participation in the relevant socially shared practices.[20] As Hart's analysis of the concept of law reveals, the relevant practices can be quite complex and their analysis might require expert-knowledge. The important point is that conceptual analysis proceeds by understanding the use of the concept in the relevant practices.

---

18 An early modern analogy of the Cartesian concept of action with respect to language would say roughly that a meaningful utterance is "the production of certain sounds caused by (or associated with) a mental state".

19 See, e.g., Austin (1979b), (1979c).

20 See Wittgenstein (1958), § 150: "The grammar of the word 'knows' ('wissen') is evidently closely related to that of 'can' ('können'), 'is able to' ('imstande sein')". For further discussions see, e.g., Anscombe (1985), Hanfling (1989), Wallace (2009). – A characterization of our competence of understanding agency as practical knowledge, of course, does not exclude that we can conceptualize our understanding in terms of knowing that or knowing what. The philosophically important point, nevertheless, is that the analysis of agency better proceed by ways of an analysis of the relevant social practices rather than an investigation of the states of minds of agents.

1.2.2. "Rules" and Normativity in Human Agency

To conceive of human agency as embedded in social practices which are constituted by complex sets of rules, is not meant to suggest that human agency is *determined* by rules.[21] However, it holds that most spheres of human agency qualify as thoroughly normative, because rules *qua* rules qualify as normative.[22]

The normativity of rules might be best explained by contrasting "rules" with "regularities" and "causal relations". Rule-guided activities, as well as behavioral regularities, manifest a certain degree of uniformity of conduct, but differ from causal relations, because the terms "rule" and "regularity" are usually applied to intentional activities which agents could have avoided or decided not to perform. But whereas rules justify *normative* expectations that persons will act in a certain way, regularities warrant *prognostic* or *predictive* expectations that they will do so. The difference is this: observation of non-compliance with rules is generally accepted as a justification for criticism or even sanctions on non-compliant behavior, whereas the observation of irregular behavior is generally understood as falsifying a prognosis and requiring a correction of the opinion of the observer.

To illustrate the point: it can be predicted in a prognostic sense that most customers in a cafe will constantly check their mobile phones. Under normal circumstances, however, a customer who abstains from checking her phone, or even does not have one, will not therefore be criticized. By contrast, customers in a cafe are normatively expected not to put their feet on the table and start their pedicure. If they do so, they will be asked to stop or to leave the premises.

Normativity is a ubiquitous feature of human agency, because human conduct is only marginally driven by instincts. The important point to notice, however, is that normativity is nothing but a social mode of human agency. That is to say that normativity is not something ontologically separate, or metaphysically different, from agency. It manifests itself in particular modes, or patterns, of agency, in attitudes towards other agents, and in socially shared expectations concerning agency. The normativity of

---

21 Many rules facilitate certain forms of activity, but do not determine individual behavior. Think, e.g., of the rules of economic exchange and the use of money, which, obviously, leave individuals with a lot of discretion concerning their economic behavior.

22 See Rawls (1955).

rules – moral rules, as well as non-moral rules – elucidates why appeals to rules qualify as action- and judgment-guiding practical reasons.

It is important to recognize that the ubiquitous normativity of human agency in no way implies that all social practices are morally justified or acceptable. In fact, social life is full of amoral and immoral practices. First, not all normative practices are morally relevant. Language is a normative social practice too, and the rules of grammar are certainly normative, as can be seen by the fact that non-grammatical speakers are corrected. But grammatical rules have no obvious moral dimension. The same holds for many laws and rules of etiquette. They too are normative in the relevant sense, but not necessarily morally required, or even morally justifiable.

Second, in order to understand how moral normativity differs from other forms of normativity, one has to explore the special function of morality within the system of normative social rules. In this respect, I will follow Baier, who suggests that the special role of morality within the overall system of normative rules is a critical one.[23] Morality, to put it simply, asks whether social practices are right or wrong, i.e., whether they qualify as valid or acceptable in accordance with standards of genuinely *moral* justifiability, such as universalizability, impartiality, or assessments from a moral point of view. Morality, accordingly, is special not because it is normative, but because it employs special standards of justification.

I will also follow Baier in construing a moral point of view as a standard for normative assessments of rules that assign citizenship and regulate migration. Unlike Rawlsian constructions of an original position, which tend to focus on the perspective of the least well off group of representative persons, Baier's construction of a moral point of view presents an impersonal point of view that assesses alternative social arrangements from the position of all representative groups of affected persons.[24]

1.2.3. Two Problems of Rule-following

The problem of rule-following, as I understand it, has two sides. The first concerns the cognitive aspects employed in following a rule. I will side with those theorists who maintain that rule-based agency exhibits a

---

23 See Baier (1965); see also Koller (2017) for Baier's distinction of legal and moral normativity in contrast to Kelsen's and Hart's separation of the two spheres of normativity.

24 For more details, see chap. 6.

genuinely practical form of practical knowledge. The practical nature of practical knowledge manifests itself in the way in which persons acquire it, namely, by being trained in the relevant social practice and in being able to proceed or to go on.[25] More important in the present context, however, is the second problem of rule-following. It concerns philosophical reconstructions of our understanding of human agency (or language) from a third person perspective, and especially from the perspective of scholarly analysis. In this respect, I will side with theorists who start from the observation that socially shared practices, unlike mental states, are not "in the minds of agents", but are in the public[26] space of the social world. Unfortunately, theorists disagree widely about the analysis of the public and social aspects of social practices.

According to the practice account employed here, the key to understanding social practices is the concept of a "rule", as analyzed above. Socially shared practices are public insofar as they are structured by rules, which – unlike mental states – are overt and cognitively accessible from a third person perspective. It is important to note, however, that participants need not have explicit analytical knowledge of the relevant rules. Few agents, I assume, understand the economic factors that determine the value of a currency, but most are familiar with the everyday use of money and concepts such as "exchange rate" or "inflation". In any case, agents must have some practical understanding of how to participate in the relevant practices; otherwise the practice would not exist.

The crucial point is that rule-guided agency is an essentially social phenomenon. As Wittgenstein pointed out in his criticism of the philosophical idea of a private language, no single person could follow a rule, and no person could follow a rule unilaterally.[27] Saying that rule-guided practices are "socially shared" does not imply that we can always identify a well-defined group of agents whose members participate in a certain practice.[28] Nor does it imply that participation in socially shared practices invests

---

25 The standard example of practical knowledge is, of course, that of the acquisition of a first language. See also Wittgenstein's discussion of "adding 2" (Wittgenstein 1958, §§ 151–155) or Wallace's characterization of a norm – which is equivalent to the concept of a rule as analyzed above – as "a learned activity that is taken to be an appropriate way to proceed in a certain domain" (Wallace 2009, p. 33).

26 "Public" here is opposed to "private" as in "private mental states".

27 Wittgenstein (1958), §§ 244–271.

28 Such a misunderstanding appears to underlie some communitarian analyses of normative terms; see, e.g., McIntyre (1995) and Walzer (1994).

agents with a kind of knowledge that is inaccessible to outsiders,[29] nor that all participants affirmatively endorse the relevant rules whole-heartedly. We might think of the "world community of mathematicians" as being engaged in a socially shared practice that provides participants with an understanding of mathematical concepts, techniques, and standards of proof. The essential point of the emphasis on the social nature of social practices concerns the appropriateness of philosophical and scientific re-constructions of how we can *understand* (and should study) language- and agency-related phenomena in a very general sense: i.e., by becoming familiar with the relevant rules and background rules. The thesis that rule-following exhibits a genuinely practical form of practical knowledge in no way excludes the possibility of reconstructing our understanding of agency in terms of theoretical knowledge ("knowing that"), by providing systematized accounts of the various sets of rules, their internal function-ing, or their interrelatedness.

Thus, a rule-based analysis will always start from a descriptive analysis of normative practices. However, it cannot be reduced to a descriptive account of what those practices are. Philosophical analysis is not satisfied with descriptive reconstructions of socially shared practices, but aims at systematizations of the principles and mechanisms that are at work in the constitution of social practices, their internal logic, and the factors that drive dynamical changes.

Some rule-guided practices, however, are social also in an additional sense: they are obviously conventional. That is to say, it is obvious to participants that the rules could be different from what they are. In the latter respect, the analysis of language and agency differ.[30] It seems fair to assume that both the cognitive competences that drive the acquisition of a first language, as well as the patterns that drive the dynamical changes of languages concerning, e.g., rules of conjugation and declination, are facili-tated by cognitive competences of which the speakers are rarely aware, and which they rarely subject explicitly to criticism and intentional attempts at improvement or correction. The overwhelming majority of agential practices, by contrast, is subject to constant normative criticism. Norma-tive criticism can be moral or non-moral.[31] Although critical standards

---

29 See Winch (1958) for such a claim.
30 See also Daniels (1980).
31 I will say more about moral criticism below. Non-moral criticism appeals, e.g., to standards of pragmatic efficiency, systemic coherence, cost-benefit-optimization, etc.

are not entirely absent in language-related phenomena, they are usually much less interesting to linguists than their counterparts are to political philosophers.

The interesting question is: "What are the relevant standards for normative criticism?". From the perspective of a practice account, the answer is: "The standards that are employed in practice". Since normative criticism proceeds by appeal to interpersonal – or intersubjective – acknowledgment of the validity of critical objections to the *status quo*, it must appeal to interpersonally shared standards that allow us to distinguish *valid* criticism and *valid* justificatory reasons from *invalid* ones. To the extent that rule-guided practices are open to moral criticism, those standards include socially shared standards of rightness, or goodness, or legitimacy. The social nature of normative justification will be of special importance in chapter 6 for the analysis of the concept of practical reasons and standards of impartiality.

According to a practice account, normative justification is best conceived of as a social practice too. Similar to other reflective practices, the standards of normative justification can become an object of scholarly or scientific study and contestation. The fact that standards of criticism and justification have to be socially shared implies neither that all participants are able to provide an abstract account of what those standards require, nor that all theorists agree in their analysis.

Think about an ordinary standard for moral validity, such as the "Golden Rule". The precise meaning of the Golden Rule is open to different interpretations, and contested even among philosophers.[32] But an appeal to the Golden Rule – or an appeal to any specific requirement of impartiality or universalizability – qualifies as a valid criticism or a justificatory reason, *because* the Golden Rule articulates at least one of the socially accepted *prima facie* standards for the *validity* of moral criticism or moral reasoning. Further widely held standards are requirements of universalizability, impartiality, or acceptance from a moral point of view.

Social practices of intersubjective justification can be quite sophisticated. They often reflect ideals of scientific or philosophical reasoning, and are self-reflective, in the sense that they often include abstract reasoning about what can or should be expected from standards of intersubjective justification. In the end, however, the abstract reasoning cannot but rely on socially shared practices of justification, because any normative theory

---

32 See, e.g., Reiner (1948).

of justification would itself have to be justified. How could it be justified if not by socially shared standards of justification?

1.2.4. The Normative Justification of Social Institutions

A proper understanding of the concept of a rule is also important for the analysis of sociopolitical and legal institutions, and their justification. Sociopolitical and legal institutions are standardly analyzed in terms of positions and offices, which are defined by complex social practices and complex systems of rules.[33] Such analyses include the specification of institutional powers and their attribution to the persons who represent those offices and positions.

An institutional account of political and legal competences is far from new. It dates back – at least – to philosophical reconstructions of the idea of a social contract in Thomas Hobbes, John Locke, and Jean-Jacques Rousseau. Breaking with philosophical traditions of natural law theories, those theorists tended to highlight the social and conventional nature of institutions by presenting them as being generated by contracting acts, or some expressive form of consent or "authorization". It seems fair to say that in most instances the terminology is merely a metaphor which is supposed to emphasize the non-natural quality of sociopolitical practices. Unfortunately, metaphors can develop a life of their own, and metaphors of contract, consent, and authorization continue to nourish voluntaristic and purely procedural accounts of normative justification in political and legal philosophy.

The particular innovation that modern reconstructions of the idea of a social contract, such as Rawls's, add to the tradition is that they translate the metaphor into systematic accounts of normative justification – e.g., Rawls's appeal to a *reflective equilibrium* –, and that they highlight the impersonal quality of institutional powers and arrangements. Following Hart, I will analyze sociopolitical and legal institutions in terms of a unity of primary and secondary rules, i.e., as an impersonal system of intertwined rules that define public offices and positions, and the political and legal competences and responsibilities assigned to them. Roughly, the function of primary rules, in Hart's terminology, is that of guiding action, whereas the function of secondary rules is that of regulating the making,

---

33 *Locus classicus* is Hart (1961/1997). See also Rawls (1958), fn.1, and Rawls (1971), § 10.

changing, abdicating, and validating of primary rules. A special element of the set of secondary rules is the so-called *rule of recognition*, which articulates a standard of validity for primary and other secondary rules.[34] Hart's analysis underlies Rawls's account of justice as a virtue of social institutions, which detaches issues concerning the generation or actual construction of social institutions from issues concerning the normative justification of their purposes and substantive contents.

From the perspective of a practice account, the moral justification of institutions and of the substantive contents of institutional rules has to meet standards of moral justification that are shared in practice. Such standards usually combine a heterogeneous plurality of justificatory demands, e.g., morally substantive requirements, formal requirements, and often appeal to standards of procedural legitimacy. Not all standards are equally adequate in all contexts, and they do not always amount to an integrated harmonious composition. They are partly competing, and philosophers sometimes tend to prioritize one standard over the others.

From the perspective of a practice account, voluntaristic and purely proceduralistic accounts of justification, which are still rather widespread in theories of democracy and citizenship, are unsatisfying, because they fall back to the mentalistic paradigm, and because they tend to focus on the traditional context of domestic (liberal) society. Generally, it should not be expected that any framework of normative justification that was developed for assessments of the legitimacy of domestic institutions can be "applied" without serious modifications to challenges that occur at the transnational level, because both the problems and the institutional background systems differ in morally important respects. Employing a practice account that aims at disclosing the latent content of rules of citizenship assignment will help us to assess the proper role of standards of procedural justice and consent with respect to new phenomena of migration and transnational citizenship. The general standard of justification employed throughout, however, is coherence, in the sense of achieving a *reflective equilibrium*.

---

34 The rule of recognition can be either a single rule or a plurality of rules, an unwritten or a written constitution. The rule of recognition, thus, can consist in a comparatively "simple" rule, e.g., the rule that new law breaks old law, but it also can consist in a highly complex sets of rules, such as the constitution of the United States or of Germany.

1.2.5. A Few Caveats

In light of Searle's analysis of the constitution of the social world, I want to emphasize that the practice account that I propose does not maintain that social practices are constituted and constantly re-constituted by *intentional* actions of individual agents.[35]

In light of the many postmodern versions of practice accounts, I also want to emphasize that the conventional nature of social practices does not imply that they are only constructions upheld for ideological reasons or prejudices. In addition, the institutional conventionalism that I propose makes no claim concerning the nature or perception of non-social reality,[36] although – for obvious reasons – it conceives of scientific research as a social practice.

The practice account defended here explicitly acknowledges that, due to their conventional nature, social practices are open to moral criticism. It also defends the view, however, that moral criticism is, and ought to be, guided by socially shared standards of justification.

1.3. *Voluntary Migration as a Transnational Phenomenon*

The second major building block of my theoretical framework concerns the specific phenomena, I am primarily interested in: transnational forms of migration.

When I speak of migration in the following, I will always speak, first, of migration across state borders, and second, of so-called voluntary migra-

---

35 Searle's analysis of the constitution of the social world appears to suggest that social practices are constantly re-constituted through individual acts. This, at least, is how I understand Searle's claim that social reality is constituted by intentional acts that are characterized by having two directions of fit (world-to-mind and mind-to-world); see John Searle (1995), Searle (2010), Searle (2001). As far as concerns Searle's paradigm example, the use of money, it certainly has to be conceded that most agents who use paper money or electronic credit cards are entirely unaware of the fact that they are participating in a social convention that would not exist if all simultaneously withdrew from it. They just understand (i.e., have practical knowledge of) how to proceed within the practice. I also think that the value of a currency, and also of stocks, etc., is an outcome influenced by a multiplicity of factors within a plurality of social practices, which is so complex that ordinary agents are in no position to understand the influence, or even relevance, of their individual actions within the conventional practice.

36 See Boghossian (2006) for a criticism of postmodern versions of constructivism.

tion, unless indicated otherwise. I will assume throughout that voluntary migration is motivated by economic interests or biographical reasons,[37] and I will not address issues concerning refugees and asylum seekers unless explicitly mentioned.

Since most mainstream contributions to an "ethics of migration" focus on issues concerning refugees and their normative status, I would like to point out how issues concerning transnational migration differ from those concerning refugees.

First, from an ethical point of view, it makes a big difference whether migration is "involuntary" in the sense of being a last resort for the protection of life and liberty, or whether it is "voluntary" in the sense of being motivated by economic, cultural, or biographical interests. Although it is true that voluntary migration is not always literally voluntary, the exposition of the ethical challenge in cases of voluntary migration is different from that concerning humanitarian support for refugees. Chapter 3 will explore in detail the structure of the normative challenges raised by voluntary migration.

Second, also the issues that are relevant for assessing the moral status of voluntary migrants differ from those related to the moral status of refugees. It is commonly assumed that humanitarian support of refugees is a duty of assistance, that refugees will stay only temporarily, and accordingly ought to be provided with shelter, basic education for children, and means of subsistence, but not with work permits, residency rights, democratic inclusion, etc. Voluntary migration, by contrast, concerns options of social and economic participation, temporary or permanent residence status, change of citizenship, acquisition of dual citizenship, etc. These are the topics in which I am interested in this book. They are worth an investigation in their own right.

Third, phenomena of transnational migration might appear a marginal phenomenon at present, but can be expected to become more important in the short and medium run. Given political reality and the current dynamics of migration, the distinction between refugees and voluntary migrants becomes increasingly blurred in practice. On the one hand, the assumption that refugees will stay only temporarily is no longer warrant-

---

37 The term "biographical reasons" is meant to cover life-plan-related interests tied to education, career, or professional training, as well as familial reasons of migrants who do not qualify as refugees. Unfortunately, it is impossible to get information about migrants' motivations, because to the extent that relevant data exist, they are protected by privacy regulations.

ed.[38] Accordingly, the expectation that refugees will ask for nothing but temporary shelter and means of subsistence is no longer adequate.[39] On the other hand, it is arguable that an increasing number of persons who ask for recognition as refugees, especially in Europe, do so mainly because it is the only viable option for immigration. It can reasonably be assumed that many of them would not appeal for refugee status if they had other viable options. Transitory migration and migration for certain biographical phases can be expected to meet the interests and needs of many migrants in that respect.

A major objection to the transnational approach is the claim that the institution of statehood is either practically obsolete or morally indefensible. A post-national world would or ought to be a world without borders. In such a world, issues concerning citizenship and migration would be obsolete or, at least, raise entirely different question concerning citizenship than in the world as we know it.

Personally, I agree with the conclusion, but have serious doubts that the empirical premises are warranted. I simply do not observe a dissolution of statehood in the real world, or its replacement by international governance or a global empire. Quite the contrary, the real-world consequences of failed states prove the point that centralized structures of government, bureaucracy, and administration are essential for the well-functioning and political self-determination of political associations.

Unfortunately, adherents of open borders usually avoid addressing the question how collective political self-organization should – or could – be organized in a borderless world. From a normative point of view, I see no alternative to the present state system that could be realistically expected to facilitate democratic forms of government and to preserve the social and normative preconditions for the practice of democracy.

Whatever the benefits of technocratic governance and international cooperation in global institutions are supposed to be, it is a (sad) fact that only a minority of political associations currently live up to the normative

---

38 Think about generations of Afghan refugees in Pakistan, or third generations of Palestinian refugees in Arab countries.

39 In many cases, the internal conflicts and wars that force people to flee are not temporary eruptions of violence, but signs of the collapse of statehood or governance, and thus pose problems rather different from those that the current humanitarian refugee regime was originally set up to deal with. It is far from clear whether the present regulations of international law concerning the status of refugees and asylum seekers are still appropriate for the practical challenges at present.

ideal of democratic government, or to even less demanding normative ideals, such as, e.g., the rule of law or accountability of administrative offices. It is a matter of fact that not all societies are democratic. Accordingly, an analysis of citizenship concepts has to reflect the fact that state citizenship does not necessarily coincide with democratic citizenship.

From a normative point of view, nevertheless, liberal political philosophy is committed to the normative ideal of democratic government and the principle of popular sovereignty. At present, the organization of the world in a heterogeneous plurality of distinct and separate states continues to be the only viable option for guaranteeing that those societies that endorse democratic ideals can also practice it. I consider this to be a strong normative reason for the acceptance of the present organization of the world in distinct and separate states. The normative values and ideals related to democracy appear to be widely shared also by quite a few citizens of non-democratic societies, since they often motivate migration and the choice of preferred host societies.

That brings me to the last building block of the present book: the broader normative framework that I employ.

1.4. The Normative Framework: Philosophical Liberalism

It appears quite common, nowadays, for each philosopher or theorist to promote her own grand theory of justice or normative ideal of political philosophy. As a result, most grand theories are highly contested even among philosophers.

My own proposal is much more modest. I will only draw on three rather general principles which I think are widely accepted in contemporary political philosophy of the analytical tradition.

This tradition has been shaped by three normative commitments, which are characteristic for the paradigm of normative justification developed in the philosophy of enlightenment: (1) ethical individualism, which is a substantive metaethical principle; (2) institutional conventionalism, which comes closest to what could be called a social ontology (if one does not take the concept of ontology too literally); and (3) the principle of individual normative self-determination, which articulates a substantive and genuinely liberal moral principle. Whereas ethical individualism and institutional conventionalism are hardly contested, the principle of normative self-determination is indeed contested by, e.g., utilitarians, some communitarians, and most culturalist theorists.

Ad (1): Ethical individualism articulates a metaethical principle for theories of normative justification. It requires that sociopolitical institutions and practices must in principle be rationally justifiable, i.e., justifiable by general and impartial reasons, which individual persons who participate in those institutions and practices could accept if they were to consider the relevant issues from a moral point of view. Another way of saying the same thing – in my view – is to say that ethical individualism is committed to the view that all individual persons ought to be granted an equal moral status, and that all differences in social, civil, and legal status must be justifiable by general and impartial reasons which rational persons could accept from a moral point of view that denies them information of how they personally would be affected by those inequalities.

As already indicated, ethical individualism does not single out one unique theory of normative justification, but rather a family of theories revolving around similar ideas, such as universalizability, impartiality, consent, contractarianism, which may be differently construed by different theorists. Ethical individualism, however, is incompatible with theories of justification inspired by Plato's search for ideal concepts, as well as with epistemic accounts of normative justification inspired by correspondence theories of truth that assume that norms and values are thing-like entities, which exist somewhere and wait to be discovered. Ethical individualism also conflicts with teleological and theocratic theories of justification.

Given that requirements of rationality, impartiality and generality can be construed differently, I want to add a few clarifications of my own interpretation of what ethical liberalism is about. First, ethical individualism is first and foremost an account of justification that applies to sociopolitical and legal *institutions*, and more precisely to *public* institutions and practices that are supposed to be upheld for long-term periods of time. That restricts the scope of issues to questions concerning *norm*-like requirements of *justice*, which apply generally to all relevant persons in all typical situations.

On the other hand, normative challenges that are generated by repeated *acts* of injustice, or corruption, or abuse of institutional powers require more complex frameworks of moral assessments, because, first, they must address issues of moral responsibility for unjust acts and, second, they usually require more information about empirical circumstances than do normative assessments of general norms. Moral challenges that are generated by repeated acts of injustice are better discussed case by case.[40]

Second, speaking of sociopolitical and legal institutions is meant to include not only state institutions and domestic systems of law, but also inter- and transnational institutions and international law. Given that the phenomena of migration in which I am interested all take place against the background of a world organized in distinct and separate states, I will not question the existence of the general order of statehood, but will re-examine theoretical conceptions of some of its basic rules and principles, and their legitimacy from a moral point of view that represents the perspectives of all affected persons.

Third, with respect to standards of rationality, I personally subscribe to coherentist standards of justification, such as *reflective equilibrium*, i.e., justification in the form of a coherent set of arguments backed up by reasons that a) reflect standards of moral reasoning, b) build on a practice account of conceptual analysis, and c) are informed by evidence concerning the relevant empirically contingent conditions and circumstances of the practical problems under discussion.

My characterization of ethical individualism as a metaethical principle implies no commitment to an individualistic or reductionist social ontology. It neither denies the existence of holistic phenomena, e.g., intergenerational entities such as states and societies, nor does it *per se* exclude the possibility that the normative status attributed to such holistic entities – the "moral standing of states" in Walzer's terms[41] – has a *sui generis* quality, in the sense of being irreducible to the moral status of individual persons. Chapter 3 will develop my position in more detail, and will also show why a practice account supports a holistic quasi-ontology that violates neither the principle of ethical individualism nor the right to individual normative self-determination. Ethical individualism simply demands that if sociopolitical institutions (such as states and societies or separate branches of government) are granted a moral status *sui generis*, then the attribution of such a status must be justifiable by impartial reasons that grant equal weight to the normative standing of all affected persons, considered as individuals.

Ad (2): Institutional conventionalism concerns issues of the analysis of sociopolitical institutions and social practices. It applies to phenomena,

---

40 In Rawls's terminology, acts of injustice fall into the domain of non-ideal theory;
    see Rawls (1971).
41 See Walzer (1980).

such as statehood and the practice of international law, but also to social institutions, such as the family, which is of special interest for the analysis of rules of sociopolitical inclusion. In a nutshell, institutional conventionalism conceives of sociopolitical institutions as artificial and changeable, even if they derive from longstanding historical traditions. Institutional conventionalism articulates a presupposition of ethical individualism, because sociopolitical institutions are open to normative criticism (and revision) only if they are conceived as neither representing (natural) facts, nor (natural) properties, nor causal consequences of natural facts or properties. However, institutional conventionalism does not coincide with a commitment to ethical individualism, because institutional conventionalism does not *per se* rule out teleological sociopolitical ideals.

Ad (3): The principle of normative self-determination articulates a substantive normative premise, which is endorsed especially by philosophers of a liberal tradition in the enlightenment sense of the term, but not necessarily by collectivistic or anti-liberal theorists. The principle maintains that persons – conceived of as individuals – have a right to hold and pursue the normative opinions, religious confessions, and justified interests that they choose according to their own discretion, within the general constraint that all persons can equally enjoy that right. I understand normative self-determination to include the freedom to disagree with the moral beliefs and political opinions of other members of one's own society, as well as members of other societies. However, a right to individual normative self-determination cannot be entirely unrestricted if it is supposed to apply to all persons equally. Respect for the moral status and justifiable interests of *all* persons, including their right to normative self-determination, restricts to some extent the range of morally acceptable opinions, convictions, and interests. In light of the fact that individuals cannot but live in social contexts, considerations concerning social compatibility and requirements of mutual acceptability can articulate justified restrictions on individual normative self-determination.

Thus, the exercise of individual normative self-determination in the public sphere and in political agency will unavoidably be constrained to some extent by requirements of fairness concerning the exercise of *collective* self-determination. Nevertheless, respect for individual normative self-determination excludes teleological, theocratic and totalitarian sociopolitical ideals, because it is committed to sociopolitical ideals that are compatible with social pluralism and reciprocal respect for the principle itself.

The important point in the present context is that in a world of heterogeneous and pluralistic societies, those constraints can differ in substance from society to society. There is no reason to expect that constraints such as social compatibility and mutual acceptability will result in similar social norms in all societies alike. Normative self-determination, therefore, is committed to the acceptance not only of social pluralism in the domestic sphere, but also to inter-societal pluralism at the inter- and transnational sphere.

In order to avoid a frequent misunderstanding, I want to add that the principle of *normative self-determination* should not be confused with *moral relativism*, which is a *metaethical* position and, actually, incompatible with ethical individualism. Moral relativism is most commonly understood as saying that ethical beliefs are essentially tied to cultural and social ways of life, which are transculturally incommensurable and beyond normative criticism. Moral relativism is actually incompatible with both ethical individualism and the right to individual normative self-determination.

If the principle of normative self-determination is combined with the principles of ethical individualism and institutional conventionalism, the broader normative framework can be characterized as "liberal" in a broad philosophical sense. In my view, endorsement of the three principles implies a commitment to the normative ideal of social pluralism and democratic forms of government at the domestic level. But I will not assume that those three principles are unanimously accepted in all societies.

As far as I can see, all liberal accounts in contemporary political philosophy endorse ethical individualism and institutional conventionalism; that includes most current versions of communitarianism, republicanism, nationalism, and multiculturalism. The interpretation of the right to (individual) normative self-determination, by contrast, is contested. It is not shared by mono- or multiculturalist theories nor by communitarian positions which argue that the moral standing of communities is prior to that of its individual members.

In my opinion, one cannot endorse ethical individualism and institutional conventionalism without also endorsing the principle of normative self-determination. In order to subsume the combination of the three principles under a common label, I will call it "philosophical liberalism". Unless indicated otherwise, the terms "liberal" and "liberalism", in the following refer to positions which subscribe to those three abstract principles; the terms are not meant to carry a political meaning or to stand for the affiliation with any political party.

Chapter 2. State Citizenship and Transnational Justice

Ethical assessments of migration overwhelmingly appeal to ideals of distributive justice that have been developed for the context of domestic societies. Before I present my own normative argument, which defends an individual liberty right to migration, I would like to raise some general objections to distributive-justice approaches.

One of the most influential arguments on citizenship and migration is Joseph Carens' "non-ideal argument" for open borders.[42] In a nutshell, the argument says that border control is unjust because it denies potential migrants fair access to social opportunities which are unequally distributed among societies. The argument qualifies as *non-ideal* for Carens, because it starts from the real-world *status quo*, i.e., the fact that social opportunities are unequally distributed among states.[43] According to Carens, the unequal distribution of opportunities, or more precisely the unequal access of individual persons to social opportunities, is unjust.

Carens' non-ideal argument attributes no intrinsic value to migration. He defends open borders as an instrumental means or rather as a remedy for a current state of injustice. At the center of his criticism is the current practice of birthright citizenship.[44] Famously, he maintains that the present practice of border control is as inherently unjust as feudal society, because it makes individual access to social opportunities dependent on the morally arbitrary fact of one's birthplace.

Despite its prominence in the literature, Carens' argument is actually rather weak. Due to its instrumental structure, it is open to the objection that migration might not be the best, or even a plausible, instrument for promoting equal access to social opportunities. Political measures that

---

42 See Carens (1987) and Carens (2015).

43 Carens' ideal argument, by contrast, assumes that social opportunities are roughly equal in all societies, and defends open borders as an intuitive extension of the right to free movement within the territory of any state. I will address freedom of movement arguments in chap. 3.

44 The only morally acceptable criterion for the assignment of citizenship, according to Carens, is social integration. It is not clear whether his views on migration and citizenship are mutually coherent. After all, migration could hardly start if integration were required, because most migrants are integrated into the social environments of their countries of origin.

improve the availability and distribution of social opportunities "at home" would most likely be more efficient and also reduce the social and moral costs of access to social opportunities, because domestic improvements would make migration unnecessary.

Most criticisms of Carens' defense of open borders focus on either his cosmopolitan ideal of justice or the analogy of birthright citizenship and feudalism. In order to move the debate forward, I will propose a general account for the analysis of citizenship concepts that allows us to address questions concerning the legitimacy of citizenship assignments quite generally, and I will suggest an important revision to mainstream conceptions of sociopolitical justice. For the sake of argument, my first proposal takes Carens' theory of cosmopolitan justice for granted, but it rejects the idea that the assignment of state citizenship by birth is a "fact", and as such "morally arbitrary". My second proposal criticizes the purely consequentialist structure of Carens' cosmopolitan ideal of justice, and his general disregard of the role that *political agency* plays in the production of social opportunities.[45] Acknowledgment of the relevance of political agency will show why inter- or transnational *and* particularistic conceptions of sociopolitical justice are not mutually exclusive, but need to be combined.

2.1. Why Birthright Citizenship is Not a Fact: The First Objection to Carens

Carens' reference to "birthright citizenship" is best understood as concerning what I call *state citizenship (nationalité)* in its way of including in national society all descendants of citizens. My first objection, then, is this: although birth – or "being born as a child to citizens of a particular society" – is a fact, the assignment of citizenship status by birth is not a fact, but a rule.[46] Like all rules, birthright citizenship is inherently normative *qua* rule, and therefore categorially different from facts. Conceived of as a status concept, citizenship is also normative in substance. It defines the

---

45 I will use "political agency" as an umbrella term for both official policies concerning domestic and foreign policy issues in a broad sense, as well as the social practices that constitute the political culture background of collective decisions at the domestic level that influence the options and the performance of political agency, such as adherence to, and efficiency of, the rule of law, degrees of civic and economic trust, degrees of corruption, etc.

46 Also in feudal times, the assignment of social status by criteria of birth was not a fact but a rule-based assignment, as can be seen by the variations of status of children within and out of wedlock with respect to title, inheritance, etc.

legal and political status of individual persons *vis-à-vis* the institutions of political government and co-citizens. Conceived of as a rule, birthright citizenship – like all conventional rules – is open to moral criticism with respect to both its validity as a rule and its normative substance and implications. In this chapter, however, I will be exclusively concerned with matters of conceptual analysis.

Once we conceive of birthright citizenship as a rule, the assignment of citizenship to descendants of citizens is not arbitrary at all, but quite reasonable, because states and societies are commonly understood as intergenerational entities. Short of proposals for a global society, on the one hand, and radical libertarian criticism of the concept of society, on the other hand, I am not aware of anybody who actually argues that "society" is a theoretically obsolete concept, or that organizing human life in societies is morally unacceptable, or that all societies ought to be dissolved. Carens himself would not defend such a claim. He argues that social integration is the only morally acceptable criterion of citizenship, and social integration certainly presupposes the existence of societies in some sense.

Currently, societies are individuated as distinct and separate entities through the institution of statehood.[47] As long as the world is organized in distinct and separate states, we will have to speak of societies in the plural. Notwithstanding Carens' cosmopolitan aspirations as far as it concerns requirements of sociopolitical justice, his argument presupposes that the world is, and will continue to be, organized in distinct and separate societies. I will take such an assumption, accordingly, for granted in my criticism of him.[48]

Pointing to the basic rationale for assignments of citizenship by birth reveals that birthright citizenship is embedded in the larger background system of rules that constitutes the institutional order of statehood. Within the context of that order, it is indeed highly reasonable to assign citizenship to descendants of citizens. Accordingly, birthright citizenship is not *per se* morally defective. It is morally objectionable only if, and as long as, it is considered to be the sole rule for assignments of state citizenship. As far as the current practice is concerned, it actually is only one rule among others.

---

47 This, of course, is not necessarily the case; think about social organizations in the institutional form of the *polis*, or the empire.

48 Questions concerning normative assessments of the legitimacy of the international system of statehood will be addressed in chaps. 3 and 5.

2.1.1. Birthright Citizenship as State Citizenship

Conceiving of birthright citizenship as a rule immediately reveals that the inclusion of descendants of citizens is not in fact the only rule for the assignment of citizenship. It is the most wide-spread rule of citizenship inclusion in international practice, because states and societies are generally conceived of as representing diachronically continuous and intergenerational social associations. The inclusion of descendants of state citizens who are born within the territory of any particular state, therefore, is a reasonable default rule. It is, however, generally accepted in international practice and theoretical discourse that citizenship also be assigned by additional rules. These rules include, besides *ius sanguinis*- and *ius soli*-regulations, immigration policies and regulations concerning family-(re-)unification.

From the perspective of a practice account, it is worth emphasizing that the practice of citizenship assignments actually acknowledges a plurality of such rules, that those rules are heterogeneous, and that they are meant to apply to quite different types, or classes, of individuals and situations. Besides the case of the descendants of citizens within the territory of states, there are also descendants of parents with different state citizenships, descendants of citizens born abroad, and non-descendant family members of citizens. Some states also have rules concerning every person born within the territory, irrespectively of the citizenship-status of their parents. In addition, there are rules for immigrants, and for long-term residents (*ius soli*), etc. This list is not meant to be exhaustive. It just illustrates the variety of cases that make it practically necessary to employ a heterogeneous plurality of rules. To make a long story short: Carens' attack on birthright citizenship is a red herring.

As a matter of conceptual analysis, a rule-based account of citizenship neither identifies state citizenship with democratic citizenship, nor does it exclusively apply to liberal-democratic societies. As far as concerns conceptual analysis, this is an advantage, because it reflects the fact that concepts of state citizenship apply also to citizens of non-liberal states, internally divided states, failed states, etc., and also the fact that even in liberal-democratic societies not all persons who are assigned state citizenship qualify for democratic citizenship.[49]

---

49 See, e.g., Bosniak (2008) and Spiro (2018) for the need for more diversified citizenship concepts in current debates.

It should also be noted that the legal status of individual persons in state-contexts is not exclusively determined by the assignment of citizenship. Human rights requirements and requirements of the rule of law are standardly conceived to apply to all persons irrespectively of their citizenship status. The status of state citizenship, however, is usually more encompassing than the status transferred by human rights; the legal standing of citizens and non-citizens thus overlap, but need not fully coincide.

A rule-based conception of state citizenship reflects the actual international practice. As I will argue, it also helps to settle some notorious recurrent problems in citizenship debates.

2.1.2. State Citizenship and the Universal Right to Citizenship

Considered as a rule, birthright citizenship is an apt implementation of the normative requirement of universal citizenship. From the perspective of ethical individualism, every person ought to be granted state citizenship, because ethical individualism is generally committed to the idea that all persons *qua* individuals ought to be granted a sociopolitical status. From a liberal point of view, the right to citizenship status articulates a "universal" right, i.e., a right that ought to be granted to *all* persons. The relevant status guaranteed by the universal right to citizenship, however, concerns state citizenship, in contrast to statelessness.

Birthright citizenship automatically assigns state citizenship to the vast majority of persons, and thus rather effectively promotes universal (state) citizenship. The moral weight attributed to the recognition of the moral and legal status of individual persons discloses the reason why withdrawal of (single) state citizenship requires special justification, and why justification of inclusion and exclusion can be asymmetric.

As far as it concerns the equality of the substance of citizenship status, the principle of ethical individualism implies that all persons who are citizens of the same state or society ought to be granted an *equal* legal and sociopolitical status. The defense of a claim that the legal and sociopolitical status of citizens must be identical in substance across all societies, however, would require further argument, because it conflicts with respect for the right of societies to collective self-determination, which articulates a basic principle of international law.[50]

---

50 See chap. 3 for a normative assessment of the principle.

Democratic citizenship cannot as easily be defended as a universal right, although it is morally highly desirable from the perspective of ethical individualism that political associations practice democratic forms of government. However, it cannot be demanded that all societies endorse democracy, because from a transnational perspective, all societies ought to be granted a right to collective self-determination. In addition, even if an ideal-theory argument could be made that all societies ought to endorse democracy, the ideal argument would be of little practical value, because the practice of democracy presupposes that citizens actually endorse democratic values and ideals, which currently is not the case.

It has to be noted that voluntary migrants are not deprived of their universal right to state citizenship when they are denied immigration or naturalization in a host society, because they hold citizenship of their country of origin. *Pace* Carens, issues of migration should, therefore, be distinguished from issues concerning the assignment of state citizenship. (Voluntary) migration concerns issues such as residence without citizenship, or changes of citizenship, or the acquisition of dual citizenship, democratic inclusion, etc. Acknowledgment of a universal right to state citizenship does not settle those questions. Any theoretically acceptable answer will have to take account of the normative purposes of citizenship, the normative value and function of societies as spaces of social agency, of social membership in general, and of the social preconditions and adequate measures of the implementation of various conceptions of collective social self-organization – in the case of liberal states, of democracy and social pluralism.

2.1.3. Involuntary Citizenship: A Normative Justification

Recognition of a universal right to citizenship requires that every person be assigned state citizenship in some state or another. However, it does not grant persons an individual right – more precisely: a moral or legal power – to choose state citizenship unilaterally according to their personal discretion. Both, democratic citizenship and state citizenship are relational concepts, insofar as they determine the status of citizens not only *vis-à-vis* state-institutions, but also *vis-à-vis* co-citizens. Concepts of citizenship are essentially linked to the role of individuals as members of a particular society or, as I will also say, of a *political association*. At present, the dominant institutional form of organization of political association is statehood. The concepts of political association and statehood, however, are not synonymous, because statehood is an institutional model for organizing political associations, whereas the concept of society (political association) is meant to refer to the exercise and practice of interpersonal socioeconomic and political activities.

It has been widely noticed that sociopolitical membership is not a matter of the discretion of any person or any group of persons. Persons usually are not asked – or allowed – to voluntarily agree to their citizenship assignment, but simply have it assigned. This is the most noted difference between sociopolitical membership and other forms of membership, e.g., membership in a club. A rule-based account of citizenship not only explains why citizenship assignments do not require individual consent – citizenship is assigned in accordance with general rules –, but also elucidates the conditions under which this form of involuntariness is morally justified: the rules must meet general standards of moral justification. According to ethical individualism, not even societies considered as institutional entities have morally unconstrained discretion to choose whatever rules of inclusion (or exclusion) they want to endorse. Rules have to be a) general and b) justifiable by impartially acceptable reasons to all relevant parties[51] in order to qualify as morally acceptable.

A rule-based account of citizenship thus shows why one rather prominent philosophical conception of sociopolitical membership in the liberal tradition is inadequate for dealing with the problem. This is the idea of membership through voluntary consent. A rule-based account of citizenship provides a theoretical alternative to voluntaristic accounts of normative justification in terms of "individual consent", and can elucidate why voluntaristic accounts are inadequate as standards of legitimacy for citizenship assignments – at least, if justification by consent is taken as literally requiring actual consent of concrete empirical individuals.

Notoriously, voluntaristic accounts of citizenship are haunted by the following problem. If sociopolitical inclusion has to be based on (unanimous) interpersonal consensus, then we obviously have to identify in advance the persons whose consent is relevant.[52] That presupposes that we have already settled the question, who should be included. The same paradox also arises for theories of normative justification based on purely

---

51 Since the latent content of conceptions of state citizenship is related to the organization of the world in separate and distinct states, impartial acceptability implies that the relevant rules must be acceptable as a general structure of the overall system of statehood. The relevant issues will be addressed in chap. 3.

52 See, e.g., Nasström (2007).

procedural conceptions of justification, such as, e.g., discourse ethics. The specification of who defines morally acceptable rules of social inclusion and exclusion must be either "all" members of the global population or remain obscure.[53]

A rule-based account of citizenship reflects the fact that – in most cases – state citizenship is neither chosen nor voluntary, but is assigned according to general rules that apply to all relevant persons equally. No doubt, those rules are open to moral criticism. But voluntary consent – or lack of voluntary consent – is not the right standard of normative justification. Sociopolitical inclusion should reflect the special nature of sociopolitical membership. From the perspective of a rule-based account, the main normative question concerning sociopolitical inclusion is, "What is the normative purpose, within the international system of statehood, of political association as such, and what makes it valuable?" Before I approach the question, I would like to revisit three traditional answers to it: voluntaristic consent-based accounts of association, (libertarian) exchange-based accounts of association, and (liberal) justice-based accounts of association.

(1) Consent-based Accounts of Political Association

The forefather of consent-based accounts of political associations is Jean-Jacques Rousseau.[54] For Rousseau, the true object of the social contract is the constitution of "the people". His social contract requires the unanimous consent of all future citizens. Once unanimity is achieved, a moral

---

53 See, e.g., Benhabib (2001) for a discussion of whether all members of the global population must be included as participants in the relevant discourse, or only democratically minded persons.

54 Rousseau (1762) disagrees in this respect with Hobbes (1651) and Locke (1690), for whom the purpose of a social contract concerns primarily the determination of the legitimate powers and competences of the office of political government *vis-à-vis* individual citizens – in the language of the period: the determination of the rights and duties of sovereigns and citizens. For Rousseau, by contrast, a social contract is required for the constitution of "the people", i.e., for the constitution of the political association – in the language of the period: the transformation of a multitude of independent individuals into a unified political body. The traditional Hobbesian and Lockean alternative to Rousseau concerning the latter question is the view that the unity of society is constituted by the institution of statehood. See, e.g., Chwaszcza (2008), Chwaszcza (2009), Owen (2018).

transformation takes place: the contracting parties are no longer natural persons, but moral persons. In other words: sociopolitical unity confers a normative status on the members of the people. According to Rousseau, the moral transformation is motivated by the idea that the contracting parties have exchanged their natural independence for (collective) political freedom, civil liberties and duties, and the protection of their rights through the common power of the political association. This transformation, according to Rousseau, is actually the only one that requires unanimous consent.

Although theories concerning the constitution of the unity of society or the unity of the people that follow Rousseau are more common in discussions concerning secession and minority group rights, they are not entirely absent in discussions of migration either. The most prominent proponent of such an account is probably Christopher Wellman.[55]

A common objection to consent theories of sociopolitical association is the unanimity requirement, which is frequently criticized as utopian. The true problem, however, is different. It is the idea that normative validity necessarily requires voluntary consent. That idea is theoretically unconvincing if it is understood in a voluntaristic sense, because it makes *all* normative requirements dependent on individual consent. In the present context, the requirement of individual consent conflicts with the recognition of a universal right to citizenship and yields implications which are unjustifiably exclusivist. Generally speaking, the shortcoming of voluntaristic versions of consent-based justification consists in the fact that they reject the recognition of any moral obligation that is not self-imposed. If we believe that at least some moral relations and obligations are not self-imposed, then voluntaristic consent-based justification cannot be an exclusive standard of normative justification.

To illustrate the point: imagine a multitude of ten socially disconnected persons, nine of whom are willing to accept every other person as a member of the unity, and one who disagrees with the inclusion of one particular other. The other nine, then, can decide whether they want to exclude the dissenting person or the person the dissenter rejects. Either decision, however, would be entirely arbitrary from a moral point of view.

If citizenship is a normative status which should be granted equally to all persons, then it cannot be withheld for no reason or for merely arbitrary reasons. Even in Rousseau the morally substantive considerations that

---

55   See Wellman's position in Wellmann/Cole (2011); see also Joppke (2010), who speaks rather vaguely of social contract accounts of citizenship.

support the participation in the very creation of the unity of the people (political liberty, protection of individual rights, etc.), are considered to be objectively good and the same for all participants. Lack of consent of one of the relevant parties *per se*, accordingly, is not a reason that carries enough moral weight to outweigh a universal right to citizenship.[56] One can reject another person as a friend for no other reason than that one does not want to befriend her. But one cannot deny another person the status of citizenship – a moral status – for no reason.

The moral and the rational validity of the ways in which citizenship status is assigned cannot be a matter of voluntaristic consent, because the reasons for the moral determination and desirability of citizenship status are tied to morally substantive reasons for having political associations, and are interlinked with the normative purposes and pragmatic functions of political association – at least from the perspective of ethical individualism.

(2) Voluntary-exchange-based Accounts of Political Association

Notoriously, libertarians maintain that political membership is not different at all from membership in a club or private union.[57] They tend to argue that there is "no such thing as society", and actually no significant sphere of politics beyond the purposes of the minimal state. According to libertarians, political associations are constituted by interpersonal agreements among private individual persons who are conceived of as property owners, whose joint real estate defines the territory of the political association. As Hillel Steiner argues, nobody could object to migration if migrants are invited to settle on the property by property owners.[58] As Steiner's proposal shows, however, even for libertarians individual consent can only be a necessary but not a sufficient criterion for civic association, because consent must be mutual.

---

56 Another problematic implication of consent theories is that they allow individual persons to opt out, i.e., to practice "individual" anarchism, because they do not recognize a *general* moral duty "to leave the state of nature" in order to establish legal relations with other individuals, as, e.g., Kant (1793) demands.

57 Libertarianism is not a philosophically arcane position in migration debates. Not only theorists, but also practitioners regularly float the idea that citizens of failed states should be granted the option to buy themselves into protected cities as an alternative to migration.

58 See Steiner (1992).

If we consider the exclusionary potential of libertarian conceptions of association, it is evident that it fails as a morally acceptable standard for sociopolitical inclusion – at least from the perspective of ethical individualism. The exclusion of *non*-invited persons without real estate is morally unacceptable because recognition of the moral status of persons ought not depend on whether or not they own real estate. Property is a social institution itself, and thus cannot be accepted as a precondition for the acquisition of civic status.

(3) Justice-based Accounts of Political Association

For liberal theorists such as Rawls, political association is special. It differs from private associations, such as churches or clubs, insofar as it does not serve a common purpose or shared aim, but ought to be organized according to principles of justice. Co-citizenship is conceived of in terms of the horizontal normative relations that ought to hold among co-citizens, rather than in terms of shared aims or goals. According to Rawls's political liberalism, principles of justice require that citizens mutually recognize each other as free and equal persons, and thus accept the fact of normative pluralism.[59] Rawls therefore defends a "freestanding conception of the political sphere". "Freestanding" means that citizens agree that the purpose of political association is the organization of the social life for persons who have a right to pursue diverging personal life-plans, and who accept that none of them can simply impose her own normative ideals on other co-citizens. A freestanding conception of political association, thus, implies a normative commitment to democratic forms of government (besides recognition of certain constitutional rights).

Voluntary consent plays no role in Rawls's conceptions of sociopolitical membership. To the extent that agreement is required, it is restricted to what Rawls calls the "constitutional essentials", which are justified according to general standards of rational justification (*reflective equilibrium*) rather than individual consent in the voluntaristic sense.

As far as it concerns standards of justification, I find Rawls's view the most plausible one. But it obviously is deficient for a discussion of political association from a transnational point of view, because Rawls restricts it to the domestic sphere. I therefore suggest that we adjust the justice requirements to the relevant background institutions of the system of

---

59 See Rawls (1993a).

statehood, and investigate the normative value of political associations as distinct and separate institutional entities from a transnational perspective. A rule-based account of citizenship provides a first step towards such an investigation, but many further issues will have to be addressed in chapters 3, 4, and 5. In the remainder of this section, I will address a few remaining issues of a rule-based account of citizenship

2.1.4. The Procedural Element in a Rule-based Account of Citizenship

There is one important limitation of a rule-based account of citizenship assignments, which seems to bring back voluntarism through the back door, but actually does not.

A rule-based account of citizenship assignments adequately reflects the conspicuous fact that citizenship assignment is in most cases "involuntary": it has simply been assigned to persons who never asked for it. Normative assessments of the legitimacy of citizenship assignment, accordingly, should focus on the moral justifiability of the relevant rules of inclusion and exclusion in accordance with morally substantive requirements of domestic and transnational justice. However, if we assume that there exists a heterogeneous plurality of rules of inclusion and exclusion that apply to different groups of persons and different conditions, and which thus need to be combined, then it is reasonable to assume that the range of justifiable combinations of rules is *morally underdetermined*. It should be expected that general moral considerations will exclude some rules and some combinations of rules, but will yield a plurality of possible combinations that equally qualify as morally justifiable. The final choice of any particular set from the range of permissible combinations, therefore, will leave a space of discretion that has to be closed by decision.

That raises the question, "Who is *authorized* to make that decision?". This question asks not for voluntary consent of individual persons, but for a specification of the institutional position or office that (*morally*) ought to be granted the *legal authority* to make the final decision. In democratic societies, as I will argue in chapter 3, the authority ought to be assigned to the legislative branch of government.

The final selection, thus, will have to be settled by a collective decision. But the legitimacy of the collective decision rests not on individual consent, but on the authority invested in political associations considered as collective entities, as represented by the legislative branch of government.

It should also be noted that the normative function of a requirement of (democratic) legislative decision is quite different from the function of individual consent in voluntaristic theories of normative justification. The concession that some normative questions have to be settled by means of (democratic) political decisions for pragmatic reasons, because they are morally underdetermined, is entirely different from the idea that individual consent is a necessary and sufficient criterion of normative justification.

Acknowledgment that a rule-based account of citizenship assignments requires a procedural element has an important implication for aspirations about what philosophers can contribute to the relevant debates. For it seriously limits aspirations as to what philosophical investigations can be expected to accomplish. Philosophers must be satisfied with the modest ambition of articulating some general constraints – in my view, mainly of the type of arguments that are valid in the relevant debates. But they cannot (and ought not) impose their personal ideals on the citizens and legislators of political associations in the real world.

2.2. *Political Agency and the Limits of Cosmopolitan Consequentialism: The Second Objection to Carens*

As pointed out at the beginning of the chapter, Carens' non-ideal argument defends open borders as a means to an ideal of cosmopolitan justice. Structurally, his argument is strictly consequentialist. He proposes a morally desirable end-state-result for the distribution of access to social opportunities. Thus, he sidelines issues concerning the generation of social opportunities and normative requirements related to those issues. Accordingly, Carens bypasses all questions concerning the social conditions that, positively or negatively, influence their generation and intra-social distribution. As a result, he ignores all questions concerning requirements of justice related to the social conditions that facilitate the production and intra-social distribution of social opportunities. Social opportunities, after all, are neither naturally given nor randomly distributed among different societies.

The theoretical exclusion of considerations concerning the production of social opportunities raises serious methodological problems. For social opportunities are products, or fruits, of "political agency", and to a large part – though not necessarily entirely – of domestic political agency, such as economic policies, political decisions concerning middle- and long-term investments in, e.g., socio-economic development, infrastructure, education, as well as general sociocultural practices related to political and administrative agency. The special point about political agency is that it is categorically different from what Rawls calls "the basic structure of society". As I will argue in more detail in the following chapters, political agency constitutes a *sui generis* source of requirements of political justice, besides and beyond Rawls's focus on social institutions. Right now, the important point is that social opportunities have to be produced through political agency, which is – largely, though not necessarily entirely – influenced by the social practices and the political culture in which political agency is embedded.

It is a notorious fault of consequentialist arguments that they are often silent about the means or instruments that are supposed to be employed for achieving the ends or goods that they promote. Unless one is ready to either take a full-blown fatalistic stance towards sociopolitical and socio-economic environments, or to assume that the distribution of social opportunities is an unintended, spontaneous consequence of global economic forces, one can neither completely discount the theoretical relevance of political agency for the generation of social opportunities, nor the fact that the contributions of political agency are ambivalent, because the actual practice of political agency is not always successful, just, or undistorted by flaws such as corruption, incompetence, mismanagement, etc. The point is not only that past and present political agency – at the domestic as well as the international level – has an enormous influence on the socio-economic *status quo* of distinct and particular societies, but that political agency is the only and the best means we have for maintaining, changing, and improving the *status quo* within any society.

Since voluntary migration can be assumed to be motivated by inter-societal differences in access to social opportunities, normative assessments of voluntary migration cannot abstract from political agency, because social opportunities are largely generated and shaped by political agency. True, political globalization has not kept pace with economic globalization, but that cannot mean that normative political philosophy can ignore the theoretical relevance of political agency.

Given the empirically contingent nature of political agency and its consequences, it is easy to see why normative theorists prefer theoretical frameworks that focus on morally desirable end-states rather than the means for, or obstacles to, their achievement. But the advantage here comes at the cost of rendering the entire approach methodologically implausible, because it misrepresents both the genuinely *social* quality of social opportunities, i.e., the fact that they have to be socially generated, not only distributed according to standards of social justice, as well as the fact that distinct and separate societies continue to be highly important spaces for the exercise of political agency.

2.2.1. The Theoretical Relevance of Political Agency

In order to explicate my criticism better, I would like to recall a distinction between two classes of primary social goods, made by Rawls in his *Theory of Justice*. Paradigm examples of primary social goods of the first class are basic rights and liberties. They ought to be distributed equally, according to the first principle of justice. Equal distribution is a reasonable requirement, because the first class consists of goods that require nothing but (mutual) recognition of the moral status of individual persons. In practice, these goods need to be implemented and enforced by social institutions, and the establishment and maintenance of those institutions consumes social and financial resources. But their "availability" requires nothing but *mutual recognition*. I therefore find it misleading to call them primary social "goods". Recognition of basic rights and liberties presents something like a "hexis", or rather an attitude that citizens ought to take towards other citizens as moral persons.

The second class of primary social goods related to the difference principle, by contrast, are goods that have to be produced: access to education, to health services, etc. The availability of those "goods" depends on the conditions and costs of their production. Since Rawls explicitly argues that the difference principle is not meant to regulate the distribution of bundles of goods, but the structural conditions of individual access to those goods, the difference principle is best understood as concerning social positions, i.e., social opportunities. According to the second principle, it is not unjust if these goods are distributed unequally, as long as it is guaranteed that inequalities concerning access to those goods are to every citizen's advantage.

My criticism of Carens in the present context concerns not the difference principle, which is notoriously contested, but the fact that the introduction of a second principle is considered necessary due to the difference between social goods of the first and of the second class. The generation of social opportunities consumes not only social and financial resources at the level of their implementation. They also have to be socially produced. Considered as "goods", social opportunities on the one hand, and rights and liberties on the other hand, differ in morally important respects. The availability of social opportunities requires more than mutual recognition; it requires a collective effort in the form of political and social agency. Performance of political and social agency also requires an institutional space for collective activities, and such spaces continue to be largely domestic even within a supra-national political union, such as the European Union.

The normative value of the rights and duties that are characteristic of liberal conceptions of democratic citizenship certainly derives not least from the normative value attributed to the option of participating in collective political agency at the domestic level. Nevertheless, domestic political agency cannot be reduced to the recognition of individual rights and duties, because it is (i) an activity that is (ii) essentially collective and (iii) empirically contingent. Carens' non-ideal argument, however, is set out in a way that eliminates the collective dimension of the social circumstances of political agency, and the (empirically contingent) social preconditions for the successful generation of social opportunities or social obstacles to it.

Carens' consequentialism is typical of a current tendency in liberal political philosophy: it conceives of politics exclusively as a means for the realization of morally desirable aims. Besides the fact that political agency cannot be reduced to a pragmatic measure for the realization of requirements of global justice, it is also a basic norm of international law that states are granted a considerable degree of autonomy as concerns domestic politics. Being an activity, political agency falls into the sphere of empirically contingent phenomena with a historically diachronic dimension, and thus constitutes a sphere of justice quite different from considerations concerning the basic structure of society (or of international law).

The main theoretical challenge is this: How can theoretical frameworks be adjusted in such a way that they reflect the practical and normative relevance of political agency. I suggest that we conceive of societies not merely as abstract institutions, but primarily as spaces for collective activities, including political agency. In the last section of the present chapter, I will outline some of the normative consequences that such an adjustment has for theories of inter- and transnational, or global, justice in general.[60]

Since Carens defends a cosmopolitan ideal of justice, I only want to add that one can, of course, speculate about what the requirements of global political justice would be *if* the present system of statehood, and the organization of political associations into distinct and separate societies, were abolished. But it should be evident that the problems of migration

---

60 Chap. 3 will further advance those points.

and political justice in such a world would be totally different from those in the actual world.

2.2.2. The Normative Relevance of Political Agency

Political agency obviously differs with respect to its normative dynamic and logic from considerations concerning the justice of the basic structure of sociopolitical institutions. First, it generates *special* normative relations among those who qualify as participants (in liberal democratic societies), or as directly affected subjects (in non-democratic societies). Second, unlike abstract normative considerations, agency-based requirements of political justice are usually path-dependent and do not apply universally to all persons or institutions in the same way, but only to the particular group of persons addressed by particular performances of political agency.

In analogy to Rawls's claim that the role of justice as fairness concerns the distribution of advantages and benefits of social cooperation at the level of the basic structure of society, one could say that the role of moral requirements generated by political agency concerns the distribution of benefits and burdens of political decisions, economic policies, etc. among participants. Many of these consequences are intended to be long-term intergenerational projects, e.g., social investments in education, infrastructure, health care, etc.; and many have long-term economic implications, e.g., economic policies, tax-regulations, labor laws, etc. Since long-term political decisions affect justified interests of different groups of participants differently, they often generate requirements of justice of a genuinely particularistic kind.

A crucial difference between a conception of justice as concerning the basic structure, and justice as deriving from political agency, is that the former is essentially oriented towards a normative ideal about what the basic structure ought to be, whereas the latter, unfortunately, is an empirically contingent phenomenon, which very often is non-ideal and can in many ways fail or be distorted. Requirements of agency-based political justice, therefore, often require rectification or compensation of present or past injustice. The normative consequences of political agency, therefore, are ambivalent. They can generate particularistic scenarios of justice as well as injustice.

A last point of clarification. As I understand the term, political agency is not restricted to the domestic sphere of political associations. It also takes place at the level of international inter-state relations and of transnational relations between states and non-state agents, e.g., economic actors, development agencies, NGOs, INGOs, etc. From a normative point of view, the special relations that derive from inter- and transnational political agency are no less relevant than are those that derive from political agency at the domestic level. They differ in exactly the same way from considerations concerning the basic structure of the present world order and international law, as political agency at the domestic level differs from considerations concerning the basic structure of political associations.[61] Given the fact that the present *status quo* of inter- and transnational relations actually continues to be regulated more by political agency than by norms and procedures laid out in a global basic structure, it seems to me absurd to ignore the relevance of political agency.

The important point to notice is that requirements of justice that derive from political agency are categorially different from requirements of justice concerning the basic structure, and that they derive from collective decisions and activities that are empirically contingent phenomena. They articulate morally relevant considerations that arise independently of considerations related to the justice of the basic structure. Against the background of the political reality of statehood in the world as it is, it is obvious that political agency and social practices, first, vary widely among different societies, and, second, are normatively ambiguous because they generate spheres of particular justice and injustice – both domestically and inter- or transnationally.

2.2.3. Non-ideal Theory: Why Consequences are Not All that Matters

Carens' lack of concern for the theoretical and normative relevance of political agency, it seems to me, reflects partly a general tendency towards consequentialism in current theories of global, or cosmopolitan, justice,[62]

---

61 In light of the common claim that Western colonialism is one of the most relevant factors for the unequal distribution of social opportunities among states, I would add that the question whether this is the case or not, is an empirical question. If it is, it certainly is normatively relevant – not only with respect to Western colonialism but also to non-Western colonialism, communist expansionism, etc. Since I will propose a theoretical alternative to remedial justice arguments in chap. 3, however, I will not pursue the issue further.

62 See, e.g., Beitz's afterword to the second edition of Beitz (1979/1999) for a defence of consequentialism in theories of international justice. See also Goodin (1988).

and partly a theoretical blind spot in theories of justice remotely influenced by Rawls. Rawls construes the theory of justice as fairness as an ideal-type theory, i.e., as a normative theory that is based on two assumptions: (1) the assumption that all agents are moral persons endowed with a sense of justice who voluntarily comply with requirements of justice, and (2) the assumption that societies are not "burdened", i.e., do not suffer from a lack of socio-economic development or other disadvantages.[63] The collective and empirically contingent dimensions of political agency are evidently not of primary relevance in an ideal-theory framework that focuses mainly on justice as a primary virtue of institutions. An exposition of the challenge of migration as triggered by differences in the availability of social opportunities, however, conflicts with the second assumption, and cannot employ the first, because it has to take account of the differences among states as they exist in political reality.

In order to avoid a misunderstanding, I want to emphasize that my defense of the theoretical and normative relevance of political agency is an issue entirely different from the controversies among Rawls and his cosmopolitan critics, such as Charles Beitz or Thomas Pogge, about whether the concept of social justice is primarily restricted to domestic institutions – as Rawls maintains[64] – or also applies to international institutions – as Beitz[65] and Pogge[66] argue. I consider these controversies to concern mainly empirical and explanatory questions, and my personal conviction is that there is overwhelming evidence that domestic institutions, while crucial for the implementation of principles of social justice, are not explanatorily sufficient for the socioeconomic *status quo*, because non-domestic factors such as international trade regimes (GATT, WTO), policies of international institutions (IMF, World Bank), and transnational economic activities are relevant factors too.

My objection to Carens, by contrast, raises an entirely different issue. It concerns the neglect of the theoretical and normative relevance of political

---

63 Non-ideal theory in Rawls (1971) is supposed to address problems that arise from non-compliance, such as a theory of just punishment or civil disobedience. Rawls's account of international justice, however, qualifies according to Rawls's own judgment almost entirely as non-ideal. Issues concerning citizenship and migration definitely fall into the area of non-ideal theory. Carens actually appears to agree with Rawls, because his ideal argument for open borders assumes that in an ideal world, migration would at most be a marginal problem.

64 See Rawls (1993b).

65 See Beitz (1979/1997).

66 See Pogge (1989).

agency for assessments of domestic, international (or cosmopolitan), and transnational justice, and the ways in which the three spheres of justice are interrelated. Carens' non-ideal argument, in my view, is highly idealistic in an unacceptable way: it announces an ideal endpoint of cosmopolitan justice, but is conspicuously uninterested in moral questions concerning the instruments and means for its realization. The main challenge, in my view, consists not in prioritizing one sphere of sociopolitical justice – cosmopolitan or domestic – over the other, but in elucidating how the various sphere of sociopolitical justice – domestic, international, and transnational – interact and can be coherently combined.

Chapter 3. Migration as a Problem of Transnational Justice: The Moral Status of Individuals and Societies

This chapter will lay out the structural contours of the normative challenge raised by transnational migration.

It starts with an argument for the recognition of a *prima facie* individual liberty right to migration and an analysis of the current structure of the conflicts raised by migration. As concerns the latter point, I will assume that ethical assessments of migration must address three sources of conflicts: (i) competition among different groups of migrants who request access to a small number of preferred host societies; (ii) competition among potential host societies for particular groups of migrants; and (iii) conflicts of interests between individual persons – be it citizens or migrants – *vis-à-vis* societies conceived of as holistic entities.

Whereas the first and the second conflict are obvious, the relevance, or even existence, of the third source of conflict is ignored by quite a few theorists, because they reject the idea that societies have a moral standing *sui generis*, and maintain rather that the moral standing of societies must be entirely reducible to the moral standing of the individuals who constitute them. I will label all such claims "normative reductionism", but I would like to emphasize in advance that normative reductionism exists in a variety of versions. The major part of the present chapter will criticize two versions: contractarian accounts of global justice, which defend the logical priority of individual rights – natural rights or human rights – over rights of states and societies, and Goodin's criticism of particularistic accounts of (domestic) social justice. I will also indicate why rejecting normative reductionism does not commit theorists to communitarianism or liberal nationalism, but is fully compatible with ethical individualism as characterized in chapter 1, and with the recognition of universal moral or human rights.

In my view, universal and particularistic conceptions of justice are not mutually exclusive, but mutually supplementary. Following David Hume, the role of justice might roughly be specified as providing principles for the settlement of standard types of interpersonal conflicts of justified interests as they occur among participants in rule-based sociopolitical practices.[67] This includes inter- and transnational sociopolitical practices, and conflicts of interests that arise at the level of inter- and transnational relations.

Since the rules of inter- and transnational sociopolitical practices are quite different from those of domestic institutions, it makes little sense to transfer conceptions of justice that were developed for the domestic level unmodified to inter- and transnational levels. Many current accounts of post-national justice, unfortunately, do just that, and remain "methodologically statist".[68] Statist accounts are of little help for normative assessments of migration, first, because migration is a transnational phenomenon, and, second, because the relevant conflicts concern standards and practices of social life, not the institutional framework of statehood. In order to explore alternative lines of theorizing post-national justice, it will be necessary to rethink some of the main arguments concerning the normative purpose and the value of political association as such,[69] and to take account of the relevance of political-agency-based aspects of social justice.

Let me add two qualifications concerning the scope of the chapter. First, in principle, assessments of the moral status of societies should have to consider not only (potential) host societies, but also societies of origin. I will, however, focus on potential host societies, because I will take the premise for granted that individuals have a right to emigrate. I will also leave out issues related to problems such as *brain drain* and *brain waste*, because they depend strongly on empirically contingent factors, which are so divers from case to case[70] that very little can be said about them at a general level.

Second, my criticism of normative reductionism will be supplemented in the next chapter by a criticism of two non-Rawlsian arguments against the recognition of an inter- and transnational dimension of sociopolitical justice.

---

67 See Hume (1777). Rawls's definition of the role of "social" justice draws on Hume, but focuses on social justice as the primary virtue of institutions.

68 I borrow the phrase from Wimmer/Glick Schiller (2003).

69 I will speak of "societies" or "political associations", when I refer to the very purpose and function of political associations in contrast to "statehood" as a special arrangement for the institutional organization of political associations, such as abstract models of the nation state, the legal state, constitutional democracy, etc.

70 See, e.g., Boeri et.al. (2012), and Özdem/Schiff (2006).

3.1. Is There an Individual (Human) Right to Free Movement Across Borders?

Should we acknowledge an individual right to migration? The answer very much depends on whether such a right is considered to be a claim right or a liberty right.

Arguments for an individual claim right to free movement across borders tend to build on already accepted individual rights, but are rarely worked out in detail. As far as I can see, the most prominent line is the pragmatic argument to the effect that an individual right of immigration is a practically necessary corollary to the human right to leave any country.[71]

An alternative individual rights-based argument is Carens' "ideal argument" for open borders.[72] Carens' ideal argument, however, is not really an argument, but an appeal to intuition. According to Carens the value that liberals attribute to the human right of free movement within the territory of any country,[73] also applies to freedom of movement across borders. I will not directly respond to Carens' intuition, because I count myself among the theorists who maintain that intuition cannot replace argument.[74] The following considerations will indicate *passim* why Carens' intuition cannot be upheld from a reflective moral point of view.

The right to leave any country articulates a universal human right. Although not universally respected in practice, it is uncontested in liberal political philosophy. The right qualifies as a right that individuals hold against any government, i.e., the government of the country of origin as well as any other country, *ceteris paribus*.[75] It generally prohibits governments from denying individuals the freedom to exit the territory of the state, and thus establishes an unrestricted right to emigrate.

---

71 Cf. UDHR, Art. 13 (2): "Everyone has the right to leave any country, including his own, and to return to his country."

72 Carens' ideal argument is *ideal*, insofar as it is meant to apply to a world in which social opportunities are roughly equally distributed among different societies. Curiously, Carens assumes that under such ideal conditions the number of potential migrants would be negligible, because individuals would prefer not to exercise their liberty of movement. If Carens' intuition is coherent, the intrinsic value attributed to the liberty to cross-border movement cannot be very great, if only few persons would pursue it.

73 Cf. UDHR, Art. 13 (1): "(1) Everyone has the right to freedom of movement and residence within the borders of each state."

74 See Miller (2016) for an explicit criticism of Carens' intuition.

75 As always, the right is not valid absolutely, but exemptions and conditions of application are irrelevant for the present discussion.

The right to leave one's country, however, is generally understood as articulating a liberty right. As such, it does not establish a right to immigrate to any country, with the notable exception of one's country of origin.

The pro-immigration argument, accordingly, is based on a pragmatic consideration. It maintains that the exercise of the right to leave one's country is practically worthless unless it be combined with a (claim) right to immigration.

From a practical point of view, emigration is indeed impossible without the possibility of immigration, because the world is fully divided into states. There is no non-state-territory, even considering the contested political status of a few territories and the status of Antarctica as the common heritage of mankind. The argument that the practical value of the freedom of exit requires an accompanying right of immigration appears *prima facie* promising as a starting point for the defense of a right to immigration[76] – at least as long as we consider emigration as an exceptional move or measure.

Secunda facie, however, and once we consider the question whether the recognition of a claim right to immigration should be accepted as a general rule, it becomes clear that acknowledgment of a universal claim right to immigration is implausible, because it would transform sociopolitical membership to a matter of purely individual discretion. It thus would be incompatible with the very conception of political *association* of – as far as I can see – all traditions of political philosophy, ranging from communitarianism to libertarianism.

An unqualified – i.e. unrestricted – *claim* right to immigrate to any country of one's choice, therefore, is too strong a claim.

This, however, is not the end of story. The rejection of a claim right to migration rules out unrestricted immigration, but does not tell us much about either the legitimacy of restrictions on immigration or the empirically contingent conditions under which those restrictions apply. According to a rule-based account of citizenship, rules of both inclusion *and* exclusion must be generally justifiable by impartial reasons. That means that rules of exclusion cannot be declared on the basis of mere discretion either.

---

76 See, e.g., Huemer (2010), and Cole's position in Wellman/Cole (2011).

3.2. *Beyond Claim Rights: Freedom of Migration as a Requirement of Transnational Justice*

I suggest that rather than starting from a justification for a right to immigration, we should start with the question whether immigration can be categorically denied, or denied for morally arbitrary reasons. Let's therefore see what is at stake.

Voluntary migration, it was assumed, is motivated by economic or biographical reasons. From a liberal point of view, such reasons qualify as justified interests, as long as no criminal, vicious, or malignant intention speaks against recognizing them as justified.

Justified interests are core elements of personal life plans which, from a liberal point of view, persons ought to be granted the liberty to pursue within the restrictions of roughly two qualifications. First, the contents of personal life-plans must be compatible with granting every other person an equal liberty of doing so; and, second, the ways and measures of their pursuit – "the rules of the game" – must meet requirements of social compatibility and reciprocal acceptability. Call these the equality and the social compatibility condition.

In my view, there is no doubt that the pursuit of economic interests and biographical reasons qualify as justified interests. After all, the promotion of individual and collective economic interests is one of the most often cited reasons for the establishment of political institutions.

If the basic line of reasoning is correct, I simply fail to see any reason why recognition of such a liberty right should be restricted to co-citizens. The contents of the right are not tied to or dependent on the civil or legal status of citizenship, but are attached to the recognition of the status of individuals as moral persons. It thus should make no difference, whether the relevant individual is a co-citizen, or a resident foreigner, or a potential migrant. As far as the liberty to pursue justified interests is concerned, *all* persons are morally on a par.

I also fail to see any reason why promotion of individual and collective interests should not be taken to be a standard of legitimacy for the institutional structure of the organization of the world in distinct and separate states. If we explore the question impartially from the perspective of the principle of ethical individualism, the first question to ask is this:

(1) "Could an institutional organization of the world in separate and distinct political associations be justified by impartial reasons to all possible parties if the arrangement denies persons the option to pursue their justified interests abroad?".

The main difficulty of the first question consists in the specification of the relevant parties. Taking a transnational perspective, I suggest that the relevant parties are best conceived of as representative persons, i.e., as individuals in their role as resident members of societies (state citizens), and as individuals in their role as potential migrants. After all, (almost) everybody is a member of society somewhere, as well as a potential migrant.

If pursuit of justified interests ought to be acknowledged as legitimate, a world of closed borders cannot be justified, unless it can be shown that one of the conditions mentioned above, i.e., either the equality condition or the social compatibility condition, is violated. This, of course, is a possibility that cannot *a priori* be excluded. But whether one or the other condition is violated depends partly on empirically contingent social, political, and economic factors, and partly on how migration is organized. The answer to the first question therefore is: "No, unless morally valid reasons speak against the recognition, or the exercise, of the liberty right."

The answer provokes a second question:

(2) "Do liberty rights of potential migrants carry more moral relevance or less moral relevance than equal liberty rights of other relevant parties, or *vice versa?*"

The answer, obviously, is "No". *All* individuals' interests should be granted equal moral relevance. "Equal moral relevance" does not imply that all interests have to be granted equal moral weight. But it implies that the justified interests of no representative group of persons can be cancelled out. If conflicts of justified interests occur, they have to settled "justly", i.e., by weighing and balancing, or by some form of impartial decision procedure, or by appeal to substantive requirements of justice of a higher value.

The specification of the relevant parties, however, is more difficult with respect to the second question than to the first, because now we have to consider not only individual persons in their roles as citizens and members of societies, but also societies conceived of as holistic entities.

Regardless of how we specify the relevant parties, a third question addressing possible counter-reasons is this:

(3) "Do individual liberty rights trump all other moral claims?"

The answer, again, is obviously "no". First, no moral principle is absolute, and, second, quite a few moral claims carry more moral weight than liberty rights. The validity of the moral force of any moral principle is always conditional on the assumption that no other moral consideration of equal or greater weight speaks against its application. If liberty rights structurally conflict with moral claims of equal or stronger weight, they either have to be modified or can be outweighed. This generally holds for all moral claims and principles. This conditionality, however, does not annihilate the moral force of a liberty right, or any other moral claim.

Once it is accepted that individuals ought to be granted the right to pursue justified interests, recognition of a *prima facie* individual liberty right to immigration is well-supported by normative argument. Three qualifications, however, ought to be mentioned: (i) *all* morally relevant persons, or parties, should be granted an equal right (equality condition); (ii) accordingly, no such right can be unrestricted, and its exercise must be regulated by ways and procedures that all relevant parties can accept (social compatibility condition); and (iii) finally, any further restrictions of the *prima facie* individual liberty right to immigration must be backed up by normative reasons of sufficient moral weight, which means that immigration cannot be denied for no reason or for morally arbitrary reasons.

It will next be necessary to explore the structure of standard types of likely practical conflicts raised by migration.

3.3. *The Competitive Nature of Current Migration Dynamics*

Taking it for granted that an individual liberty right to immigration must be recognized as a valid claim on the side of potential migrants, it seems worthwhile to explore the types of interpersonal practical conflicts that might occur. Obviously, such an enquiry depends essentially on empirically contingent circumstances, such as the number of migrants and the range of the destinations at which they aim, and the consequences which can be expected to follow.

An interesting – and in my opinion empirically adequate – observation has been made by Alexander Somek.[77] His argument starts from the premise that societies have a right to restrict migration by considerations concerning the preservation of the stability of society, which is a standard reservation in international law, and also morally and practically reasonable. The relevant point of Somek's argument, however, concerns the empirical conditions and consequences, i.e., the (unintended cumulative) effects that the recognition of an unrestricted claim right to immigration would have, not with respect to the *status quo* of potential host societies, but with respect to the normative status of potential migrants.

---

77 See Somek (1998).

In light of the empirically contingent fact that currently several million persons would like to live and work abroad, in combination with the fact that most voluntary migrants prefer to migrate to the USA, Canada, Australia, or a state of the European Union, plus the empirical assumption that host societies' capacity for successful social and economic integration of immigrants is limited, Somek concludes that a right to immigration could not be a claim right in Hohfeld's sense but, at best, a privilege accruing to those who consume it first while excluding latecomers.

Obviously, the argument strongly depends on the assumption that the current dynamics of mass migration will continue – an assumption that appears warranted at the time of this writing. Although empirical assumptions can change, they are conceptually important for the justification of individual rights, because individual rights must meet formal requirements of generalizability: they are supposed to apply *generally* to all persons who are in morally similar circumstances. In the present context: to all potential migrants alike.

One of those formal requirement is that, which Baier calls the requirement of "not being self-frustrating": if acknowledgment of a right to x would have the effect that right-holders' interests in x-ing were frustrated if the right were generally exercised, then such a consequence disqualifies x-ing from being acknowledged as a general norm.[78]

The interesting point in Somek's argument is the observation that a normative analysis of practical conflicts generated by dynamics of mass migration cannot focus exclusively on the positions of potential individual migrants *vis-à-vis* potential host societies, but also has to reflect the fact that groups of individual migrants also stand in competition with other groups of individual migrants.

In Somek's argument, the relevant groups are first-comers and late-comers. Somek, I think, rightly hints at the point that the timing of migration qualifies as morally arbitrary. Migrants, however, can also be grouped in accordance with other criteria, e.g., highly skilled versus unskilled migrants, economically powerful versus economically dependent migrants,

---

78 See Baier (1965). In practice, it might not always be feasible to treat first-comers and late-comers equally for pragmatic reasons. But the issue here concerns the question whether general conditions for the recognition of a claim right are met. There should, therefore, be at least a reasonable expectation that equal cases can be treated equally.

family members versus unaffiliated migrants. It is not evident that such criteria are less arbitrary from a moral point of view.[79]

Somek's argument makes clear both that assessments of the moral status of individual migrants cannot abstract from the consequences that a legal regulation has for different affected parties, and that one relevant consideration concerns potential competition among different groups of migrants. As it stands, however, his argument does not rule out the recognition of a *prima facie* individual liberty right to migration.

If we look at the consequences for potential host societies, it appears that they are mixed. As Claus Offe pointed out, several societies compete for certain groups of immigrants, e.g., immigrants with special skills or certain age-groups, while trying to block other groups of immigrants.[80]

It is also warranted to assume that host societies are not internally unified or homogeneous blocks, but are internally divided by conflicts of interests among co-citizens. It is well-known that citizens of host societies disagree about the desirability of immigration policies, because, *inter alia*, they affect their economic interests, political bargaining power und representation by unions, etc. Accordingly, we cannot take for granted that the interests of each citizen coincides with the interests of society as a whole. For that reason, we will have to differentiate between interests of individual citizens and interests of societies conceived of as collective entities.

Migration, however, affects not only (potential) host societies, but also societies of origin and their individual members. Consequences, such as brain drain and waste of investment in public education or professional training of co-citizens on the one hand, and, on the other, benefits of money remitted to family members in the country of origin and their distribution among residents in the country of origin can be morally relevant too.[81]

Accordingly, the additional relevant parties that have to be taken into account in assessments of the moral status of potential migrants are the following: (i) other (groups of) migrants, (ii) (potential) host societies, (iii) individual members of host societies, (iv) societies of origin, and (v) individual members of societies of origin. For reasons mentioned above, however, I will disregard (iv) and (v).

---

79 See chap. 6 for a more detailed discussion.
80 See Offe (2011).
81 See Brock/Blake (2015) and Brock (2016).

It will therefore be necessary to start with a re-assessment of the moral standing of the relevant parties, i.e., individual citizens, individual (potential) migrants, and societies conceived of as collective entities. This task will have to be completed in chapter 6. In the remainder of the present chapter, I will explore the probably most controversial aspect, philosophically, of the exposition of the moral challenge, i.e., the moral standing of societies and political associations conceived of as collective entities.

3.4. A Criticism of Normative Reductionism I: Ethical Individualism and the Moral Standing of Persons in Institutional Contexts

The principle of ethical individualism as stated in chapter 1 articulates a metaethical principle that guides assessments of the legitimacy and moral status of sociopolitical institutions. It is neither a method for the construction of those institutions, nor *per se* committed to a particular social ontology. Unfortunately, ethical individualism is often implicitly understood to imply a commitment to *methodological individualism*,[82] which articulates either a social ontology or an explanatory framework for the analysis of social macro-phenomena.

Roughly, methodological individualism maintains that the analysis of complex social phenomena has to be given in terms of the actions and dispositions of the individual persons whose activities are constitutive of those phenomena. The amalgamation of ethical and methodological individualism maintains that the normative structure of complex sociopolitical institutions must be explicated and justifiable in terms of the normative powers and competences – in the following for short: the moral standing – of the individual persons who participate in the institutional framework.

There is at least one straightforward reason why reductionism is unconvincing from a quasi-ontological point of view. The existence conditions of states and societies do not coincide with the existence conditions of the individuals who constitute them. The reason is that states and societies qualify as intergenerational entities whose diachronic continuity exceeds the lifespans of individual persons, and also the lifespans of the persons who represent the office of government, or even the very form of governmental regimes.

---

82 This holds especially for theorists who employ rational choice theory for the analysis of social macro-phenomena.

Nevertheless, recognition of states and societies as collective entities with a moral standing *sui generis* has been challenged by several individual-rights-based approaches in political philosophy which appeal to the principle of ethical individualism. In some cases, such arguments amalgamate ethical and methodological individualism by claiming that the moral status of individuals is normatively prior to the moral standing of collective entities. Certain individual rights, i.e., "natural rights" or "universal human rights", are assumed to be prior to sociopolitical institutions and to be the very source of the normative capacities and competences attributed to states, governments, or communities conceived of as holistic entities.[83]

Such arguments played an important role, e.g., in theories of justice inspired by social-contract theories, and especially in the construction of an original position for the specification of principles of global or international justice.

A paradigm case is the controversy between Rawls, on the one hand, and Beitz or Pogge,[84] on the other hand, about how to specify "representative persons" in the construction of a global original position. Whereas Rawls argued that representative persons in a global original position ought to be taken to be "peoples",[85] Beitz and Pogge argued that they ought to be taken to be individual persons. The point at stake concerns the question not so much what, but how, normative powers should be attributed to the different levels of institutional organization of statehood.

3.4.1. Methodological Individualism in Contractarian Theories of Global Justice

Let me start with a few purely analytical considerations. In international law and international relations, it is quite common to conceive of states and political associations ("peoples" in Rawls's terminology) as "col-

---

83 See, e.g., the controversy between Luban, Beitz, Walzer and others concerning the moral standing of states and the (non-)justifiability of foreign (humanitarian) intervention in Walzer (1977), Beitz (1979), Luban (1980), Walzer (1980), Beitz (2009a).

84 See Rawls (1993b), Beitz (1979/1999), Pogge (1989).

85 Rawls use the term "people" in a very broad sense, because he wants to avoid the term "state". In my terminology, Rawls's use of the term refers to what I call "political associations", because I would like to reserve the term "people" for a democratic electorate, i.e., as equivalent to "the *demos*" as in the principle of "popular" sovereignty.

lective agents" or "collective persons", who represent particular political associations *vis-à-vis* others at the level of international relations, and who bear a special moral or legal status, i.e., a moral status that is different from that of individual persons.[86] States and political associations are thus conceived of as holistic entities from the outside, i.e., from the perspective of international relations and international law.

Prima facie, it seems natural to suppose that the moral status of states in international relations and international law must be constituted either strictly bottom-up (from individual persons to institutions of statehood and thence to international relations) or strictly top-down (from the guarantee of external sovereignty in international law to statehood to the legal status of citizens).[87] Traditionally, contractarian theories tend to conceive of states and political associations – figuratively – as constituted bottom-up, which suggests that it makes sense to conceive of international relations and international law likewise.

Secunda facie, it is obvious that neither the top-down nor the bottom-up scenario makes any sense, because the idea of a linear direction of constitution is unreasonable if taken literally. From the perspective of a practice account, it is evident that we cannot conceive of the moral status of "citizens" as something outside of, or detached from, the background rules for the institutional organization of political associations. In the same sense, it does not make sense to think of the moral status of states outside of, or detached from, the international order of statehood. The relevant norms and institutions are interlinked. The legal institution of individual rights cannot be conceived of as separate from the institution of the legal state.[88] Likewise, the very concept of statehood cannot be separated from the idea that the world is organized in plurality of distinct "sovereign" states.

This interlinkage of "normative levels" (so to speak) is most obvious with respect to the moral standing of individuals *vis-à-vis* domestic institutions, which is the traditional level of social contract theories. As far as concerns the civil, legal, and political status of individual citizens, it does not make sense to think of that status as being given by nature or as being

---

86 Although it is no longer the case that exclusively states are recognized as legal subjects in international law, it still is a standard assumption in international law that states (represented by governments) are paradigm authors, subjects and addressees of international law.

87 A top-down-view appears to have been defended by Kelsen in some of this works on international law; see Langford/Bryan (2012), and Langford/Bryan (2019).

88 See, e.g., Hart (1955) or Feinberg (1970).

determined by some inherent properties of human beings – at least if one subscribes to ethical individualism and institutional conventionalism. The normative standing of citizens is inseparably interlinked with the existence of sociopolitical institutions – which is to say that there is no state of nature that serves as a starting point for the constitution of institutions. As Rawls rightly maintains, the rights and liberties defined by the first principle of justice in his *Theory of Justice* are not natural rights in a Lockean sense, but are tied to the institutional framework of political associations.

From the perspective of ethical liberalism, it would indeed be self-contradictory to conceive of human rights, or any other class of individual rights, as "natural" (or God-given) rights à la Locke.[89] One of the most important contributions of ordinary language philosophy to practical philosophy is the insight that the analysis of legal concepts has to be undertaken against the background of the relevant rule-guided social practices – be it the constitutions of political associations, or international law. From the perspective of a practice account, it makes no sense to conceive of the normative status of individuals as detached – figuratively speaking as "prior to" or "outside of" – those institutional background institutions.[90]

It might be objected that ordinary-language style of analysis is too conservative and preserves the current normative *status quo*. Such an objection, however, misses the point. Ordinary language philosophy is not a normative position, but rather a method of conceptual analysis. It neither forestalls nor excludes normative criticism of the *status quo*. It simply reminds us that the metaphor of a social contract is a metaphor, not a step-by-step-guide for the construction of political and legal institutions – at whatever level of institutional organization.

Similarly, if we conceive of the normative standing of states within the institutional system of international relations and international law, we cannot detach internal and external aspects of state sovereignty from each other. Specifications of the normative status of states in international law, such as, e.g., the institution of external sovereignty, describe normative features that derive neither from the domestic aspects of statehood, nor from an inter-state agreement, but are part of the essence of *statehood* in contrast to, e.g., the idea of an empire. When we speak of statehood, we presuppose that there exists a plurality of politically independent states. The concep-

---

89 See Locke (1690).
90 See Chwaszcza (2011a) for an analysis of human rights as standards of legitimacy for sociopolitical institutions and the claim that their function resembles that of what Hart calls the rule of recognition.

tions of internal and external sovereignty are mutually interlinked, and are reinforced by the secondary rule that the only legitimate sources of international law are inter-state treaties or customary state practices. The organization of political associations in distinct and separate states – as it developed after the Westphalian peace – is as much an implication of the institution of statehood as the various models of the legal state, democratic state, etc.

To make a long argument short: the different institutional layers and the normative powers and competences attributed to them are inextricably interlinked; they form not a linear sequence of hierarchically ordered layers, but rather a net of interrelated normative institutions, which are in part mutually constitutive for each other.[91]

Methodological considerations concerning the *analysis* of sociopolitical institutions do not exclude the possibility of criticizing even constitutive principles of the current *status quo* of that order, including the substantive content of the legal status of external sovereignty. It should be evident, however, that the different institutional layers are interrelated. One of the challenges is to make sure that normative criticisms addressed to different layers, in the end, will amount to a coherent normative whole.

Given the interrelatedness of the moral standing of individual persons and the determination of the moral standing of states as subjects of international law, it is no coincidence that "contractarian" frameworks for the justification of requirements of international justice were largely superseded by frameworks based on philosophical theories of human rights. In light of the enormous expansion of human rights regimes in international law in the second half of the 20th century, political philosophers could no longer work around the concept of human rights, or discard it by identifying it with (pre-enlightenment) natural law theory. Hardly surprisingly,

---

91 A similar objection actually applies to *explanatory* versions of methodological individualism, which are common in the rational-choice-inspired analyses of the conventional nature of social institutions and socially shared rules. The specification of the actions and dispositions of the agents, which are considered to be constitutive for the existence and functioning of complex social institutions, cannot be specified without reference to the rules, functions and purposes of those institutions. Again, it is entirely reasonable to ask whether those rules, functions and purposes are justified from a normative point of view, and also whether the persons who represent those offices and positions of the relevant institutions are playing by the rules or abusing their powers and competences. But it does not make sense to try to specify agency embedded in institutional contexts, e.g., "legislating", without reference to those contexts.

Pogge and Beitz were among the first theorists who replaced contractarian metaphors with appeals to the idea of human rights.[92] Unfortunately, the idea of human rights is itself highly contested among political philosophers. From the perspective of a practice account, however, an analysis of the concept of human rights as "pre-institutional" or "extra-institutional" is highly problematic, because it fails to reflect the understanding of the concept of human rights in historical documents, as well as in the praxis of constitutional law and international law and the normative discourse about them.[93]

I conclude that ethical individualism is best understood not as a guideline for the construction of normative powers and competences, but as a metaethical principle for the assessment of the normative status of individual persons as members and participants in sociopolitical institutions.

---

92 See Pogge (2002), Beitz (2009b). From the perspective of a practice account, conceptual analysis should at least start with an examination of the use of the concept of human rights in practice, i.e., in historical documents and the contemporary practice of international law. Such an examination immediately reveals that the substance of "human rights" overwhelmingly concerns civil and political rights, and social, economic and cultural rights, which define the normative status of individual persons *in* sociopolitical and legal institutions, and thus cannot be detached from those institutions. It is, accordingly, much more convincing to interpret the special role of human rights, following Beitz (2009b), as protections of individual persons from threats that they standardly face in sociopolitical institutions, or, following Chwaszcza (2010), as secondary rules that articulate formal and morally substantive standards of legitimacy for sociopolitical and legal institutions. Pogge's suggestion, that we should conceive of human rights as universal rights to morally best institutions, appeals explicitly to the letter of the *Universal Declaration of Human Rights* (Pogge 2002).

93 The most common alternative to a practice-based analysis is an analysis of the concept "human rights" as "rights that persons hold *qua* being human". Two prominent defenders of such a style of analysis are Griffin (2008) and Miller (2007). According to Griffin, the concept of human rights is best interpreted as deriving from a universal property of human beings, "personhood". Human rights are supposed to apply to concerns that are different and separate from issues of sociopolitical justice. A similar distinction between the concepts of sociopolitical justice and the idea of human rights is defended by Miller. Unlike Griffin, however, Miller suggest that human rights serve the function of (exclusively) protecting basic human needs. Both proposals defend a minimalistic account of human rights, and maintain that normative requirements which correspond to human rights are entirely different from requirements of social justice.

3.4.2. Ethical Individualism and the Holistic Nature of Social Institutions

The principle of ethical individualism *per se* entails no commitment to normative reductionism. As I will argue in the present subsection, ethical individualism is not only fully compatible with the recognition of a *sui generis* moral standing of collective entities, such as states and societies (political associations), but actually provides one of the strongest reasons for such a view. The argument is well-known, but its implications are not always sufficiently appreciated in discussions of post-national political philosophy: political government is a normative *institution* – at least according to ethical individualism. One of the main powers of political government is the *right* to issue generally binding laws. No natural person has such a right. Legislative rights are assigned to offices and positions, not to persons.

The artificial nature of legislative powers is one of the aspects that marks the difference between political government and the exercise of mere force or coercion. The powers and competences which are constitutive for political government, and also the procedures for their assignment and their exercise, are constituted and specified by (normative) background rules that also define the relevant institution. It follows that there is no legitimate form of government outside institutional settings and rule-based practices.

According to ethical individualism, the relevant background rules qualify as legitimate to the extent that they can be justified by general and impartial reasons. Since ethical individualism maintains that all persons have an equal moral status, there are no reasons that could possibly justify why one particular person, or any particular group of persons, should be granted the right to rule over others due to their moral status. Accordingly, liberal conceptions of political government reject the idea of government as the rule of *persons* over other persons. Government qualifies as an *impersonal* institution, i.e., a system of offices and positions with special normative competences and responsibilities. True, offices and positions have to be represented by persons who were appointed to them, but those persons hold and exercise the relevant powers only in their role as representatives of the relevant offices.

The transfer of political powers and competences to institutions, in my view, is an *essential* aspect of the normative *raison d'être* of the concept of popular sovereignty, because no person – conceived of as a natural person

– "deserves" a right to govern over others.[94] The idea that sovereignty is assigned to a natural person (called Rex I, Rex II,...) has been devastatingly criticized by Hart.[95] Nevertheless, it might be worthwhile to recall that the very same arguments apply to the complex institutional arrangements, which are common in systems of representative democratic government. Parliament, obviously, is an institution. Less obviously, also, "the people", to which the principle of popular sovereignty refers, is not simply a multitude of individual persons, but a political institution – as some want to say: a legal fiction – which stands for the totality of all those persons who have the normative status of democratic citizenship and bear active and passive political rights.[96] "The people", as I will use the term, is equivalent to "the *demos*", not identical with "the population" or even Rawls's use of the terms "peoples", which includes non-democratic political associations.

Given the normative nature of the *right* to political government, ethical individualism provides us with very strong normative reasons for opposing the idea of normative reductionism. The principle of popular sovereignty can only be exercised collectively. Also the power of jurisdiction is standardly assigned to collective agents, as can be seen, e.g., in the naming convention of criminal matters in US courts: "the State of Maryland versus John Doe."[97]

The principle of ethical individualism, accordingly, has explicitly anti-reductionist implications. Its metaethical point manifests itself in the requirement that the background system of rules that specifies the relevant powers and their exercise, as well as the offices and position to which they are assigned, meet certain standards of normative justification. It does not rule out, however, that the powers and competences assigned to sociopolitical institutions have a *sui-generis* quality that makes them irreducible to the normative status of the individual persons who constitute them.

---

94 For a recent defense of the idea that no natural person has the right to govern or rule any other persons, see also Kolodny (2014) or Viehoff (2017). My own argument, however, differs from theirs insofar as I emphasize the institutional nature of normative powers.

95 See Hart (1961/1997).

96 See Chwaszcza (2011b).

97 In German courts the pronouncement of judgments always begins "Im Namen des Volkes,...", which would best be translated as "In the name of the people...".

3.4.3. The Idea of Government by Authorization: A Non-voluntaristic Interpretation

The general idea of the principle of ethical individualism is often identified with the claim that the right to political government has to be based on "authorization" – as, e.g., in the metaphor of a social contract. It is important to keep in mind, however, that the metaphor is nothing but a metaphor. It is just another way of saying that political government is a normative institution that is legitimate only if it is backed up by the right sort of normative background rules, i.e., rules that can be justified by impartial reasons to citizens.

How then should we interpret the idea of "government by authorization" if normative reductionism is rejected and if voluntaristic accounts of normative justification are ruled out? The most reasonable suggestion, in my view, is that we identify the idea of government by authorization with certain morally substantive requirements that constrain the legitimate scope and exercise of political government. These include a) substantive requirements concerning secondary rules – most importantly, a commitment to democratic forms of government and the rule of law – and b) the recognition of the institution of individual (constitutional) rights.

True, the substantive content of individual rights, and their range and constitutional function, are contested among liberal, republican, communitarian, and libertarian theorists. Moreover, implementations of democratic forms of government are normatively underdetermined. But the claim that the idea of government by authorization manifests itself in substantive normative requirements, which constrain the normative validity of primary and secondary rules (as one might say following Hart), or in the substantive contents of principles for the arrangement of the basic structure (as one might say following Rawls), is far from new, and is theoretically more convincing than either voluntarism or normative reductionism.[98]

---

98 The general criticism of voluntaristic ideals of normative justification is supported by considerations concerning the normative limitations of actual consent. If it happens – as history informs us, it can be the case – that "the people" agree to replace the principle of popular sovereignty with a principle that requires obedience to a leader, the new regime does no longer qualify as "government by authorization", even if the new regime were unanimously consented to by citizens and office-holders.

3.4.4. A First Interim Conclusion

To sum up: the metaethical principle of ethical individualism does not require that the moral status of collective agents, such as states and societies, must be identical with, or reducible to, the moral status of individual persons. It does require that the institutional organization of the normative powers, competences, and purposes of political government meet certain substantive moral provisions that protect the moral status of individual citizens, including the institution of individual (human or constitutional) rights. From the perspective of ethical individualism, it must also be accepted that external aspects of the normative standing of political associations must be justifiable by impartial reasons to non-members, in their roles as (potential) migrants, as well as members of distinct and separate political associations.

In the context of discussions concerning citizenship and migration, which analytically presuppose the existence of a plurality of states and societies, recognition of the holistic nature of the institutions of states and societies implies that states and societies must be granted a normative status that is – at least to some extent – *sui generis* and different from the normative status of individual persons. I thus conclude that not only individual persons – be they citizens or migrants –, but also political associations – conceived of as collective entities – must be acknowledged as morally relevant parties of practical conflicts with a normative standing of their own.

The next subsection will address another line of criticism of the holistic nature of states and political associations, i.e., criticisms of the idea that political associations generate particularistic requirements of sociopolitical justice. Probably the most famous argument is Goodin's denial that the normative relations that hold among co-citizens – "fellow countrymen" – are special, because political association is just a means for the implementation of universal requirements of justice.[99]

3.5. A Criticism of Normative Reductionism II: How to Reconcile Universalistic and Particularistic Conceptions of Justice

Goodin's rejection of particularistic conceptions of sociopolitical justice is, in my view, another example for the general neglect of the relevance

---

99 See Goodin (1988).

of political agency in theories of sociopolitical justice. As I will argue, universal and particularistic conceptions of sociopolitical justice are not mutually exclusive, but mutually supplementary. The theoretical challenge will be to show how the two can be coherently thought together, once the normative relevance of political agency is acknowledged, and to specify the moral implication that follow from the acknowledgment of particularistic spheres of justice for issues concerning citizenship and migration.

Goodin's argument combines a consequentialist account of moral reasoning with the claim that requirements of justice are universal. Originally, the argument appears to have been opposed to Rawls's account of justice as fairness, which explicitly restricts social justice to the domestic sphere by construing it as special normative relations that hold among the members of closed and autarchic political associations.[100] It applies equally, however, to other strictly domestic conceptions of sociopolitical justice, such as, e.g., Miller's liberal nationalism, which I will discuss in more detail in chapter 4.[101] To the extent that the controversy is not merely a verbal dispute, Goodin's characterization of the normative relations that hold among co-citizens is highly relevant also for normative theories of democracy.

3.5.1. Goodin's Argument against Moral Particularism

For Goodin, requirements of sociopolitical justice are universal requirements that have to be acknowledged to be internationally or globally valid. The main purpose of statehood, according to Goodin, is a purely pragmatic one: states are administrative units that facilitate the implementation of universal requirements of justice. The present organization of the world into distinct and particular states is nothing but a "division of moral labor" with the aim of optimizing state-based protection of universal moral rights of individuals.

In political reality, obviously, not all states live up to Goodin's demand, and few would share his aspirations of universal justice. Goodin's appeal to

---

100 In this respect Goodin appears to side with Barry (1995).

101 Neither Rawls nor Miller deny that international relations ought to be guided by normative principles, and both acknowledge the institution of universal human rights in a minimalistic sense, but both argue that questions of international justice raise issues quite different from those of domestic sociopolitical justice. – See Rawls (1999) and Miller (2007).

universal requirements of justice, however, does not justify the stipulation that relations among fellow countrymen may not also manifest special moral relations, over and above the universal normative relations that anyone has with regard to non-compatriot human beings from a moral point of view. The moral relations among citizens cannot be reduced to considerations concerning the pragmatic efficiency for the realization of universal requirements of justice because, from a liberal point of view, co-citizenship has a normative purpose or value in and of itself.

Similar to Carens' cosmopolitan account of justice, Goodin's defense of moral universalism is pure consequentialism. By taking a purely instrumental – or technocratic – attitude towards state institutions, he loses sight of the fact that the *modus operandi* of governmental activities, i.e., political agency, generates *sui generis* spheres of justice in and by itself of a genuinely particularistic sort. Goodin's argument in a curious way eliminates politics from political philosophy.

It might be worthwhile to recall in advance that the particularistic nature of political-agency-based requirements of justice derives from the *exercise* of political agency. As such, political-agency-based requirements are not restricted to domestic spheres of political agency, because political agency can also be exercised at the international level, in which case it generates particularistic spheres of international justice. I thus maintain that political agency *generates* special normative relations among the relevant participants, because its exercise generates particular normative relations.

3.5.2. Political Philosophy without Politics? – A Criticism of Goodin

Goodin is, no doubt, not the first philosopher who conceives of political agency as an exercise in "applied" moral philosophy. His argument, however, suffers from its strictly consequentialist focus. He appears to conceive of political agency merely as an instrument for the implementation of moral demands, not as an activity, which is itself based on and inherently regulated by moral requirements. His perspective on government activities is strictly outcome-oriented – which, in my view, coheres with his defense of an epistemic theory of democracy that attributes a primarily instrumental value to democratic procedures and deliberation.[102] His argument thus recalls the utilitarian ideal of technocratic government – with the notable

---

102 See, e.g., Goodin (2003), Goodin/Spiekermann (2018), and List/Goodin (2001).

difference that Goodin is interested in the optimization of justice rather than utility.

Nevertheless, state governments are not bureaus of technocratic master-calculators of justice, and state citizens are not passive recipients of weekly or monthly doses of justice treatments. Even if we accept the premise that the facilitation of conditions of justice is indeed one of the primary (though not exclusive) purposes of state institutions, it is evident (i) that the implementation of requirements of justice is not fully determined by *universal* norms, (ii) that universal requirements can conflict in practice, and (iii) that the legitimacy of the ways and means by which requirements of justice are implemented and executed, are rarely determined by universal *principles* of justice either.

If political decisions are underdetermined by universal principles of justice, Goodin's argument is deficient in at least two respects: (1) it downplays requirements of input legitimacy; and (2) it ignores requirements concerning the fair distribution of the benefits and burdens of governmental activities and their long-term consequences among participants. From a democratic point of view, Goodin's argument might satisfy a conception of government for the people, but not conceptions of government of the people and by the people.

A purely instrumental view of political agency is unsatisfying also from a transnational perspective. Given the fact that social and economic environments continue to be largely shaped by political decisions, and that domestic institutions continue to be a primary sphere for the exercise of political agency, political agency should not be treated as a black box. It continues to have a huge impact on the socioeconomic, political and sociocultural practices that constitute the social environment of particular societies, and on the distribution of social opportunities to the persons who (inter-)act in those environments.

Requirements of justice that derive from political agency are particularistic – in contrast to universal – because collective political agency is restricted to authorized participants – at the level of democratic societies: to the members of *demos*. As long as societies continue to constitute particularistic spheres of political agency,[103] relations among co-citizens will be to some extent special, and political agency will generate particularistic requirements of justice.

---

103 Chap. 5 will address issues concerning transnational democracy.

3.5.3. Political Agency as a *sui generis* Source of Sociopolitical Justice: A Defense

Why should we recognize that political agency constitutes a *sui generis* source of requirements of sociopolitical justice that is different from, and irreducible to, the abstract norms and universal principles of justice that determine the legitimacy of the basic structure of societies? The main reason is that universal principles do not determine political measures and means. Political agency cannot be reduced to "applied" justice, for several reasons that are well-known but are worth repeating.

(1) Universal moral requirements of justice rarely determine either the items on the political agenda or the policies, i.e., the political means and measures for their implementation. This is due not only to empirically contingent differences in circumstances and options, but also to empirically contingent past choices and decisions. Given the empirically contingent nature of the circumstances and measures of political agency, it is reasonable to assume that different (groups of) citizens will be differently affected by different policies, and that their interests will diverge with respect to (i) the topics on the political agenda, (ii) the ranking of those topics, and (iii) the desirability of particular measures and means. In short, political agency is a source of practical disagreement and conflicts of interest among citizens.

(2) It is evident that in modern pluralistic democratic societies, those practical conflicts among citizens are not restricted to conflicts of interests, but also include disagreements about the substantive content of requirements of justice.[104] Even if we assume that there are at least some universal principles which are uncontested, it is evident that those principles do not determine measures and means of their pursuit in practice; universal principles also do not determine normative judgments in cases where principles have to be weighed and balanced, or where their implementation consumes scarce resources, and conflicts with the implementation of other aims. Generally, if the principle of normative self-determination is accepted, normative pluralism is not merely a *fact*, as Rawls maintains, but a normative entitlement, because individuals have the *right* to disagree on normative issues.

---

104 Normative disagreement is also highlighted by Christiano (2008b) and Estlund (2008), among others.

Taken together, the under-determination of political choices by universal requirements of justice and the right to normative disagreement both have serious implications for the mechanisms that qualify as legitimate for determining the political agenda of governments and state institutions. They reveal that in many cases recourse to uncontested substantive normative standards is not a viable option. The legitimacy of collective political choice in these cases must be generated through non-substantive standards of legitimacy, such as mechanisms of pure procedural justice, the single most important of which is the *practice* of democratic forms of government.[105]

For this reason, conditions of political legitimacy can be neither replaced by, nor reduced to, purely consequentialist conceptions of output legitimacy.

A third reason that applies not only to Goodin but also to ideal-theory accounts of international or cosmopolitan justice inspired by Rawls, is the following:

(3) Real world political agents rarely resemble Rawls's abstract concept of moral persons as being endowed with a sense of justice and willing to voluntarily comply with requirements of justice. Real-world political agents often pursue partisan aims, are corrupt, or prioritize personal interests. For this reasons, Rawls's focus on requirements for the basic structure of society is too narrow a concept of sociopolitical justice. It certainly articulates an important part of sociopolitical justice, but it cannot be accepted as exhaustive, because conflicts of interests do not stop at a constitutional moment. A theory of justice for the real world should allow us to address conflicts and problems that arise in the practice and exercise of political agency.[106]

---

105 For obvious reasons, the demarcation of substantive from procedural mechanisms of legitimacy is also crucial in debates for and against constitutionalism, such as the controversy between Dworkin (1987) and Waldron (1999). Here, however, I focus exclusively on the practical underdetermindedness of requirements of justice.

106 The reason why considerations concerning the normative relevance of political agency are widely ignored in contemporary political philosophy appear to me to derive from the focus on the justification of individual rights in Rawls (1971) and Dworkin (1977).

3.5.4. A Second Interim Conclusion

Returning to the discussion of citizenship and migration, the criticism of Goodin's version of a purely consequentialist account of global justice reveals once more why the theoretical and normative relevance of political agency should not be ignored or eliminated. In a world organized in distinct and separate societies, which constitute – at least partially – distinct and separate spheres of political agency, assessments of the normative status of potential migrants and citizens cannot entirely abstract from political-agency-based factors of the *status quo* in societies of origin and host societies.

3.6. *The Moral Standing of Societies*

Once political agency is recognized as a normative sphere of activities in its own right, the normative value of political associations and societies as spaces for collective political agency becomes evident. As long as it is reasonable to assume that societies continue to be primary and irreplaceable spaces for (democratic) political agency, they ought to be acknowledged as spheres of genuinely particularistic requirements of sociopolitical justice in addition to universal requirements of justice or requirements concerning the justice of the basic structure (even if their basic structure qualifies as fully just). We can now address questions concerning the value of societies, or rather of membership in particular societies.

3.6.1. Societies as Spaces of Political Agency

Politics is the human form of organizing social life. In modern societies, there is hardly any sphere of socioeconomic, political, and cultural agency that is not regulated by political legislation to some extent. Although it is true that many political decisions are now internationally coordinated, national political institutions continue to play a significant role, even within a supranational organization, such as the European Union.

Not all political decisions, of course, raise issues of justice. Many are meant to facilitate coordination and cooperation in a much broader sense, or to promote social goods and prevent social harms of a non-moral sort. But many do raise issues of justice. Tax laws and investments in infrastructure, education, and social security systems are obvious examples.

Since political agency is usually transformed into legal regulations, collective political decisions tend to have long-term, often intergenerational, consequences.[107] Political agency thus has a genuinely diachronic social dimension. It sets collective parameters and regulations that serve collective social projects, and apply generally to all present – or even future – members of the society.

Given the inclusive and diachronically continuous relevance of politics, the practice of politics requires some degree of stability with respect to the composition of societies. This is not only a pragmatic matter of planning, but also a question of fairness, because individuals cannot be asked to bear the burdens of long-term investments, unless these individuals can reasonably expect that sufficiently many others will bear them as well. In addition, long term investments and intergenerational policies work on the assumption that the individuals who participate in the early stages are either identical with, or socially connected to, those persons who are affected by the relevant decisions in the later stages. I assume that it would be not only pragmatically difficult in the long run to require citizens to bear burdens for the advantage of others, but also unfair, unless they are in a position to institutionally identify and restrict the range of persons who are supposed to benefit from their contributions to collective investments and policies.[108] Chapter 5 will add additional reasons, by arguing that the practice of democracy also requires a certain degree of stability and intergenerational continuity of the *demos*.

As far as issues of citizenship and migration are concerned, it has to be conceded that rules of citizenship assignment play an important role in the facilitation of the diachronic continuity and stability of societies, conceived of as spaces of political agency.

Whatever further political relations exist beyond the level of the nation state, political agency in particularistic political associations continues to play a crucial role in the organization of interpersonal socioeconomic and cultural activities and exchange. Although the conditions and preconditions for the exercise of political agency are not exclusively tied to the institution of statehood, but would be required in any other form of organization too, statehood is the one form of organization that presently prevails. I do not detect any signs of an imminent overhaul or its disap-

---

107 Legal stability (*Rechtssicherheit*) is often considered to be not only desirable but obligatory.

108 Libertarian theorists might object to the above picture on moral grounds, but very few societies endorse libertarian principles.

pearance. Quite the contrary, the number of persons who want to emigrate from failed and collapsing states proves that the institution of statehood is far from obsolete.

Although transnational phenomena of migration obviously challenge traditional conceptions of citizenship, they neither challenge statehood nor do they replace the general institutional organization of the world in a plurality of distinct and separate states and societies. The function of the institution of society as a space for political agency therefore continues to be theoretically and normatively relevant. The challenge that transnational phenomena of migration pose for political philosophy concern primarily traditional conceptions of citizenship and of the unity of society. Perhaps the social transformations that trigger migration can become so significant that the system of statehood will collapse. At that point, however, issues of migration *as we now know them and want to address them* will be eliminated as well.

Accordingly, Goodin's question "What is so special about our fellow countrymen?" has an unspectacular answer: they qualify as primary political associates. The answer, obviously, is trivial, but not therefore false.

Not trivial is the claim that this is all that normative particularism is about. At this point, I can only state the claim, because its argumentative defense must also show why two non-Rawlsian defenses of normative particularism, such as Miller's liberal nationalism and Blake's argument from coercion, are unconvincing.

3.6.2. Societies as Bearers of a Right to Collective Self-determination

As long as political associations are organized in distinct and separate states, ethical individualism, in combination with the principle of normative self-determination, strongly supports the claim that societies ought to be granted a right to collective self-determination. Although there is no logical inference that leads from respect for a right of individual normative self-determination to a collective right of political self-determination, there is a strong argument in support of the claim that (members of) political associations ought to be granted a right to non-interference in their domestic affairs, as long as they – or the relevant governments – abstain from severe violations of universal principles of justice and human rights.[109] Starting from the inter-state dimension of collective self-determination, I take it for granted that the principle of ethical individualism requires prohibiting aggression, colonialization, normative imperialism, and (morally unjustified) intervention in internal affairs.

The intra-state dimension of the right to collective self-determination is more contested. Theorists who subscribe to the principle of ethical individualism *and* the individual right to normative self-determination will strongly defend *democratic* interpretations of collective self-determination. Culturalist theorists and theorists who subscribe to metaethical relativism, by contrast, will require that peoples or cultures be granted the right to choose a form of government in accordance with their socially shared values, whether it is democratic or not. Since questions concerning democratic citizenship arise only in liberal democratic societies, I will restrict the discussion of democratic inclusion and exclusion to liberal societies. Otherwise, I will assume that not all societies are liberal-democratic, and that not all individual migrants share liberal ideals, because those assumptions reflect the transnational nature of migration in a political reality organized in a plurality of distinct and separate states invested with the right to collective self-determination.

To conceive of statehood as the currently prevailing institutional form for the organization of political associations, and of societies as spaces for political agency, is entirely different from accounts that attribute the normative value of societies to the reproduction of shared cultural values, national solidarity, or orientations towards the common good.[110] The thesis presented here focuses on the role and function of societies as spaces of political agency. It also stops there.

3.6.3. Societies as Addressees of Collective Responsibility

As already indicated in chapter 2, the normative implications of collective political agency are ambiguous. Political agency can be a successful instrument for the production of social opportunities and social justice as much

---

109 Exceptions concern the moral permissibility of so-called humanitarian intervention, which are not relevant to the discussion of issues concerning voluntary migration and citizenship.

110 For reasons to be presented in chaps. 4 and 10, I disagree with basic assumptions of such approaches.

as an obstacle to their promotion. This is one of the reasons why persons ought not to be forced to remain in their country of origin and be granted a *prima facie* liberty right to cross-border migration.

As emphasized before, the normative relevance of politics is accordingly double-sided. It can generate particularistic spheres of justice, as well as injustice, or simply dysfunctional government. There is ample evidence collected by social scientists and economists that conditions of justice depend not only on the design of the basic structure of state institutions, but also on past and present political agency, and social conditions for the implementation of policies, such as the presence or absence of civic trust, administrative efficiency, degrees of corruption and honesty, the presence or absence of violent intrastate conflicts, etc.

Since social practices and institutions are neither naturally given nor unchangeable, societies bear some responsibility for the social and political *status quo* of their society. It is obvious that no citizen *qua* individual person can be held responsible for the sociopolitical *status quo* of any society. But in light of the empirical evidence, it would be absurd to maintain that shared sociopolitical practices, governmental policies and decisions, and their administrative implementations have no impact at all on the sociopolitical *status quo*. It is therefore reasonable to maintain that neither a satisfying nor an unsatisfying *status quo* qualifies as a moral hazard, similar to a natural disaster, that does not raise questions concerning the responsibility for either its occurrence or its remedy.

Accordingly, the other side of the coin of granting societies a right to collective political self-determination is that societies must also be collectively held responsible for how they exercise this right, within the range of feasible choices open to them. Even if no person can individually be held responsible for the *status quo*, citizens should be held collectively responsible for the *status quo* of their society, at least to some degree, *qua* institutional membership.[111] Citizens are not random groups of persons, or unconnected passers-by, but are participants in an institution who must be expected to support the just purposes of the institution within the limits of their means and options. As difficult as it may be to organize collective protests or to counteract wide-spread corruption, I find it difficult

---

111 Dysfunctional social practices, unfortunately, can be hard to change, even if their dysfunctionality is publicly recognized – see, e.g., Angelos (2015) or Bicchieri (2017). But such practical difficulties do not nullify moral responsibilities for improvement. Who else should be authorized to change dysfunctional social practices if not the participants themselves?

to deny that citizens have a civic duty to support justice and to prevent injustice, if they can do so without moral sacrifice.

It might well be justifiable to assume that the collective sociopolitical responsibility of citizens for the sociopolitical *status quo* of their societies of origin is stronger in democratic societies and weaker in non-democratic or autocratic societies. But it cannot be taken to be entirely absent in the latter case either, except perhaps in the most repressive versions of dictatorship. Alternative views would have to defend one form or another of fatalism, or a strong belief in the irresistible powers of economic forces, historical laws, or a similar view. All societies therefore ought to be held to some extent responsible for their form of government and the social conditions that prevail.

3.6.4. A Third Interim Conclusion

In light of the fact that adherence to liberal principles of justice appears to be an exception in current political reality, and in light of the fact that only a minority of societies endorses and practices liberal-democratic ideals of political government, purely consequentialist accounts of global or cosmopolitan justice, such as Carens' or Goodin's, are unreasonably idealistic. Purely consequentialist arguments ignore the theoretical and normative relevance of political agency in the real world. Their focus on (ideal) outcomes pays too little attention to the means for achieving those outcomes, and the consequences that follow from them in the non-abstract, non-ideal real world. Not only is it the case that quite a few societies explicitly reject liberal ideas of justice – which, actually, is one of the reasons that drives voluntary migration –, but even if they would endorse them, it would still be necessary to address particularistic requirements of justice related to political agency and the practice of democracy.

3.7. Summing up: Transnational Justice and Normative Assessments of Rules of Inclusion and Exclusion

What are the implications of the above considerations for the justification of rules of inclusion and exclusion?

As argued above, in light of political reality it would be normatively unacceptable to force individual persons to stay and remain in their country of origin. Assuming throughout that (potential) migrants are motivated by morally justifiable interests, a commitment to philosophical liberalism demands recognition of a *prima facie* individual liberty right to migration. As I have argued, this does not imply that the justified interests of (potential) migrants are the sole morally relevant considerations. But it implies that recognition of a *prima facie* liberty right to migration articulates a requirement of *transnational (sociopolitical) justice*.

The crux of the argument, as indicated above, consists in specifying what additional considerations are morally relevant, and how – or under what conditions – those further considerations can justify exclusion. Within the larger framework of a rule-based account of citizenship, such questions concern (i) the general legitimacy of sets of rules of inclusion and exclusion, and (ii) questions concerning the assignment of the authority to select particular combinations of rules out of the larger set of morally permissible options.

Ad (i): In light of a rule-based account of citizenship as outlined in chapter 2, no person *qua* individual has a right to choose his or her citizenship. In this respect, citizens are not in a different position from migrants: their inclusion is regulated by general rules alike.

These rules must, on the one hand, coherently fit within the larger set of background rules that determine the relevant institutions and the relations between them, and they must be justifiable by general and impartial reasons to all affected persons. If we assume that inter- and transnational institutions must be justifiable to all persons who are affected by them as individuals from a transnational point of view – i.e., in their role either as potential migrants, or as non-migrating members of societies of origin, or as resident members of potential host societies – it seems reasonable to assume that the additional morally relevant considerations must reflect the perspectives of all relevant agents and roles: individuals in their roles as citizens and migrants, and societies as collective entities and particularistic spaces of political agency.

Ad (ii): General and impartial moral constraints, however, will not determine one unique set or combination of rules of inclusion and exclusion. It is reasonable that they will outline a range of permissible options for different conditions. That raises the question, who should be authorized to select a particular combination out of the larger range of permissible options. Within the framework of a practice account, this question comes down to the following: "To which institutional position should the authority be assigned to determine the final set of rules of inclusion and exclusion?"

As political authority is best conceived of as an element of the right to collective self-determination (within normative constraints), it is reasonable to argue that the authority is best assigned to societies conceived of as collective entities. The presently dominant opinion in international law and political philosophy is that the authority is an element of the institution of external sovereignty, and thus is to be assigned to the executive branch of government, which is usually considered to represent states conceived of as subjects of international law. From the normative perspective of ethical individualism, however, the right to collective self-determination implies a commitment to the principle of popular sovereignty. In democratic societies, therefore, the authority ought to be assigned to the legislative branch of government. In light of the fact that only a minority of states currently qualifies as liberal-democratic, it should be conceded that authority for selecting rules of inclusion and exclusion can be assigned to the executive branch in non-liberal states. In democratic societies, however, it *ought* to be assigned to the legislative branch.

The general outline of the crucial elements of a *transnational* account for normative assessments of issues concerning citizenship and migration have now been set out. The last section of this chapter will address a likely objection to normative particularism from an *inter-* as opposed to a *transnational* perspective.

3.8. Beyond the Model of the Nation State: Internationalism or Transnationalism?

Does the transnational perspective proposed above ignore the realities of international relations and institutions? I do not think so. All international regimes are still treaty-based, and the right to collective self-determination continues to articulate a basic norm of the entire system. The elimination of that principle would surrender a basic principle of the current system of international law. My proposal is fully compatible with the option of treaty-based international and supranational coordination, as it currently exists in form of international legal regimes or supranational organization, such as the European Union, whose member states have agreed on free movement for citizens among states (but not for citizens of third countries). It is also fully compatible with the existence of *international* legal regimes for the protection of refugees, and *international* legal regulations concerning migration, extradition, or deportation, such as, e.g., the Geneva convention, etc.

A normative requirement that follows from my claim that the authority for the final selection of rules of inclusion and exclusion ought to be assigned to the legislative branch of government, is that domestic legislative branches (i) ought to be consulted in the process of determining the legal competences that are transferred to the international level, and (ii) that they have to agree to any such treaty. This is worth mentioning, because, in practice, there are rather few societies where the legislative branch is in a position to exercise some degree of control over inter-state treaties; even in many democracies, international agreements are settled by interstate negotiations, which fall within the competences of the executive branch.

The question whether it is morally or legally desirable to establish international regimes is not easy to decide, because the answer depends on how those legal regimes are arranged and interlinked. From the perspective of philosophical liberalism, it appears highly desirable that the regulations of the different legal regimes form a coherent set. At present, this appears not to be the case,[112] especially if the relevant international institutions are equipped with international courts that have been invested with legislative powers to some extent.[113] From the perspective of philosophical liberalism, such transfers of legal powers tend to conflict with the principle of popular sovereignty at the domestic level, and to reproduce some of the normative problems of constitutionalism at the international level.[114] Thus, regulations enshrined in the Geneva convention and judgments of the European Court of Human Rights are not always coherent. States that are parties of both regimes can find themselves in a situation where compliance with one regime requires non-compliance with the other.[115] Scholars of international law speak of a "fragmentation of international law" – and still disagree about whether it is a blessing or a curse.[116] I assume the answer

---

112 See Koskenniemi (2006), Krisch (2010). See also Wilder (2012) for a historical perspective.

113 It is no secret that judges and legal practitioners are not always politically neutral but sometimes pursue a normative agenda themselves, and see international legal regimes and international courts as vehicles for the promotion of those aims.

114 See Stone Sweet (2000).

115 This happens, e.g., when a state that signed the Geneva convention is asked by another signatory state to extradite a person, but the European Court rules that the person may not be extradited, because her life in the country that required the extradition is under threat for political or medical reasons.

116 See, e.g., Hafner (2004), Koskenniemi and Leino (2002), Krisch (2011).

depends on the depth of legal integration, the degree of divergence, and the range of issues that is regulated.

Legal fragmentation, however, appears not to be inevitable. A practical response to problems of legal fragmentation and constitutionalism at the interstate level might be an arrangement that guarantees an exit option to societies that participate in international legal regimes, or the option of introducing hierarchical rankings for different regimes in cases of conflicting regulations.

A more difficult challenge, in my view, derives from the lack of normative consensus at the international level. Liberal and democratic societies are actually a minority in the international system. The drive towards international legal integration raises the danger that liberal democratic principles will be watered down in the search for international compromise. Liberal scholars and practitioners often express the hope that international legal integration will promote liberal democratic values and principles world-wide. The results so far are at best ambiguous. In addition, in political reality more powerful states have greater influence in international legal integration, and often can push their own agenda. This is often considered by less powerful states and critical theorists to constitute a form of legal colonialism. The accusation reflects once more the fact that the right to collective self-determination is not a dead letter. I therefore think that respect for the right to collective political self-determination is neither normatively outdated nor institutionally superseded. If the right to normative disagreement is a basic principle of liberal political philosophy, reasonable pluralism should be considered a virtue not only of domestic societies, but also of the international system.

Chapter 4. Normative Particularism Without Nationalism or Statism: A Liberal-democratic Account

Recognition of a *prima facie* liberty right to migration as an element of transnational justice must be defended against two prominent lines of argument that reject the idea that voluntary migration raises any requirements of (inter-, or transnational) *justice*: David Miller's account of liberal nationalism, and Michael Blake's argument from coercion. The two arguments do not reject migration *tous court*, but appear to primarily address claims, such as Carens', that border control and other restrictions of migration are *unjust*. The issue at stake, accordingly, concerns diverging conceptions of justice, arguments for the recognition of particularistic (domestic) spheres of justice, and the appropriate construction of a normative framework for assessing the moral status of migrants *vis-à-vis* host societies. Miller's and Blake's conceptions of domestic justice are the opposite extreme to Carens' cosmopolitan ideal of open borders, and are equally unconvincing for systematic reasons.

As long as political associations are organized in distinct and separate states, we will necessarily have to speak of states and societies in the plural, and to distinguish between members and non-members. What makes relations among co-members special, I have argued, is related to the role and value of societies as spaces for collective political agency. To conceive of societies as spheres of particularistic requirements of justice in no way rejects the recognition of universal and international requirements of justice. It maintains that requirements of justice derive from a plurality of sources, and that political agency constitutes a *sui generis* source of requirements of justice that differ from abstract and universal normative values, because political agency generates special normative relations.[117]

---

117 In putting the emphasis on political *practice*, the present account differs from accounts that focus on *territorial* separations of domestic spheres of jurisdiction; for the latter see, e.g., the debate among Song (2017), Cox (2017), and Blake (2017). It also differs fundamentally from conceptions of "the Political", with a capital "P", that follow Carl Schmitt's friend-enemy-distinction (Schmitt 1932/2015), which is normatively and analytically incompatible with philosophical liberalism.

The rule-based account of citizenship defended so far provides a genuinely liberal foundation for the recognition of particularistic spheres of justice different from Miller's defense of national liberalism, as well as from Blake's defense of national sovereignty.

4.1. Miller's Liberal Nationalism: A Constructive Criticism

Miller's *liberal* nationalism[118] differs from 19th-century conceptions of nationalism in substance as well as in its theoretical foundations. In the present chapter, I will focus on the latter.

4.1.1. A Brief Outline of Miller's Argument for Liberal Nationalism

Liberal nationalism, as I understand it, is an explanatory hypothesis that is supposed to elucidate why conceptions of sociopolitical justice are restricted to domestic institutions and special relations that hold among co-nationals. Miller's conception of sociopolitical justice is redistributive, and appears to be not fundamentally different from Rawls's conception of justice as fairness in substance. With respect to their theoretical foundations, however, Miller strongly criticizes Rawls's contractarian argument, and especially Rawls's concept of society as a cooperative venture for mutual advantage, as too abstract.[119] According to Miller, an adequate concept of society must reflect its cultural and sociohistorical dimensions, because the maintenance of redistributive institutions of social justice presupposes a form of civic solidarity that can flourish only if citizens share a common national culture.

National liberalism thus articulates an account of the unity of society in culturalist terms, but restricts the range of morally acceptable forms of nationalism to cultures that are compatible with liberal conceptions of sociopolitical justice. Whereas Miller's early terminology sometimes includes undertones of ethnic nationalism, his later works defend national solidarity overwhelmingly in terms of civic and political attitudes.[120]

---

118 See Miller (1995).
119 See Rawls (1980).
120 In the preface to *Strangers in Our Midst* (Miller 2016), Miller explicitly describes his theoretical motivation as reflecting practical consequences of British policies of multiculturalism.

Liberal nationalism is a theory of domestic sociopolitical justice. Miller supplements it with an account of global moral responsibility based on universal human rights.[121] According to Miller, the function of human rights is restricted to the protection of basic human needs. Accordingly, the line between the two normative spheres is rather rigid. For the present purpose, it is not necessary to go into the normative details of his account of domestic justice or human rights.[122] Within the context of discussions of migration, it suffices to mention that cultural normative particularism, in Miller's view, implies that national societies must be granted the right to control the conditions of immigration in terms of access as well as demands of social integration.

It is evident that Miller's account and the practice account proposed here overlap with respect to important normative conclusions. Both attribute to societies a privileged position for the final selection of the rules of inclusion and exclusion, and both defend the normative relevance of particularistic spheres of political justice and special relations. Whereas Miller emphasizes national solidarity, however, I argue that political philosophy should acknowledge the normative relevance of political agency. I am not certain that Miller would actually reject the latter idea, but I assume that he would find it insufficient as an account of the unity of society, due to its exclusive focus on the relevance of political agency. In my view, it is not clear whether Miller's culturalist foundation of liberal nationalism provides us with a coherent concept. If the culturalist foundations are taken seriously, they conflict with a liberal commitment to social pluralism, and if they include a commitment to social pluralism, it is hard to see what cultural aspects beyond liberal democratic attitudes can be included. The main difference between Miller's version of domestic particularism and my own is that I argue that domestic normative particularism derives from the practice of political agency, whereas Miller presents a culturalist hypothesis concerning the social preconditions of socio-political justice.

---

121 See Miller (2007).
122 The relevant point will be discussed in chap. 6.

4.1.2. National Integration and the Development of the Model of the Social State

Miller's solidarity argument appears closely related to the evolution of the model of the social state.[123] If we conceive of social justice in terms of the historical development of the model of the social state in Europe, Miller's liberal nationalism is far from implausible. Historical and sociological research supports the thesis that the development of the institutions that are characteristic of the model of the social state (in those societies that have it) was interlinked with the social integration of the so-called "third class" not only in Great Britain – as famously argued by T.H. Marshall –,[124] but also in other states.

I am not convinced, however, that this historical development has been promoted primarily by feelings of national solidarity or national sentiment. It appears to me to have been promoted by various doctrines besides nationalism, e.g., socialism, utilitarianism, fascism, and it has been facilitated by a variety of factors, among them social and economic transformations caused by the industrial revolution, an expansion of the agenda of state institutions and bureaucracies, including compulsory education, and a general shift of focus in 19th century moral philosophy from individual virtue to sociopolitical institutions.[125] Although it has to be conceded that 19th-century doctrines of nationalism have played a historically important role, I do not think that they are the whole of the explanatory story. An important supplementary hypothesis would be that the development of the institutions of the social state is closely tied to the extension of bureaucratic and administrative tasks and functions of (pre-democratic) state institutions.[126]

Even more problematic, in my view, is Miller's thesis that sociopolitical justice presupposes feelings of (national) solidarity, and that feelings of solidarity are restricted to co-nationals. Miller does not provide evidential support for his hypothesis. I am myself highly skeptical that it can be maintained *a priori* that solidarity plays such a decisive role, because I am generally skeptical that there is exactly one factor or condition that can be

---

123 Cf. Miller (2008).
124 See Marshall (1950/1992).
125 See also Somek (1998).
126 Such a hypothesis might explain some of the differences in the development of models of statehood and attitudes towards charity in Europe and the United States, but I will not pursue this point further.

singled out as an irreplaceable and necessary precondition for the practice and acceptance of social justice that applies to all persons at all times and under all circumstances. It seems to me evident that institutions of social justice have historically been supported by a plurality of different attitudes – moral, paternalistic, prudential –, as well as a plurality of sociopolitical doctrines besides nationalism, e.g., socialism, communism, and catholicism.

From an explanatory point of view, sociopolitical attitudes are much more pluralistic and heterogeneous than Miller seems willing to concede.

My main objection, however, is that the normative force of appeal to *de facto* social attitudes makes at best a very weak argument from a normative point of view. For it is a basic assumption in practical philosophy that personal and sociopolitical attitudes are open to reflection, criticism, and modification or correction through reasoning, public discourse, and moral criticism. Recourse to the explanatory hypothesis that solidarity requires some degree of cultural homogeneity as a precondition, therefore, is at best of limited weight in a normative account of the preconditions of social justice. From a normative point of view, moral discourse and criticism should have an effect on the social attitudes of persons – and, if required, provide arguments for a change of attitudes. From an empirical point of view, there appears to be ample evidence that solidarity is not at all confined to co-nationals.

For these reasons, I find Miller's liberal nationalism unwarranted from an explanatory perspective, and unsatisfying from an ethical perspective.

4.1.3. A Counter-thesis: Democratic Legitimacy vs. Liberal Nationalism

In contrast to Miller, I want to emphasize that the institutions of the model social state are first and foremost *statist*. They are mainly domestic, because their establishment and maintenance require instruments of statehood and national political agency. Most institutions of the social state function through compulsory inclusion, either by taxes or compulsory systems of social insurance, well-functioning state institutions, and a professionally minded state administration. The establishment and maintenance of institutions of the social state, in my view, are not so much founded in civic solidarity as been driven by the expansion of the administrative agenda of modern state institutions. Although many liberal theorists would defend the claim that social rights are universal in the sense that everyone should be able to enjoy them, the administrative realization of social rights has not been universal. It remains a conundrum how systems of social security could be stable and functional if people were free to opt in and out as it pleases them. That, I think, is one of the main reasons why compulsory inclusion, as well as benefits, have so far been restricted (mainly) to citizens.

A statist hypothesis concerning the development of the model of the social state fits with another historical observation of Miller's.[127] The institution of formal attestation of citizenship is comparatively recent, and seems to have developed in parallel to the model of the nation *state*. It appears justified to assume that the two developments are intertwined, not merely contingently but institutionally. The hypothesis that I would propose is that this coincidence is due to the fact that national integration has often been promoted as an extension of the political agenda, i.e., of state powers and responsibilities (e.g., compulsory inclusion of all citizens into military service, introduction of state-run poverty relief programs, compulsory education, etc.). Thus, political agency promotes social integration as a follow-up to the expansion of the political agenda in modern states, not *vice versa*. The generation of particularistic spheres of sociopolitical justice, accordingly, is a consequence of, rather than an essential motivation for, the existence of nation states.

Considered as an explanatory hypothesis, the historical interlinkage of the institutions of citizenship and of the model of social state would have at best marginal normative implications, because no explanatory hypothesis justifies a quasi-Hegelian argument to the effect that the model of the national social state is also the final end of history, or that it is the morally most desirable form of organization for the implementation of sociopolitical justice. Cosmopolitans might simply object that we ought to move on to inter- or transnational or global systems of sociopolitical justice.

The relevance of requirements of democratic legitimacy for political agency (as developed in chapters 2 and 3), by contrast, presents a genuinely normative argument for normative particularism that reflects the social conditions of political agency. Fortunately, the normative requirement is also independent of explanatory hypotheses about the cultural preconditions of solidarity.

The core of my argument – i.e., the claim that liberal theories of political justice cannot ignore the theoretical and normative relevance of political agency at the domestic level – does not prioritize any sphere

---

127 See Miller (2008).

of justice over others; it makes no assumptions concerning non-political interpersonal attitudes of citizens; and it does not draw on dubious culturalist hypotheses, but only on moral principles and arguments that support democracy and social pluralism (as I will argue in chapter 5). Thus, my counter-thesis endorses philosophical liberalism, but rejects nationalism as well as any other appeal to culturalism (as I will argue in chapter 10).

4.2. State Sovereignty and Normative Particularism: A Criticism of Blake's Argument from Coercion

Blake's defense of normative particularism is methodologically statist and quite different from Miller's. It focuses on the institution of state sovereignty in a highly abstract sense.

4.2.1. Blake on Citizenship and Coercion

Starting from a traditional concept of statehood, Blake defends a moderate form of normative particularism by – as I will call it – the *argument from coercion*.[128] This argument combines two claims. The first holds that state institutions exert legal and political coercion against citizens, and that coercion is morally wrong *ceteris paribus*. The second claim holds that the moral wrong of coercion can be justified if it is compensated by a moral good of equal weight, and that the recognition of individual rights as required by political justice is such a compensatory moral good. The relevant rights accordingly apply to citizens but not to foreigners. Although Blake acknowledges that sovereign states also exert coercion against (potentially migrating) foreigners, by denying them access to the territory of a state, this form of coercion does not require compensation in form of granting them civic rights. He also concedes that sovereign states exert coercion to foreign residents by requiring them to obey the laws, but he argues that foreigners do not deserve compensation, because they enter the territory of the state voluntarily, whereas citizens are non-voluntarily integrated into their state of origin.

---

128   See Blake (2001).

4.2.2. Beyond Coercion: Political Sovereignty Bottom-up rather than Top-down

Personally, I find Blake's argument puzzling. It relies on conceptions of sovereignty, statehood, law, and individual rights that I find hard to reconcile with ethical individualism and institutional conventionalism. Blake presents internal sovereignty as an entirely top-down and borderline authoritarian hierarchy, i.e., as a unidirectional *vertical* relation between states – or rather governments – and subjects, as if the civil and political status of citizens were a compensation for moral harm rather than a normative requirement built into the idea of government by authorization, as explicated in chapter 3. He ignores the general liberal idea that the normative *raison d'être* of those institutions is that governmental powers depend on authorization and are normatively constrained by, among other things, requirements related to the principle of popular sovereignty and the recognition of individual rights. Although the idea of government by authorization includes a duty on the part of citizens to comply with the laws and regulations that political government issues (insofar as compliance is justified), it implies that the relation between citizens and state government has essentially a bottom-up direction.

I would also object to Blake's presentation of individual rights as a device of compensation for state coercion, because it ignores the liberal idea that respect for (deontologically binding) individual rights reflects the *horizontal* normative relations that reciprocally hold *among citizens*. To use a phrase of Rawls's in *Political Liberalism*: citizens ought to recognize each other reciprocally as free and equal persons. I would also add that citizens ought to promote institutions and practices that are necessary for the realization of political justice. In my opinion, the claim that citizens non-voluntarily submit to state institutions falls back onto a pre-liberal Hobbesian account of sovereignty.

Arguably, Blake's argument is best understood as an attempt to present a non-circular argument in favor of normative particularism by focusing on abstract institutional properties of state sovereignty. Rawls's emphasis on reciprocal recognition of individual rights and duties has indeed frequently been challenged by the objection that mutual recognition of citizens' rights draws a normatively arbitrary distinction between citizens and foreigners. Cosmopolitans have long argued that persons also ought to acknowledge each other reciprocally as equal and free human beings, and ought to promote human rights through adequate inter- and transnational institutions. The argument from coercion obviously tries to go beyond the metaethical justification of individual rights claims, but I find it un-convincing, and even incompatible with the principle of philosophical liberalism as stated in chapter 1.

According to the practice account, a plurality of sources of normative requirements that support individual rights can be identified. Some indi-vidual rights articulate special requirements of justice; others articulate universal requirements of justice; and many requirements of justice are not related to either category of individual rights but derive from different sources of valid normative claims, e.g., principles for the settlement of conflicting or competing justified interests. Political agency is one such a source: in its domestic performances, it generates normative spheres of a genuinely particularistic sort tied to institutional demarcations of politi-cal associations, which coincide with state borders. Normatively relevant, however, is not the protection of national sovereignty or statehood *per se*, but protection of political associations as well-functioning spaces of political agency and its collective exercise.

I also want to recall that political agency and particularistic spheres of justice are not necessarily confined to the domestic levels of political asso-ciations. Political agency can take place at an international level as well; it then qualifies as a genuine source of particularistic spheres of political justice at the interstate level beyond universal human rights requirements. The important point in the present context is simply this: as long as political associations are organized in particularistic states, political agency continues to create particularistic spheres of domestic justice that will include some individuals (co-citizens) and exclude others (non-resident foreigners).

A comparatively recent objection to the argument from political agency is that, to the extent that domestic political agency affects foreigners, they should be integrated or allowed to participate in the relevant decisions. Transnational accounts of democratic participation and discourse-theoreti-cal arguments for transnational inclusion, however, require discussion in themselves and will be addressed in the next chapter.

For now, I conclude that the focus on the normative consequences of political agency fits neatly into the broader framework of a transnational account of political philosophy that articulates a genuinely liberal alterna-tive to both Miller's liberal nationalism, as well as Blake's argument from coercion, in three respects: in terms of conceptual analysis, in terms of metaethical principles, and in terms of a coherent extension of the norma-tive paradigm of philosophical liberalism.

Chapter 5. Pure Procedural Justice and Democratic Legitimacy

Chapters 3 and 4 have argued that normative assessments of transnational migration must pay attention to the relevance of political agency at the domestic, as well as the international level. Although philosophical liberalism has to tolerate non-democratic societies at the international level, as concerns liberal states it entails a commitment to democracy.

In the present chapter, I will propose an account of the normative value of democracy in order to explore the sociopolitical preconditions of the practice of democracy, and to indicate why democratic political agency is most likely restricted to the particularistic level of political associations. In order to do this, I will compare the normative function and value of procedural elements of democracy from the perspective of a practice approach with Jürgen Habermas' metaethical account of purely procedural justification, and arguments in favor of transnational democracy.

Let me recall the theoretical motivations of discourse ethics and of appeals to transnational democracy.

Habermas introduced discourse ethics as a general metaethical approach that addresses the problem of how *rational* normative justification is possible.[129] According to Habermas, only purely procedural methods of justification qualify as rational in post-traditional societies, i.e., under conditions when moral objectivism has been replaced by subjectivist conceptions of value and morality. For Habermas, norms and general rules qualify as normatively valid if, and only if, they are unanimously accepted – or consented to – in an ideal discourse by each person who is affected by them. The basic presupposition of discourse ethics maintains that unanimous consensus *can* be reached if all affected persons engage in a discourse under ideal conditions, because Habermas conceives of discourse as a genuinely communicative form of action that inherently aims at unanimous agreement.[130]

Discourse ethics thus transforms a universalizability-requirement into a procedural consent-based account of normative justification – partly inspired by pragmatism and philosophy of language –, but insists that

---

129 See Habermas (1983) and Habermas (1991).
130 See Habermas (1987).

consent has normative force only if it is reached under ideal circumstances. An important requirement, especially in Habermas' early writings, is the demand that the ideal discourse has to be actually performed, and has to continue until unanimous agreement is reached. Normative verdicts that have not (yet) been unanimously affirmed through an ideal discourse are not truly valid, but are at best preliminarily assumed to be valid and under critical contestation.

Since the ideal conditions required by discourse ethics are not (yet) met in practice, proponents of the account require that philosophers practice *epoche*, i.e., that they withhold normative judgment, or at least refrain from presenting their own thinking as normatively valid considerations, unless their judgments have been affirmed by unanimous consent under ideal circumstances.[131]

Discourse ethics, thus, represents a purely procedural account of normative justification. That reduces the scope of what philosophers can contribute to discussions of citizenship and migration mainly to the question "Who ought to be included in the ideal discourse?", which – in contexts of migration – is roughly identical with the world population, or least with those who are willing to participate in an ideal discourse and are also willing to accept its results.[132]

Theorists of transnational democracy, by contrast, commonly understand their project not as a metaethical program, but as a substantive requirement of political legitimacy. In light of economic globalization and legal internationalization, those theorists argue, democracy has to follow suit and has to be transnationalized too.[133] Transnational democracy, however, raises questions very similar to those of discourse ethics: "Who should be included in a transnational *demos*?". Quite a few theorists argue that all persons who are "affected" by political decisions ought to be included irrespectively of their institutional affiliation or territorial residence. Others suggest that the interests of all affected persons can also be represented by special interest groups, e.g., INGO's. Since border regimes and rules of inclusion and exclusion affect foreigners and potential immigrants, so the argument goes, those persons or their representatives must be included

---

131 See Habermas' criticism of Rawls in Habermas (1995).
132 See, e.g., Benhabib (2001) who defends such a position with the one reservation that participants must be democratically minded.
133 Conceptions of transnational democracy vary widely in important respects; compare, e.g., Held/Archibugi (1995) or Held (2006) with Dryzek (2006).

within the democratic *demos* that is vested with the authority to determine rules of immigration.

5.1. Democratic Legitimacy and the "All Affected Persons" Principle

Interestingly, discourse ethics and accounts of transnational democracy actually share a common problem because both appeal to the so-called "all affected persons" principle (AAPP). Outside of traditional theories of domestic government and municipal law, however, it is far from clear what "affected" means. Within the context of traditional theories, the range of "all affected" persons is taken to be identical with the totality of the persons who are members of the relevant institution, i.e., state government or municipal law. As David Owen rightly suggested, "affected" in this sense means "subjected" to the law of the land. He therefore suggests that the principle be better called the "all subjected persons" principle.[134]

Recourse to AAPP is best conceived of as a modified continuation of voluntaristic and republican accounts of democracy. The principle has played a major role in arguments for universal suffrage. Once the principle is detached from the domestic context, however, it is essentially an open question what "affected" means. Most theorists appear to understand the term as referring to empirically contingent consequences that political decisions have for individual persons, which is not a legal relation, such as "subjected" to the law of the land is.[135] I will not attempt to define the concept for contexts beyond traditional theories of domestic political government and municipal law, because that should be the task of those who advocate AAPP in post-national contexts. My criticism of the idea of transnational democracy is, in fact, independent from a precise definition of how to understand the term "affected" outside its traditional context.

Within a practice account, democratic membership is a normative status that is part of a normatively more complex institutional system. The practice account conceives of the idea that political government is based on authorization as a normative justification of the principle of popular sovereignty, but rejects the idea that "the people" is a pre-political unity. "The people" is considered to be a status concept that applies to the totality

---

134 Owen (2011), p. 645.
135 See Bauböck (2018) for a normative criticism of AAPP from a republican perspective on citizenship. Bauböck's stakeholder account of citizenship will be discussed in chap. 8.

of citizens with active and passive political rights, i.e., to the electorate. Thus, it makes no sense to speak of "the people" outside institutional contexts. From this perspective, discourse ethics and theories of transnational democracy focus on the wrong question. The crucial question is not "Who should be included in the *demos*?" but "What are the normative background rules and social preconditions that facilitate the practice of democracy, and are likely to guarantee its acceptability as a mechanism of legitimacy?".

5.2. Democracy as a Mechanism of Pure Procedural Justice: An Outline

Rawls distinguishes three standards of legitimacy, which he labels as perfect procedural justice, imperfect procedural justice, and pure procedural justice.[136] I find Rawls's distinction quite helpful, because the three standards differ with respect to their normative logic and the conditions of their application.

Roughly, mechanisms of perfect and imperfect procedural justice are supposed to produce results, i.e., outcomes or judgments, that conform to substantive normative standards or principles of justice that are given independently of the procedure. In cases of perfect procedural justice, the procedures guarantee that the final judgment or result meets the substantive standard of justice. In the case of imperfect procedural justice, the procedures makes it very likely that the final judgments meet the substantive standard most of the time.[137] Perfect and imperfect procedural justice thus are supposed to represent mechanisms or procedures whose application guarantees, or at least makes very likely, that the results of their application qualify as just in accordance with a normative substantive standard or

---

136 Rawls (1971), § 14.
137 Rawls (1971) illustrates perfect procedural justice by the example of a procedure, familiar from children's birthday parties: the one child who is allowed to cut the cake will be the last to take a piece; the independent, substantive normative standard that is supposed to be guaranteed by the procedure is that of an equal division. For an illustration of imperfect procedural justice, he alludes to the procedures of legal courts. The independent substantive standard for the normative assessments of the courts' final judgments is the principle that innocent persons should be acquitted and guilty persons should be convicted. Obviously, the relevant rules are quite complex and do not guarantee that their application will always yield a just result; but they do so in most cases; otherwise, they would need to be changed.

principle. The procedures do not serve a genuinely justificatory task, but are instrumental in producing an outcome that is justified by independent standards of rightness or legitimacy.

Pure procedural justice, by contrast, applies to contexts where no independent substantive normative standard exists, and where the legitimacy of the result is held to be generated through the practical application of the procedure itself.

A standard paradigm of the conditions of application for pure procedural justice are collective democratic decisions in pluralistic societies. Pluralistic societies grant citizens the right to pursue not only competing and conflicting justified interests, but also a right to mutual normative disagreement with regard to conceptions of justice that are supposed to regulate conflicts of interests. In most cases neither conflicts of interests nor normative disagreements can be overcome. Nevertheless, collective decisions have to be made, and appeals to substantive standards of justice must be replaced by standards of procedural legitimacy. Mechanisms of pure procedural justice are meant to generate legitimate results that all participating persons can accept, not for substantive reasons, but because the procedures that led to them are considered just and fair.[138] Since the legitimating force is in the procedures themselves, mechanisms of pure procedural justice unfold their legitimating potential only if they are performed. Pure procedural justice, so to speak, cannot be replaced by abstract reasoning or argument; it must be practiced.

5.3. The Moral Point of Democracy

Democratic decisions reached by majority vote are paradigm cases of pure procedural justice in Rawls's sense, but the practice of democracy cannot be reduced to majority vote. Rather, it includes an entire set of background rules and conditions that are intended to guarantee – or at least make it very likely – that all citizens have equal political and civil rights not only formally, but also roughly equal opportunities and means

---

138 As an illustration of pure procedural justice, Rawls (1971) refers to gambling, but the main object of application of pure procedural justice is the contractarian construction of an original position. Rawls (1993a) and (2001) also present democracy (within institutional constraints) as a mechanism of pure procedural justice, which is supposed to generate legitimacy in conditions characterized by normative pluralism.

to voice their interests and defend their opinions in public discourse, to assemble, to form parties, unions, or coalitions, etc.[139]

The contrast between substantive standards of legitimacy and mechanisms of pure procedural justice, therefore, should not be understood as being exclusively disjunctive. Democracy as a mechanism of pure procedural justice actually presupposes the recognition of rights, liberties, etc., that are attributed to participants on the basis of substantive standards of legitimacy. Most important in contexts of democratic political government are requirements of legal and political equality.[140] A practice account of democracy is also compatible with the demand that the application of mechanisms of pure procedural justice, i.e., the topics of the political agenda, can be restricted by substantive normative principles or standards, e.g., constitutional rights, *Grundrechte*, or human rights requirements.[141]

The normative role of democracy as a mechanism of pure procedural justice reflects the liberal principle that all citizens ought to be granted equal political powers, but it also serves a special legitimating function if three assumptions hold, and are generally accepted as holding. First, political disagreement is unavoidable in a pluralistic liberal society, because the justified interests and normative convictions of citizens in liberal democracies will often diverge. Second, liberal societies respect the principle of individual normative self-determination, and accordingly ought to respect

---

139 Here, I follow Christiano (1996).

140 See Christiano (2008b) who – I think convincingly – argues that democracy is founded on the ideal of political equality, not on individual (or collective) liberty.

141 See Chwaszcza (2011b). The range and substance of constitutional rights is notoriously contested, but even theorists who defend the priority of democratic mechanisms over constitutional rights and judicial review recognize the need to guarantee political rights and the rule of law. Personally, I agree with Waldron's contention that the pro's and con's of the debate are not purely normative. According to Dworkin, a strong version of judicial review is morally desirable, because he conceives of democratic processes as being driven entirely by self-interest, ambition, and bargaining for personal advantage, whereas judges are conceived of as committed to impartial and rational styles of argument. Whether Dworkin's picture of democracy is true or not is an empirical question. It certainly cannot be ruled out *a priori* that the political culture of a democratic society actually degenerates into such a deficient practice. As Waldron rightly maintains, however, it cannot be ruled out *a priori* either that judges are motivated by partisan political views. There is no reason to assume *a priori* that political reasoning and deliberation in well-functioning democracies are inferior to reasoning and deliberative skills of judges.

the right of citizens to normative disagreement.[142] Third, citizens accept the idea of a free-standing conception of the political (to use Rawls's phrase), that is to say, they reciprocally recognize each other as free and equal citizens, and agree that no person or group is entitled simply to impose their normative convictions on others, and they also agree that no person or group ought to be denied an equal right to pursue their justified interests.

If these assumptions prevail, and are publicly accepted as prevailing, mechanisms of pure procedural justice fulfill a crucial normative function: their performance is expected to provide a source of legitimacy for the results of collective decisions in the absence of any *substantive* normative standard that can be expected to be accepted by all participants and, especially, those who have been outvoted.[143] In other words: mechanisms of pure procedural justice provide participants with a normative reason for the acceptance of the result that is independent from whether they personally agree with the result or not. Standards of procedural legitimacy address a puzzle that haunted Rousseau – and continues to haunt theorists who, like Rousseau, think that the legitimacy of democratic procedures depends on achieving the right outcome or judgment, as in conceptions of perfect or imperfect procedural justice. Famously, Rousseau demands that members of a democratic minority, after having been outvoted, must change their opinions and beliefs and accept the result of the collective decision as "the correct" insight of an ominous *volonté générale*.[144]

---

142 Normative pluralism is not an "anything goes" position. It is constrained by requirements of *reciprocal* acceptance and social compatibility required by the principle of ethical individualism. Where the line between legitimate and illegitimate normative opinions is to be drawn is notoriously contested. The main point in the present context is, however, that democratic choice is meant to settle not only conflicts of interests, but also normative disagreement about topics of the political agenda outside of constitutional essentials.

143 A standard example would be political elections in a multi-party system. Every citizen is free to endorse the party of her choice, but in the end, the voters who find themselves outvoted by the majority must be given a normative reason for accepting that the winning party *legitimately* forms the new government.

144 Rousseau (1762), bk. IV, chap. 1 characterizes the concept of a *volonté générale* as follows:

So long as several men together consider themselves to be a single body, they have but a single will, which is concerned with their common preservation and the general well-being. Then all the energies of the state are vigorous and simple; its maxims are clear and luminous; there are no entangled, contradictory interests; the common good is clearly apparent everywhere, demanding only good sense in order to be achieved.

When a law is proposed in the people's assembly, what is asked of [citizens] is not precisely whether they approve or reject, but whether or not it conforms to the general will that is theirs. Each man, in giving his vote, states his opinion on this matter, and the declaration of the general will is drawn from the counting of votes. When, therefore, the opinion contrary to mine prevails, this proves merely that I was in error, and that what I took to be the general will was not so. If my private opinion had prevailed, I would have done something other than what I wanted. In that case I would not have been free.[145]

Theorists who conceive of democratic procedures as mechanisms of pure procedural justice, by contrast, conceive of the problem which those mechanisms address as entirely different, i.e., as non-epistemic and as deriving from an equal right of citizens to pursue personal interests and to disagree on the substance of "common good" or principles of justice. According to a practice account of democracy, the primary function of mechanisms of pure procedural justice is that of generating normative reasons *sui generis* for the acceptance of the collective decisions that are independent and distinct from the substantive contents of the decision.[146] Procedural legitimacy obviates the supposed need for a mysterious *volonté générale*.

Accordingly, democracy is considered to be valuable because it responds to the problem of normative pluralism or, more precisely, the problem of legitimacy of collectively binding choices and policies under conditions of normative pluralism. Such an understanding of the normative value of democracy departs from epistemic and discourse-ethical conceptions of democracy, both of which pursue an ideal of unanimous agreement. The first tend to conceive of majority rule and pre-choice deliberative discourse as instrumental means to find out what the *right* or *just* decision is; the latter simply stipulate that an ideal discourse would yield a unanimous consensus. Neither epistemic accounts of democracy nor discourse ethics provide a normative response to normative pluralism, but rather suggest that it can, or should, be overcome.[147]

A practice account of democracy is not anti-deliberative, but it locates deliberation in the spheres of public discourse and political culture, i.e., the everyday practice of political agency by professionals and citizens. Acceptance of social pluralism is fully compatible with requirements that

---

145 Rousseau (1762), bk. IV, chap. 2.
146 See Chwaszcza (2021) for a more detailed discussion.
147 See Lagerspetz (2010) for a comprehensive criticism of the basic epistemic assumptions of epistemological accounts of democracy and discourse ethics.

collective decisions should be made in light of the relevant evidence concerning factual matters and positions; that citizens' choices should reflect the experience not only of one's own person but also that of other participants; that opinions and votes should express well-considered judgments rather than personal preferences, egotistical bias, or impulsive desires. In a nutshell, the practice of democracy presupposes a democratic political culture. A democratic political culture, however, cannot be reduced to the rules and procedures of collective decision making. It must manifest itself in the everyday practice of political agency and requires that citizens, their political representatives, and public officials are willing to participate in rational deliberation in everyday public discourse, that they support their views by argument, and that they respect the fact that others might have diverging views, interests, and opinions.

In the present context more important, however, are some social preconditions that must be met in order for democratic forms of decision making to reveal a legitimating potential.

5.4. Democratic Legitimacy as a Social Practice[148]

The legitimacy generated by mechanisms of pure procedural justice resides in the procedures that produce the outcome, not in the outcome itself. Accordingly, those mechanisms provide a source of legitimacy only if, and to the extent that, they are actually performed. Mechanisms of pure procedural justice can be neither replaced by abstract argument, nor delegated to self-authorized experts or specialists. The actual practice of democracy is therefore essential for the realization of its legitimating potential, and to the extent that the practice of democracy presupposes that certain social preconditions are met, these preconditions are equally essential for the legitimating potential of democratic forms of decision making.

An obvious precondition is the general acceptance of majority rule. Although democracy cannot be reduced to majority rule, the acceptance of majority rule definitely represents a crucial element of democratic legitimacy. Citizens must not only accept majority rule themselves, but also have reason to believe that their co-citizens accept it too. If citizens who find themselves on the minority side with respect to a certain decision are expected to recognize the decision as legitimate, they must have some form of evidence that those citizens who find themselves on the majority side of

---

148 Some of the following ideas are taken from Chwaszcza (2012).

the vote of a decision would also accept the result as legitimate if it had turned out differently.

Accordingly, three conditions seem to be necessary for the functioning of democratic legitimacy. First, democratic forms of decision making must be exercised as a *general* practice. That means that they must be regularly exercised, and exercised across all relevant issues, in order to reinforce the mutual beliefs of citizens in the reciprocal acceptance of majority rule. Second, participants must have reliable evidence that co-citizens are willing to accept majority rule as legitimate. Third, minority and majority must not be rigid groups constituted by the same individuals with respect to all decisions.

The first and the second conditions warrant the assumption that the individuals who participate in the practice must be a roughly continuous group – perhaps not the very same group of persons every time, but definitely not a new and different group for every single issue. If the exercise of democratic practices is exceptional or confined to single issues, participants lack the evidence necessary for a justified belief that all participants are reciprocally willing to accept majority rule and democratically decided decisions as legitimate.

5.5. The Idea of Transnational Democracy in Light of the Practical Preconditions of Democratic Legitimacy

I think that both of the practical conditions mentioned above require that the overall *demos* be to some extent continuous and stable. No *demos*, of course, is rigidly stable, due to intergenerational dynamics of its membership-basis. Nevertheless, I seriously doubt that inter- and transnational extensions of democratic forms of decision making, which include all (empirically) affected persons, are likely to meet and to reproduce the preconditions of democratic legitimacy, especially if the relevant groups of participants vary across issues. If different topics of the political agenda will affect different persons abroad, their inclusion most likely produces fluid and diverse *demoi*.[149]

---

149 One could argue that all decisions affect everybody and require global democracy, or at least regional democracy. In that case, however, we would just have a territorially extended form of traditional democracy, not transnational democracy. See also La Torre (2005).

I am even more strongly inclined to think that proposals for the democratic inclusion of semi-professional representatives of affected interests, i.e., INGO's or social movements, are even more problematic. They represent *special interest groups* that usually pursue single topic agendas and are represented by spokespersons who lack public "authorization", as they are usually recruited exclusively by other members of the INGO or social movement.

My skepticism, of course, is partly based on empirical assumptions that can only be judged in light of empirical evidence. Since I am not in the position to test the correctness of my hypotheses myself, I will withhold judgment here. But the lack of success so far in constituting transnational *demoi*, or even an European *demos*, justifies skeptical reservations about the project.

On one point, however, the empirical evidence is uncontested. Given the comparatively small number of democratic societies at a global scale, the requirement of general acceptance of majority rule as a mechanism of pure procedural justice with a *sui generis* legitimating potential is highly unlikely to be met at the global level. Inclusion of non-democratic or even anti-democratic *demoi* in a practice of transnational democracy will definitely not promote democratic legitimacy; it might even undermine the sociopolitical foundations of democratic legitimacy in democratic countries, as Christiano suspects.[150]

5.6. The Limits of Metaethical Proceduralism: A Criticism of Discourse Ethics

The defense of democracy as a mechanism of pure procedural justice is entirely different from, and actually incompatible with, the metaethical program of discourse ethics. First, a practice account of democracy is not a metaethical theory, but rather an analysis of the normative and practical conditions which sustain and reproduce democratic attitudes in liberal pluralistic societies. Second, it attributes a special role to pure procedural justice, but does not regard it as a comprehensive account of normative justification, or even as an entirely freestanding standard of legitimacy. As mentioned above, majority vote functions as a mechanism of pure procedural justice only within a rule-based framework that guarantees that participants have equal political rights, and roughly equal resources for their exercise. Third, the practice account of democracy conceives of indi-

---

150 See Christiano (2017) and Christiano (2008a).

vidual voting rights not as a vehicle for achieving unanimous consensus, but as a protection of the right to normative disagreement.

Incompatible accounts cannot be compared, but only contrasted by making the differences explicit. I simply want to recall that, so far, no theorist has succeeded in reducing the plurality of standards of legitimacy to a single one, and that I find it even theoretically undesirable to try to do so, because different practical problems require different standards of legitimacy. Pure procedural justice certainly would not only be unnecessary but also inadequate for the justification of, e.g., the right to physical integrity. The distinction between substantive standards of legitimacy and procedural mechanisms of legitimacy is not meant to be exhaustive. It is simply meant to elucidate the reason why mechanisms of procedural legitimacy are indispensable in pluralistic, liberal societies. Normative disagreement cannot be wished away by liberal theorists, because it is not merely a fact but a normative implication of the right to individual normative self-determination, which itself is a morally substantive principle.

Considered as a method of analysis, practice accounts always take a starting point that is inherently normative, not morally agnostic. This difference between practice accounts and discourse ethics partly reflects the different theoretical motivations that drive them. For Habermas, discourse ethics is supposed to provide a theoretical remedy for moral skepticism, as well as a practical (political) program. Ordinary language philosophy, by contrast, often aims at showing that philosophical skepticism is the result of bad philosophical methodology and is unwarranted in practice. Unfortunately, according to Habermas no norm, claim, or principle qualifies as normatively valid before it has been unanimously accepted by the participants of an ideal discourse. Since the ideal discourse, so far, has not even started, nobody can be certain which norms, claims, or principles will be morally valid. I consider this a rather devastating result for a bulwark against moral skepticism.

The practice account presented here, by contrast, starts by exploring the logic of the normative structure of the sociopolitical and legal institutions of statehood and citizenship, and confronts it with an analysis of the practical problems and challenges as they exist in political reality, in order to construct a moral point of view from which current practices can be critically assessed and normatively revised. The metaethical accomplishment at which the practice account aims is that of a critical reassessment and correction of rule-guided practices, not an original constitution of normative validity. From the perspective of a practice account, normative assessments concerning citizenship and migration do not have to be postponed until a transnational unanimous consensus to guide such assessments has been reached.

There is obviously something unsatisfying about metaethical disputes that start from entirely different perceptions of what the problems are, and of what an acceptable account of normative justification would have to accomplish. However, the proof of the pudding in such cases is in the eating. A metaethical theory of normative justification that requires that we practice *epoche* until an *ideal* discourse has successfully taken place in practice, appears to me more discouraging than the threat that some of our current moral beliefs might be unjustified or mistaken. Moral beliefs, unlike abstention from judgment, can at least be critically challenged and improved by *ordinary* moral discourse in accordance with socially shared standards of moral justification.

Chapter 6. Citizenship and Immigration from a Transnational Moral Point of View

The most important implication of a rule-based account of citizenship is this: like all rules, the rules for the inclusion and exclusion of citizens are open to moral criticism. The present chapter will propose a moral point of view – roughly along the lines developed by Baier[151] – that provides us with standards for normative assessments of rules of inclusion and exclusion. These assessments won't yield concrete substantive conclusions, because moral considerations need to be supplemented with empirical evidence, the provision of which is beyond the scope of the present book. The moral point of view, however, will provide standards for normative assessments of general arguments employed in debates on citizenship and migration.

Let me start with a brief summary of some conceptual and methodological conclusions which have been reached in chapters 2 to 5, and which entail the constitutive elements of a transnational moral point of view.

First, I have argued that recognition of a *prima facie* liberty right to migration articulates a requirement of transnational justice. I have also argued that the recognition of such a right provides a more convincing starting point for normative debates about citizenship and migration than are discussions of the scope of sociopolitical justice and the distribution of social opportunities.

Second, I have argued that normative issues concerning citizenship and migration are best understood as assessments of the moral validity of rules of inclusion and exclusion from the perspective of all affected parties, i.e., (i) potential migrants, considered as (groups of) individual persons, (ii) individual members of potential host societies, and (iii) potential host societies, conceived of as collective entities. In principle, societies of origin[152] and their individual members also qualify as relevant parties, but an

---

151 See Baier (1965).
152 See Brock (2016) and Brock/Blake (2015) for an informative discussion of issues of brain drain; the relevance of problems of brain-drain is also emphasized by Dauvergne (2016). Fernando Tesón, by contrast, defends the claim that brain drain, if it indeed causes harm, does not cause morally objectionable harm, because societies do not "own" their talented citizens, according to libertarian

exploration and evaluation of their interests requires access to empirical evidence beyond the scope of the present book.

From the perspective of a rule-based account of citizenship, neither rules of inclusion nor rules of exclusion can be accepted as being a matter of mere discretion, but have to be justifiable by impartial reasons in accordance with the principle of ethical individualism. Given the fact that roughly 97 % of the world's population has no intention of migrating, respect for the universal right to citizenship justifies accepting birthright-citizenship as a default rule for assignments of state citizenship, on the condition that it be supplemented with additional rules of inclusion. A reasonable moral requirement is that the final set of rules be neither over-inclusive nor over-exclusive.[153]

Third, I proposed an exposition of the normative problem raised by migration (a) as a problem of transnational justice from an institutional point of view, and (b) as involving two dimensions of competition of interests from an empirical point of view. The transnational nature of migration requires that normative assessments both include considerations of justice that derive from the practice of political agency, and coherently integrate particularistic and non-particularistic requirements of justice. Normative assessments, accordingly, cannot be reduced to ideal-theory-based requirements concerning the basic structure of domestic societies or international law, but must include the particularistic requirements of justice that derive from the practice of political agency within and among various political associations in the real world. I have also shown that normative arguments cannot be based on purely consequentialist assessments of morally desirable end states, but have to reflect both the moral nature of ways, means, and measures for the achievement of those end states *and* the moral responsibilities for the morally deficient *status quo*.

---

conceptions of self-ownership (Tesón 2008). I consider it a matter of collective self-determination, whether societies decide to endorse a libertarian conception of self-ownership. I want to point out, however, that the argument from self-ownership is of restricted relevance if the development of talent is promoted by public policies and education programs financed by taxes or development programs.

153 Especially Bauböck has repeatedly argued that each of the common rules of inclusion can be over-inclusive and should not be taken to be unrestrictedly valid. For more extensive discussion see Bauböck (2018). See also Joppke (1999) and Shachar/Hirschl (2014). As Lindahl (2018) rightly points out, rules of inclusion and exclusion are not mutually exclusive, because every rule of inclusion includes certain groups of persons and excludes others.

From an empirical point of view, it appears justifiable to assume that current migration dynamics are characterized by two layers of competition, as potential host societies compete for certain groups of immigrants[154] but would prefer to exclude others, and different groups of potential immigrants compete for the access to comparatively few potential host societies, as it seems at present, the USA, Canada, Australia, and member states of the European Union.[155] The second assumption builds on the empirical assumption that the total existing number of potential migrants is larger than the number of immigrants that potential host societies are able to integrate socioeconomically.

I would like to recall that the special focus of attention of the present book concerns voluntary migration, i.e., migration for economic or biographical reasons, and that I will assume that many (potential) migrants aim not at naturalization or a permanent change of citizenship, but intend to stay and work abroad temporarily. As always, intentions may change as life goes on. In order to address transnational phenomena of migration in particular, I suggest that we distinguish access to temporary residence, educational training, or work permits, from permanent residence, naturalization, and democratic inclusion. The different levels of inclusion are best conceived of as possibly, but not necessarily, consecutive steps.

In light of these three preliminary results cited above, I consider it a requirement of transnational justice that societies respond to justified interests of potential migrants in morally adequate ways. In my opinion, this requires publicly announced regulations that facilitate legal immigration under conditions in which potential immigrants can securely apply for immigration. If interests in voluntary migration qualify as justified, and if the principle of ethical individualism applies to the present organization of the world into distinct and separate societies, migration must be practically feasible. Access can only be denied if denial is backed up by impartial reasons.

---

154 The groups are not rigidly defined, but are identified by case-relative or economically relevant distinctions. A standard distinction is that between highly skilled and unskilled migrants; sometimes the distinction is even narrowed down to certain professions, e.g., medical personnel, investors, artists, athletes.

155 It should not be omitted that in practice there is also migration to many other societies, e.g., Oman, United Arab Emirates, South-Africa, China, Vietnam, which are not all liberal societies. Since the normative arguments that I explore are decisively liberal, I will only consider liberal host societies. It also should not be forgotten, when we look at the reality of statism, that liberal societies are the minority.

In a nutshell, I maintain that *all* societies ought to adopt immigration laws and establish legal paths for the handling of applications, which potential immigrants can reach without having to risk their lives, freedom, or physical integrity.

Writing from a European background, I want to emphasize that the current practices of human trafficking – not only of refugees, but also of migrants who will not qualify as refugees but have no option to apply for immigration other than applying for refugee-status –, the new slave markets, the systematic raping of women and children, and the inhumane conditions in traffickers' camps are not an unavoidable *tragedy*, but an *expectable and foreseeable consequence* of the migration policies of the European Union and its member states.[156] If the suffering as well as the sheer number of victims of human trafficking can be expected to be reduced by opening formal procedures and channels for potential migrants to apply for access from their countries of origin, it is morally imperative to do so.[157]

The first section of the present chapter will introduce the account of normative justification which I will employ. The second section will discuss requirements of fairness concerning different groups of migrants, and their normative ranking. Then the third section will propose three general standards for weighing and balancing of justified interests of the different parties with respect to access to host countries. The main issue here will concern the moral permissibility of preferential treatment of different groups of potential immigrants.

6.1. Impartiality as a Standard of Moral Justification

There is, presently, no shortage of proposals for accounts of normative justification in terms of practical or impartial reasons. But different theorists

---

156 The situation in other parts of the world appears to be not entirely different, but unlike many European states, traditional immigration societies such as the USA, Canada, and Australia *have* immigration laws, even if their details are politically contested.

157 The objection that the establishment of legal paths will consume large amounts of financial and human resources is certainly descriptively correct, but not as such decisive from a moral point of view. At the moment, it is the immigrants who are supposed to pay all the costs, and for many that means sacrificing their life, liberty, or physical integrity.

use the terminology quite differently. In order to indicate how I use it, I will start with a few terminological clarifications.

6.1.1. Practical Reasons

The concept *practical reason* is taken to stand for considerations that are generally accepted as valid and relevant elements in processes of reasoning and deliberation. *Generally accepted* means that those considerations conform to *socially shared standards* of practical rationality.[158] I will say more about *considerations* in a minute, but I want to illustrate, first, what I mean by *standards*. Standards determine which kind of considerations are relevant and valid in processes of practical deliberation about what to do, and how to rank competing considerations. There is a plurality of such standards. Uncontested standards include, e.g., appeals to prudence, i.e., the advice to give greater weigh to long-term interest, if long-term interest compete with short-term interests; other widely held standards are cost-benefit-efficiency, means-end-coherence, etc. Given the plurality of standards of practical reasoning and their heterogeneity, all practical reasons qualify as *prima facie* reasons. Final judgments almost always require additional practical deliberation.

From the perspective of a practice account (as outlined in chapter 1, section 2), also considerations that appeal to rules qualify as practical reasons.[159] In the present context, that includes the normative background rules of sociopolitical institutions, and moral rights and duties that derive from them. The concept of practical reason employed here thus differs from Humean conceptions of practical rationality as proposed by, e.g., Bernard Williams and Michael Smith,[160] as well as from rational-choice-based accounts of practical rationality.

What, then, are relevant considerations? Like most philosophers, I want to include ordinary facts – i.e., states of affairs of the world – as well as

---

158 Here too, I follow Baier; see Baier (1978). Since reasons are frequently identified with "facts", I want to illustrate the point with the help of an example: it is a fact that bicycles roll better if one regularly greases the chain, but the fact is a *relevant* reason only for bicyclists, and even then only if we assume that greasing the chain is conducive according to some standard of rationality, such as means-end-efficiency.

159 See Chwaszcza (2017) for a more detailed analysis of practical reasons in contexts of social agency.

160 See Williams (1981), Smith (1987).

psychological facts, such as desires, and preferences, and most important in the present context, personal interests – *if*, and *to the extent that*, those psychological facts are generally accepted as relevant and valid considerations. Thus the mere occurrence of a psychological facts does not *per se* imply that those mental states also qualify as reasons. *Vice versa*, non-awareness of an interest or false beliefs can imply that an agent has a practical reason of which she is unaware. From the perspective of a practice account, reason-making considerations also include (among other things) present or past acts of agents; general duties and obligations; and normative expectations related to the rule-based socially shared practices.

Since not all personal interests which qualify as rational also qualify as moral, I will reserve the term *justified interests* for those that qualify as rational *and* moral.

6.1.2. Moral Reasons

Not all practical reasons qualify as moral reasons,[161] and even some that do so in certain contexts may not qualify as moral in all contexts.[162]

As concerns standards of normative justifications, most current accounts revolve around ideas of impartiality, universalizability, contractarianism, contractualism, etc., which share a certain degree of family resemblance but differ in the details. I suggest that we adhere to a standard of *impartiality*. Impartiality, as I understand it, requires that the background rules of social practices and sociopolitical institutions can be accepted by all *representative persons* who participate in those practices and institutions. Representative persons are not identical with any particular empirical person or group of empirical persons, but are *average* persons, or *typical* persons: they have average interests, values, expectations, etc., similar to interests and expectation that, e.g., administrators ascribe to pedestrians, bicyclists, and car drivers when they evaluate different options for how to reorganize traffic routes through the city.

The account of impartial reasons endorsed here thus differs significantly from utilitarian constructions of the figure of an impartial spectator. First,

---

161 To illustrate the point: it might be prudent, i.e., in the long-term interest of an agent, to break a promise, but such an interest would normally not qualify as morally acceptable.

162 Even an appeal to the rule that promises ought to be kept can be outweighed by other circumstantial considerations of higher moral weight.

utilitarians compare actual psychological states of empirical persons (at least in theory) without appeal to socially shared standards of rationality. Second, utilitarians ascribe no intrinsic normative value to rules, norms, and institutions, individual rights or deontological obligations or duties, whereas I do.

If a practical reason qualifies as morally justified, it has to be accepted as a morally valid reason irrespectively of who the person is who has it, whether the person is a potential migrant or any other morally relevant party.

Within the framework of philosophical liberalism, the substance of considerations that qualify as valid impartial reasons is not terribly difficult to determine. Impartial reasons derive mainly from three normative sources.

(1) One source consists of substantive values and principles that can be backed up by the principle of ethical individualism and the right to individual normative self-determination.

(2) Another source includes appeals to sociopolitical institutions or their background rules that can be backed up by those two principles, plus socially necessary pre-conditions for the maintenance or implementation of those institutions or rules. In the present context, the second class of impartial reasons includes: (i) conditions and considerations related to the functioning of societies as spaces of (democratic) political agency; (ii) recognition of societies as diachronically continuous spaces of intergenerational relations of political justice at the domestic level; (iii) particularistic relations of justice at domestic, inter- and transnational levels; and (iv) social preconditions for the socioeconomic integration of residents and migrants.

(3) Finally, there are personal interests and other considerations that can be expected to be *reciprocally* acknowledged as justifiable if the relevant persons were to think the matter through calmly and from an impartial point of view. In order to distinguish the third class of reasons from the first and the second, I will speak of "morally substantive claims" with respect to the first and the second class, and reserve the term "justified interests" for the third class.

Even though practical reasons are not merely facts, it is obvious that many practical reasons – especially personal interests, the conditions of their realization, and the consequences of their pursuit – depend on assumptions concerning empirically contingent facts. That means that many of the following arguments and considerations will be conditional, insofar as they depend on empirically contingent facts and circumstances. Thus, morally valid reasons, although generally valid, might "apply" to some societies and some potential migrants but not to others. Conditionality in this sense does not undermine the validity of the general requirement that similar cases ought to be treated equally, but it acknowledges that dissimilar cases can require different treatment.

6.1.3. Impartiality and the Construction of a Moral Point of View

Different theorists propose somewhat different constructions of the impartiality requirement: besides moral point of view accounts, Rawls's construction of an original position and universalizability requirements are probably the most prominent models. The present account draws on Baier's explication of a moral point of view: practical reasons qualify as morally valid or justified if they can be defended from a moral point of view that represents an *impersonal perspective*. The impersonal perspective is characterized by two features. First, it compares different possible normative arrangements of sociopolitical institutions[163] with regard to their impact on the social conditions for the pursuit of individual life-plans, from the perspective of all representative persons under the assumption that they do not know which position in society they occupy.[164] Second, representative persons in the present context are the affected parties identified above.

Impartiality, as I understand it, is neither a substitute for the epistemic ideal of "truth", nor an anything-goes metaethical principle, but rather a moral standard that is closely tied to philosophical liberalism. It reflects ethical individualism, and it respects individual persons as "self-authenti-

---

163 In principle, requirements of impartiality can also be applied to particular acts and situations, but since the main object of normative assessments will be general rules of inclusion and exclusion, I will adopt an institutional and norm-oriented perspective.

164 The standard of impartiality outlined above is not very different from Hart's and Rawls's *principle of fairness*, which is a standard of justifiability that demands that individuals who benefit from the normative arrangement of sociopolitical institutions must also be willing to accept the burdens and costs that those institutions impose on participants. That is to say, the normative considerations ought to have the form of *generally* binding rules, and must be acceptable as such, irrespective of whether their application in a concrete case is beneficial or disadvantageous to one's own person. Unlike Rawls, however, I think that the principle of fairness is not confined to domestic institutions, but also applies to the recognition of transnational rules and the normative status of individual persons in the international system of statehood.

cating sources of valid normative claims".[165] It thus requires that justified interests of representative persons are compatible with the principles of philosophical liberalism.

The standards of moral justification outlined above are widely shared in liberal political philosophy, despite some differences in the details of their interpretation. Disregarding verbal disputes concerning the concept of sociopolitical justice, I hold that the main difference between the moral point of view presented here and positions, such as Carens' or Miller's, concerns the exposition of the practical conflicts raised by voluntary migration. Those differences derive mainly from two points of disagreement: first, my diagnosis that new forms of migration have a genuinely transnational quality, and, second, my claim that normative assessments must reflect the theoretical and normative relevance of political agency. In order to do that, a transnational moral point of view conceives of societies – political associations – as collective entities that function both as spaces of political agency, and as bearers of a right to collective self-determination.

6.1.4. Normative Reasoning

Recognition of the theoretical relevance of political agency and its empirically contingent nature, unfortunately, precludes aspirations to grand-theory-theorizing, because it excludes the preferred strategy that enables it, which is ideal-theory-theorizing. Rawls's employed an ideal-theory-theorizing strategy, when he developed a theory of justice under the assumptions (i) that all participants are endowed with a sense of justice that guarantees that they voluntary comply with fair principles of justice, and (ii) that societies are autarchic and economically well-developed ("unburdened"). Whatever the methodological advantages of such a strategy of theorizing are, the assumptions on which it builds are not warranted for assessments of issues concerning citizenship and migration, because the reasons that drive migration are related to the fact that those assumptions are not fulfilled. The general theoretical framework has to pay tribute to the fact that the international order of statehood, as it exists in political reality, is characterized by imperfect justice and lack of justice, if not outright injustice, at all institutional levels.

In addition, the fact that final judgments depend on empirically contingent conditions and circumstances curbs aspirations concerning the

---

165 See Rawls (1980).

contribution that philosophical analysis can offer for concrete practical judgments, solutions, and policies. Accordingly, normative reasoning from a moral point of view will not yield concrete solutions to practical problems, but only standards for the assessment of the *normative validity of arguments*, as employed in current debates.

A third reason for theoretical modesty is the fact that recent movements of mass migration in the context of an international order of statehood are a rather new phenomenon. Moreover, questions concerning transnational justice are largely unexplored normative territory, because the *de facto* existing legal organization of transnational relations is still in *statu nascendi*. Explorations of requirements of transnational justice thus differ from theories of sociopolitical justice at the domestic level. Rawls' developed his *theory* of justice against the background of moral and empirical evidence concerning standard problems in domestic societies, which have been discussed in philosophy, law, and the social sciences for decades. That made it possible for Rawls to focus mainly on his criticism of utilitarianism, and on the normative justification of a deontological conception of individual (constitutional) rights, which had already been implemented in practice and whose consequences and implications were well known. Issues concerning inter- and transnational justice still have to explore the territory, and cannot consult consolidated experience and historical evidence.

6.2. Requirements of Fairness concerning Different Groups of Migrants

6.2.1. Equal Respect: Why the Least Well Off Should Not Always Have Priority

The demand that basic sociopolitical arrangements should contribute to the benefit of *all* representative persons requires us to consider all groups discretely and in their own right. Ever since Rawls presented his difference principle, however, political philosophers have tended to prioritize the group of least well off persons, whereby that focus is often presented as a normative requirement of justice.[166] I think that this focus is morally unjustified. From an impartial moral point of view – and also from Rawls's

---

166 Besides Carens, Shachar (2009) is probably the most prominent theorist who applies Rawls's difference principle to normative questions concerning citizenship and international justice; Shachar, however, defends not open borders, but rather redistributive financial transfers.

construction of an original position – the perspective of all representative persons ought to be equally considered.

In contexts of migration, the group of least well off persons is commonly assumed to be either refugees or extremely poor persons.[167] Although I fully agree that claims of refugees have moral weight in their own right, I do not think that that fact is a sufficient justification for ignoring the justified interests of voluntary migrants. Even in Rawls's *Theory of Justice*, the focus on the least well off group was originally introduced as a theoretical simplification of the requirement of equal respect for *all* relevant (representative) persons. The focus on the least well off group of persons thus served as a methodological short-cut, in light of the assumptions that the different social positions are interconnected and that any improvement of the social position of the worst off group will also improve the position of every other social group. There are good reasons to assume that Rawls's empirical assumptions are unwarranted even in the domestic case. They are definitely unwarranted in contexts concerning migration. If we assume that host societies' capacities of integration are limited, and that the number of refugees continues to increase at the same level as it has in the last two decades, lexicographical rankings will tend to entirely ignore justified interests of voluntary migrants. Such a consequence would be extremely unfair, because it would require that voluntary migrants forego their justified interests for the benefit of refugees.

In his later works, Rawls defended the difference principle as "reasonable", i.e., as justified for *moral* reasons, but conceded that alternative principles might be equally justifiable within his own framework of justification. Since the difference principle has been criticized on moral grounds as well, it should not be taken for granted as a normative starting point or established truth.

My main objection to the focus on refugees is that the practical challenge in the case of refugees concerns not requirements of sociopolitical justice, but rather the mitigation of harm and injustice which is inflicted upon persons by "third parties". Transnational refugees, I would like to recall, are overwhelmingly victims of war, civil war, ethnic cleansing, or the consequences of bad government or failing states. Accordingly, the

---

167 Social scientists frequently emphasize that the poorest people usually lack the means and opportunities for migration as well as the skills necessary to improve their situation through migration. My objection to focusing on the group of the least well-off persons, however, is a matter of principle not an assessment of pragmatic options and conditions.

conditions that cause refugees to flee do not resemble a moral vacuum, but derive from acts of injustice. Whatever the global or international responsibilities to address these dire situations are, one has to admit that the overwhelming majority of individual voluntary migrants do not directly contribute to the causes of refugees' flight.[168] It would be *unfair* to demand from voluntary migrants that they sacrifice the pursuit of their justified interests in order to remedy acts and events of injustice for which other agents are morally responsible. A claim to the effect that the justified interests of voluntary migrants have no moral validity in their own right, would either neglect their moral status or demand a supererogatory sacrifice from them.

Moreover, although it is widely accepted that everybody has a duty to counteract injustice and to assist victims of injustice, such duties are usually understood as being limited by what counts as reasonable burdens for those agents who have those duties. In the present case, it must be recalled that such duties amount to a collective responsibility, which ought to be shouldered not by individual persons but by what is sometimes euphemistically called "the community of states",[169] i.e., all those states which are in a position to give support in their role as collective agents or subjects of international (humanitarian) law.

If the justified interests of all affected parties ought to be considered equally valid, regulations of immigration may foresee quotas for different groups of immigrants and for refugees. Accepting quotas does not imply that the number of accepted immigrants from each group must be equal. Quotas should, however, guarantee that the justified interests of all representative groups are equally taken into account. Equal respect for justified interests can be compatible with attributing unequal moral weight to claims and interests of different groups of potential migrants, in light of morally substantive considerations. However, it rules out fully discounting justified interests of any group.

---

168 Below I will address objections to the present line of argument that claims of refugees ought to be granted more weight than justified interests of voluntary migrants. Here, I am only concerned with counting all justified interests as *equally valid* moral reasons.

169 Cf., e.g., Beitz (2009b).

6.2.2. The Moral Status of Voluntary Migrants: A Justice-based Criticism of Miller

Prima facie, the requirement that societies offer public and safe paths of immigration looks similar to Miller's demand that potential host societies provide potential immigrants with a reason for denying them access. *Secunda facie* it becomes apparent that the moral justification of the demand from a transnational perspective is quite different from Miller's.

Miller's defense of formally and publicly announced immigration procedures rests on his distinction of three types of sources of moral duties: human rights, which generate international duties of justice; social justice, which is confined to domestic spheres and generates particularistic duties of justice; and also a class of unspecified requirements, which generates duties not of justice but of what appears to me to be best called "general decency". Miller introduces the distinction between the first and the third source in an argument by analogy that compares two scenarios. In the first scenario, a well-equipped traveler in a desert encounters a person who is dying from thirst. According to Miller, the issue at stake in the first scenario concerns a basic human need, and *therefore* involves a human rights-based duty, which imposes a transnational moral responsibility to the effect that the traveler has to share some of his water with the dying person. In the second scenario, the person asks the traveler not only for water but also for one of her books. The second request is neither backed up by a basic human need, nor does it, according to Miller, generate requirements of sociopolitical justice, because the traveler and the person whom he encounters are not co-nationals. Miller accordingly concludes that the traveler is not under any justice-based duty to fulfill the second request. The traveler should respond and explain her decision, but she does not have to offer a *moral* reason for it.

> Return for a moment to the stranded hiker in the desert who urgently needs water. Since her condition places her human rights in jeopardy, and I am the only available source of remedy, I have an obligation to give her the water she needs, assuming I have a surplus. But now, her need to drink satisfied she asks whether I could give her one of the books I am carrying in my pack, since she's run out of reading matter. No human right is at issue in this case, and there is no obligation on my part to hand over a book. But I think that I must at least consider her request, and if I decide that I have no book that I can really spare, I should explain why. In other words, I owe her some consideration: it's a perfectly reasonable request, and I should respond to it with reasons

of my own. I don't exactly have to *justify* myself to her if I refuse, but I need to say something.[170]

For reasons developed in chapters 3 and 4, I find Miller's objection to the notion of inter- or transnational justice theoretically unconvincing. In light of the principle of ethical individualism, the duty to respond to the justified interests of potential migrants is not a matter of general decency among strangers, but a requirement of transnational justice. According to the practice account, the denial of the exercise of the liberty-right to pursue justified personal interests falls into the sphere of transnational justice. It requires a moral argument, which in most cases is something different from considerations that motivate a personal decision.

Miller's argument is obviously intended to respond to Carens' cosmopolitan defense of open borders by proposing an alternative account of sociopolitical justice. It is evident, however, that Miller's distinction between human rights, domestic social justice, and general decency is no less contested than Carens' ideal of cosmopolitan justice. The more modest proposal of a moral point of view, by contrast, has the advantage that it appeals to normative principles that are widely accepted.

I find Miller's exposition of the problem of migration by means of the two scenarios theoretically unsatisfying in another respect as well. The analogy presents issues of migration as an emergency situation. Although Miller seems not to draw too much normative potential out of the emergency situation, besides the recognition of human-rights-based requirements of justice in the first scenario, other theorists do. I will therefore address the issue explicitly.

6.2.3. The Deficiency of Arguments from Emergency

Emergency arguments are rather prominent in contributions to the ethics of migration, regardless of whether it concerns refugees or voluntary migration. Their popularity, it appears, derives from the assumption that they justify the imposition of general duties towards persons to whom the duty-bearer stands in no morally or institutionally significant relation. The assignment of duty is based instead on the properties of the *situation* that characterize it as an emergency. A standard example is that of a child who is drowning in a shallow pond while an adult person walks by. Standardly,

---

170 Miller (2016), p. 37; emphasis in the original.

the example is understood to justify attributing to passers-by a duty to save the life of the child, simply due to the random fact that she passes by and can provide help without significant cost to herself. Both Miller's desert scenario and the drowning baby scenario differ fundamentally from scenarios that cause flight or migration.

It is worthwhile to start with arguments from emergency concerning refugees, because they are closer to the life-threatening circumstances to which emergency scenarios usually appeal. As mentioned before, forced migration in the overwhelming number of cases is triggered by war, civil war, ethnic cleansing, government failure, or autocratic repression – that is to say, by unjust human agency. The life-threatening situation of refugees, accordingly, is not a moral hazard as the analogy with the case of the drowning baby suggests. It rather resembles situations, where somebody continues to push babies into the water in order to get them out of her way. Moral duties towards refugees, therefore, are remedial duties – and often only second best solutions – based on general duties, such as the duty to palliate harm, to promote good, and to counteract injustice if possible. Unlike moral hazards, for which nobody can be held responsible, injustice results from human agency and therefore raises questions about who ought to be held morally responsible for it. The morally best solution would be the prevention of injustice, and the punishment of wrongdoers.

In addition, the moral status of refugees as regulated in the practice of international humanitarian law attributes a collective responsibility for the protection of refugees to the member states of the United Nations. Although refugees often tend to flee to neighboring states, because they do not want to move too far away from their homes or region, neighboring states are not the only agents who qualify as duty-bearers (as supposed in Miller's scenario or the passers-by scenario, where there is only person close by). Non-neighboring states are supposed to support those states in their task, which manifests itself in the practice that other states or the UNHCR are supposed to organize financial and logistic support.

In light of the dynamics that have triggered recent refugee crises, it can be questioned whether (remedial) humanitarian law is still an adequate response to the conflicts and policies that cause those crises. A serious discussion of alternatives to humanitarian support, however, would have to address issues beyond the scope of the present book, and I will not pursue the issue further.

As I have mentioned before, moral assessments concerning the status of refugees pose problems quite different from those concerning the status of voluntary migrants *vis-à-vis* societies, such as access to work permits, or questions concerning democratic inclusions. The common assumption might no longer be warranted, because conditions of violent conflicts and civil wars linger on, and because state institutions might break down or fail for other reasons. Such developments might make it impossible for refugees to build anything like a personal life-plan around the supposition that they will return to their country of origin in due course. If that is the case, refugees might simply have to apply for long term residency or naturalization in other countries, and ought to be granted such an option. The moral weight of the cause of their application can then justify some degree of preferential treatment as compared to other groups of migrants with respect to access, socioeconomic integration, and naturalization – especially if we consider second and third generations of refugees, who were born abroad and spend no continuous period of their lives in the country of origin of their parents or grandparents. However, I find it evident that moral claims of refugees in such cases do not qualify as an emergency, but rather point to a systemic failure of the humanitarian regime for assisting refugees. Obviously, a lot depends on the empirically contingent conditions and circumstances. I am therefore not categorically denying that certain circumstances can justify giving priority to (second and third generations of) refugees, but I deny that the least well off persons must in principle be given priority.

What I am denying is that such cases or developments resemble emergency scenarios that justify the attribution of duties due to contingent situational circumstances.

If we consider voluntary migration, it is even more evident that the analogy to emergency situations breaks down, because *per definitionem* voluntary migration is neither triggered by threats to life or human rights, nor does it resemble a situational emergency in any other respect. The moral challenge of migration concerns the normative status of individual persons within the international system of statehood. Assessments of the moral status of individual persons must be based on considerations which can justify general norms. It should again be noticed that in contexts of voluntary migration we are speaking about a scenario where the totality of the approximately 198 distinct states and societies might function as potential host societies. It is obvious that the position of any one society to which a potential immigrant appeals does not single it out as a unique addressee of a liberty-right to migration.

The main structural difference between emergency situations and the normative challenge raised by voluntary migration is that normative assessments of the moral status of potential migrants *vis-à-vis* potential host societies ought to be articulable as general rules, preferably diachronically stable general rules. Respect for a *prima facie* liberty right to migration differs from contingently attributable duties due to situational circumstances. For that reason, arguments that appeal to emergency situations present a misleading exposition of the problem.

6.3. Three Standards for the Settlement of Conflicts of Morally Substantive Claims and Justified Interests

In this final section, I would like to propose three general standards for the weighing and balancing of justified interests of different parties, as concerns denial of access to (potential) host societies and preferential treatment of particular groups of (potential) migrants.

Notoriously, there are hardly any standards that are both *general* and *informative* for the weighing and balancing of conflicting or competing reasons. That does not mean, of course, that weighing and balancing is arbitrary, but that what is decisive is the substantive content of the relevant considerations and their weight in the particular constellations. Three problems of weighing and balancing in the context of the present inquiry, however, can be addressed at a general level that allows us to identify at least three normative standards for weighing and balancing. The first applies to conflicts between morally substantive claims and justified interests; the second, to the settlement of conflicts of justified interests at the intra-social level; and the third, to the settlement of conflicts of justified interests of individual immigrants, on the one hand, and, on the other hand, of societies considered as collective entities.

The first standard is based on the distinction between morally substantive claims and justified interests in section 6.1.2 above. It is reasonable to expect that morally substantive claims, as defined above, include claim rights of individuals, as well as the right of societies to collective self-determination. The pursuit of economic, cultural, and biographical interests, by contrast, has been characterized as a normative basis for the recognition of a *prima facie* liberty right.

It is commonly accepted that claim rights weigh more heavily *ceteris paribus* than justified interests, even if the latter support the recognition of *prima facie* liberty rights. For liberty rights do not impose corresponding duties on other parties beyond reciprocal recognition of their validity. Although interference with the exercise of liberty rights is ruled out, no one has a duty to promote or support liberty rights over and above not providing an obstacle to their exercise. Exceptional constellations are always possible, and it cannot be categorically excluded that justified interests under some circumstances trump claim rights; but exceptional circumstances are not the norm.

The distinction between morally substantive claims and justified interests is often an analytical one. It is reasonable to assume that the considerations that qualify as relevant on the side of all affected parties will often combine them. To give an illustration: if we assume that the pursuit of educational training or a professional career abroad qualifies as a justified interest in migration, and if we also assume that no particular society is obliged to offer education and work permits to all potential aspirants, some aspirants might be in a situation of comparative moral disadvantage with respect to other aspirants, e.g., because they are women immigrants from societies of origin that deny women access to higher education. To be sure, potential host societies are not *obliged* to rectify the domestic injustice in the society of origin. But I fail to see any reason why immigration regulations ought to exclude such considerations *tout court*. It should be morally permissible to give more weight to the interests of persons who are morally disadvantaged in addition to having a justified interest.

The second standard for the weighing and balancing applies to conflicts of interests among co-citizens of host societies. As argued in chapter 5, the institution of democratic government provides us with a mechanism of procedural justice for settling such conflicts.

If we assume that different groups of citizens have different interests with respect to granting access to certain groups of immigrants, e.g., unskilled workers, where one group has an interest in cheap labor and another group an interest in reducing competition for themselves, then the conflict between the two groups ought to be settled by democratic procedures. If we assume that the second group holds not only justified interests, but is also entitled to some form of compensation by standards of domestic political justice, then the second group is justified in demanding compensation *within* their society, if the first group wins the votes of the majority. Their entitlement, however, derives from the recognition of *special* requirements of particularistic justice against their co-citizens, not from the assumption that interests of citizens of host societies have greater weight than those of foreigners.

For reasons also outlined in chapter 5, recourse to a mechanism of procedural justice for the settlement of conflicting interests is not an option at the transnational level, because there is no transnational equivalent to the social and normative preconditions of the practice of democracy that would preserve the legitimating potential of majority rule.

As concerns weighing and balancing in conflicts of justified interests of individual immigrants, on the one hand, and of societies conceived of as holistic entities, on the other hand, I suggest a third standard: justified interests of collective agents, especially when they are backed up and filtered by democratic procedures, should be granted more weight than justified interests of individual persons. Two reasons speak in favor of granting more weight to democratically legitimated interests of societies (considered as collectives) than to justified interests of individual persons. The first is that attributing greater weight to collective interests is standard-ly accepted at the intra-social level – as the very practice of democratic decision making implies it. We standardly expect citizens to accept the result of majority vote as legitimate, even if the decision conflicts with their personal interests. If interests of societies considered as collectives bear more weight than those of individual persons in cases of intra-social conflicts, it appears reasonable to assume that the same standard also applies to cases where justified interests of societies conflict with justified interests of foreign individuals.

The second reason is that interests of societies, considered as collective entities, have a normative pedigree that adds to their moral weight as compared to mere interests. They are closer to morally substantive claims, because they carry a form of "legitimacy by authority" that derives from the recognition of societies as bearers of a right to collective self-determi-nation. As argued above, potential host societies cannot fully ignore the justified interests of non-citizens, or deny them access for no reason. But if societies function as indispensable spaces for collective political agency, and ought to be granted a right to collective self-determination, it is appro-priate to attribute special weight to justified interests of societies conceived of collective agents within the international system of statehood.[171]

---

171 This proposal evidently does not apply to cases of inter-*national* conflicts of justified interests, that is, the collective interests of one society as conflicting with the collective interests of another society, where we consider both societies as collective entities.

6.4. Fairness of Access: A Preliminary Conclusion

If I am right that potential host societies ought to pay equal respect to the justified interests of all groups of potential migrants, there definitely exists an upper bound for prioritizing interests of societies considered as collectives. Societies can be justified in treating some groups of migrants preferentially, but they are not justified in totally ignoring the justified interests of the remaining groups of potential immigrants. Thus, I assume that societies are not entitled to select potential immigrants *exclusively* on basis of the society's own interest, and invite exclusively certain groups (e.g., economic investors, highly skilled professionals, or immigrants with preferred professional skills). They ought to pay respect to the justified interests of the individual members of other groups of migrants (e.g., unskilled migrants, economically non-self-sufficient persons, dependent family members) as well, and ought to accept a fair share of persons from other groups too, for reasons of fairness that apply to circumstances of competition among different groups of (potential) migrants.

The next two chapters will address normative assessments concerning democratic inclusion of voluntary migrants. Closing the present chapter, I want to recall that certain pro-immigration arguments, e.g., demographic reasons or arguments concerning the preservation of the socioeconomic *status quo*, attribute a purely instrumental value to potential immigrants. Kant's dictum that one should regard other persons not exclusively as means but always also as ends in themselves, also applies to immigrants.

Chapter 7. Migration and Selective Exclusion from Democratic Citizenship

Intentions often change. Non-citizen residents who originally intended to stay temporarily might want to change their status and apply for naturalization or democratic inclusion. How shall liberal societies respond?

Quite a few liberal theorists argue that (liberal) rules for citizenship assignments ought to be *universal*, in the sense of being non-discriminatory all-inclusive.[172] Other liberal theorists argue that all residents *qua* residency (*ius soli*) ought to be democratically included.[173] The present chapter will address the first line of argument with regard to democratic inclusion. The following arguments do not necessarily apply to questions concerning access and temporary residence.

The rule-based account of citizenship assignments distinguishes state citizenship from democratic citizenship, and classifies the universal right to citizenship as applying only to state citizenship; it also takes a transnational perspective on migration that grants societies a right to collective political self-determination. The latter right obviously applies to all societies, not only to liberal-democratic societies. I take this right to include measures for the preservation of sociopolitical stability and the exercise of political agency according to a society's own standards of political legitimacy. In the case of liberal societies, sociopolitical self-preservation includes the preservation of social pre-conditions of democratic government, and is (as argued in chapter 4) essentially restricted to the preservation of liberal-democratic political institutions and social pluralism.

Arguments concerning democratic inclusion obviously apply to liberal-democratic societies only, not to autocratic or oligarchic regimes. The same holds for arguments that defend the principle of non-discrimination, which is a basic principle of philosophical liberalism but is not universally endorsed by all societies and political ideologies. From a transnational perspective, only a minority of societies qualifies as liberal-democratic, and thus is morally sensitive to objections based on the principle of nondiscrimination. The normative perspective in the following is thus genuinely

---

172 See, e.g., Joppke (2005).
173 See chap. 8.

liberal, but it is not ideal, insofar as it does not assume that liberal ideals are universally shared and respected.

As I am interested in voluntary migration, I will assume throughout that immigrants who apply for naturalization or democratic inclusion already hold state citizenship of their state of origin, and ask either for change of citizenship, dual citizenship, or democratic inclusion on a non-citizenship basis.

7.1. The Case Against Discrimination

From the perspective of liberal political philosophy, non-discrimination is the default rule, because the principle of ethical individualism is committed to the principle of formal equality, unless unequal moral status can be justified by impartial reasons. Recourse to the principle of non-discrimination, in fact, implicitly presupposes a distinction between justified and unjustified discrimination, because not every form of differentiated treatment is morally objectionable. The principle of non-discrimination, therefore, more precisely prohibits *unjustified* discrimination, i.e., discrimination for reasons that would not be acceptable from a moral point of view.

Historically, the principle of non-discrimination was one of the driving forces for democratic inclusion and universal suffrage in liberal societies. It thus is hardly surprising that many liberal scholars seem to take it for granted that the principle ought also to apply generally in contexts of migration. Actually, some social scientists have even argued that recent dynamics of immigration rules in many states are best explained as being driven by an increasing acceptance of (equal) "universal" individual rights.[174] It has to be said, however, that, as far as I can see, some of those

---

174 See, e.g., Joppke (2011) for the thesis that citizenship regulations have become increasingly non-discriminatory and individual-rights-oriented. The empirical evidence that Joppke cites in support of the universalization thesis concerns assignments of citizenship to children of parents with different citizenship. Previously it was a common practice for states to assign state citizenship exclusively in accordance with the citizenship of the father. An increasing number of states have changed the relevant rules, and now also foresee assignment of citizenship in accordance with the citizenship of the mother. See also Soysal (1994) for a trend of individualization, and Rubio-Marín (2014) for an advocatory legal assessment of human rights of migrants. The trend towards (moral) "universalism" in liberal societies, however, should not be overestimated, because it is counteracted by opposite trends such as multiculturalism as, e.g., Shachar

studies focus on developments within liberal-democratic societies.[175] My impression of the practical *status quo* outside of liberal-democratic states is that the above hypotheses concerning the acceptance of universal human rights are overly optimistic. I find it hard to tell whether the concurrence of changes concerning citizenship and naturalization rules even in liberal states are motivated by a moral consensus, or rather are driven by political interests as liberal states compete for the same groups of immigrants.[176]

Endorsement of the principle of non-discrimination, however, cannot in and by itself determine rules for naturalization and democratic inclusion, because further moral considerations are relevant. It is, in fact, generally accepted that no normative principle is *absolutely*, i.e. unconditionally, valid, because practical problems usually arise when a plurality of conflicting normative rules and principles are in play. It is therefore worthwhile to take a closer look at what is at stake.

7.2. Democratic Citizenship and Justified Discrimination

The most conspicuous background of actual controversies concerning discrimination of immigrants with respect to democratic inclusion is the immigration of large numbers of Muslim immigrants to democratic societies, which has raised concerns about the compatibility of so-called *fundamentalist* versions of Islam and the stability of democratic practices in liberal host societies.[177] In light of the present preoccupation with rules of political correctness in public and scholarly debates, however, the topic is more often addressed tongue-in-cheek, if not silenced or rejected as illiberal.[178] Nevertheless, I think it is better to address the issue openly, because discrimination against individual persons on the basis of their religious faith – at least *prima facie* – appears to violate one of the core principles of philosophical liberalism, i.e., the individual right to normative self-deter-

---

(1998) points out in her discussion of the delegation of authority for determining membership to indigenous peoples in Canada.

175 See Koopmans/Michalowski (2017) for a comparison of immigration policies of 44 states across continents.

176 Dauvergne (2016) suggests that the convergence of immigration law in liberal economically well-advanced societies reflects their competition for the same groups of immigrants (highly skilled professionals, economic investors, etc.).

177 See, e.g., Joppke (2014) und Joppke (2015).

178 See, e.g., Dauvergne (2016) for the view that fear of Islamic fundamentalism is "the" driving force of the rise of "securitization" issues in migration debates.

mination. In order to avoid some notorious objections, however, I would like to start with three preliminary caveats concerning the empirically contingent assumptions underlying the following arguments.

7.2.1. Discrimination on the Basis of Religious Belief

(1) Three Caveats

A first caveat is that one must avoid falling prey to the unfortunate tendency of unwarranted generalizations, promoted by so-called identity politics, concerning personal identity. Identity politics is overwhelmingly committed to theories of group identity. The following discussion, by contrast, concerns individual persons. It makes no assumption about group identity. Quite the contrary, I find it important to keep in mind (i) that personal identities are rarely determined by just one cultural factor, e.g., religion;[179] (ii) that almost all societies are non-homogeneous, and that individual members of any society need not hold uniform social attitudes, and political or religious views;[180] (iii) that not everyone who was born or raised into a particular religious environment is herself religious; (iv) that migration to liberal-democratic societies is often pursued because individual immigrants share liberal principles and democratic values that are not publicly accepted in their society of origin. As mentioned before, only a minority of societies currently qualifies as liberal-democratic. The constitutive principles and values of liberal-democratic forms of government in fact appear to be among the factors that make them so attractive to many migrants.

The incompatibility fear, therefore, concerns exclusively individual persons who endorse one of the particular versions of Islam that are often labeled as *fundamentalist* because their proponents endorse a combination of three convictions: (a) they subscribe to a literal interpretation of the Quran (literalism); (b) they maintain that their religious doctrines articulate ultimate standards of legitimacy for the organization of sociopolitical life and public law that are superior and supreme to the institutions of host societies (anti-secularism); and (c) they neither accept religious tolerance (not even towards non-fundamentalist versions of Islam) nor normative

---

179 The point has frequently been made by Sen (2006).

180 See also Vertovec (2007) who speaks of a new "super-diversity" of immigrants in Britain.

pluralism as a principle for the organization of social life, and are ready to promote fundamentalist transformations of their host societies (anti-pluralism). Fundamentalism in this sense, of course, is not a peculiarity of Islam. There are fundamentalist versions of other religions as well. The following arguments are supposed to apply to all fundamentalist religions equally. But since current public debates as well as scholarly literature focus on fundamentalist versions of Islam, I will do so as well.

A second caveat is to keep in mind that there are various forms of Islam, and that none of them can claim to represent an "orthodoxy" in a manner familiar from other religions, because there is no religious authority in Islam that would be entitled to define an orthodox view. It is not quite adequate to portray Islamic fundamentalism as an *inter*-religious challenge; it is also an *intra*-religious one, because not all versions of Islam are fundamentalist. Neither all individual Muslims, nor all societies and governments which are organized in accordance with certain sociopolitical principles of Islam, such as Sharia law, qualify as fundamentalist.

A last caveat concerns the question whether the phenomenon of Islamic fundamentalism exists, i.e., whether there are individual persons who hold such views. In fact, quite a few social scientists and theological experts argue that fundamentalism distorts the true doctrine or meaning of Islam. That may well be the case. But the question whether there exist persons who hold fundamentalist views, who they are, and how large their number is, is an *empirical* question, not a matter for theological dispute. In light of movements like ISIS, or Boko Haram, or radical versions of Salafism, it can simply not be denied that there are individuals who subscribe to fundamentalist views. A crucial question, therefore, is whether (potential) immigrants and non-citizen residents who appeal for naturalization or democratic citizenship hold such views.[181] This is one of the cases where empirical evidence cannot be replaced by academic, theological, or scholarly consensus about the true doctrine of Islam, because the opinions and views of the expert participants in those debates are not necessarily representative of the beliefs and convictions of non-expert persons in the real world. If the actual numbers are very small, fundamentalist beliefs

---

181 Unfortunately, the number of empirical investigations of these questions, as summarized, e.g., in Koopmans (2015) and Koopmans (2017) is still small, and the comparative scope of empirical studies is rather limited, because differences in immigration patterns in different societies make comparative studies difficult.

might be practically irrelevant. But I find it unhelpful to deny *a priori* that such views exist.

(2) What is at Stake? The Moral Weight of Freedom of Religion in Arguments for Democratic Inclusion

It must be emphasized in advance that the problem at stake only apparently concerns freedom of religion, which is also recognized as a human right in liberal-democratic societies. What is at stake rather is the moral weight that should be granted to justified interests of potential migrants *vis-à-vis* justified interests of liberal-democratic host societies. Potential immigrants are not denied freedom of religion, as far as it concerns the individual and collective exercise of religious practices, when they are denied naturalization or democratic inclusion. Also, the issue at stake concerns not the universal right to state citizenship, because immigrants are supposed to hold state citizenship in their country of origin. The issues at stake concern change of citizenship, or acquisition of dual citizenship, and democratic inclusion in host societies.

Nevertheless, it will be useful to start with a more principled discussion of the norm of freedom of religion within pluralistic versions of liberal democracy. Freedom of religion is essentially guaranteed by the right to individual normative self-determination. In the context of non-ideal-theory normative reasoning, however, the normative weight and significance of that right depends on additional normative considerations.

First, although the principle of normative self-determination requires that persons ought to be granted an individual right to freedom of religion, liberal political philosophy is equally committed to normative pluralism as far as it concerns regulations and rules of social life, on the basis of the very same principle. Freedom of religion thus is never fully unconditional.[182] It is restrained by further principles – most importantly, compatibility with human rights requirements, and respect for the law of the society, as well as a requirement of reciprocity, which demands that the members of distinct religious communities be willing to respect the freedom of religion – and more generally, the right to normative self-deter-

---

182 Widely discussed issues concern compatibility of religious views and human rights, the protection of children's rights, the right to change one's religious confession, and the right to exit the religious community.

mination of those co-citizens who endorse different religious beliefs or are atheists.

In a nutshell: although liberal political philosophy is committed to respect the right to individual normative self-determination, the social implementation of that right requires the preservation of conditions that facilitate social pluralism. *Pluralism* must not be confused with *metaethical relativism*, i.e., the metaethical view that moral practices are determined by homogeneous local social practices, which are generally considered to be immune from rational criticism and objections from outsiders. Metaethical relativism is often appealed to in support for the claim that all moral and sociopolitical systems ought to be regarded as equally valid. Philosophical liberalism rejects such a view. The right to individual normative self-determination is a morally substantive principle that articulates a morally substantive position. The three principles of philosophical liberalism are incompatible with anti-pluralistic and anti-secular ideals of sociopolitical association. The exercise of normative self-determination, therefore, is morally justified only to the extent that it is compatible with the practice of normative pluralism and democracy in the public sphere.

Second, liberal political philosophy requires that sociopolitical and legal institutions respect a plurality of diverging religious practices, because normative pluralism is not merely – as Rawls says – a fact, but a moral requirement for the protection of the right to individual normative self-determination. Philosophical liberalism is not a sociopolitical anything-goes position. The principles of normative self-determination and of ethical individualism constrain the legitimate purposes and arrangements of sociopolitical institutions. Acknowledgment of those principles has consequences for the understanding of the legitimate purposes and demarcations of public institutions and the basic structure of society. The principles therefore articulate for public institutions a standard of legitimacy that is special and distinct from personal normative orientations, and ought to be thought of as separable from any personal values or normative orientations that guide citizens' pursuit of personal life-plans.

In Rawls's terminology, a liberal conception of the public sphere conceives of it as "freestanding".[183] Unlike theocratic and totalitarian conceptions of politics, which see politics as an instrument for the promotion of predefined sociopolitical goals, liberal conceptions conceive of politics and the organization of the public sphere as the art of organizing social life for persons who have the right to disagree, and actually often do disagree, on

---

183 See Rawls (1993a).

ultimate ends, highest values, sociopolitical ideals, and even conceptions of political justice. Acceptance of the political sphere as "freestanding" is probably the most important difference between fundamentalist and non-fundamentalist religions.

Standards of *political* legitimacy thus articulate normative standards that differ from evaluative standards for personal life-plans. A freestanding political sphere presupposes that a line can be drawn between private spheres and the public sphere, and that citizens can agree that there is and must be such a line. Diverging personal religious commitments and normative values may be fully compatible with liberal standards of political legitimacy as long as the persons who hold them are willing to agree that standards of *political* legitimacy are special.

Although the borders between the public sphere and private spheres are notoriously hard to define, it is evident that philosophical liberalism opposes any sort of demand that implies that citizens must uniformly subscribe to the very same normative beliefs. Sociopolitical institutions, therefore, qualify as legitimate only to the extent that they respect and facilitate social pluralism, and one of the basic preconditions of social pluralism is that all participating individuals and parties respect the right to individual normative self-determination reciprocally, and tolerate other confessions.[184]

For this reason, liberal accounts of justice are committed to toleration of religious *pluralism* – including atheism –, but they are not committed to acceptance of intolerant religious confessions. Practically viable commitments to tolerance of religious pluralism can never be unconditionally non-discriminatory. The practice of religious tolerance is always restricted to religious doctrines that reciprocally respect pluralism themselves, or are entirely a-political. The reason is that the practice of (intra-social) religious

---

184 Notoriously, the implications of religious tolerance are contested. In my opinion, tolerance is better served by a truly secular state than by equal protection of religious confessions. But for historical reasons, different societies have developed different arrangements. Since Rawls's idea of an overlapping consensus is tailored to address problems of religious pluralism, I want to recall that Rawls's historical scenario of how such an overlapping consensus might evolve, fits roughly the *democratic* history of the USA, but definitely not the history of non-democratic European states of the same historical period, where most societies were subject to autocratic governments that followed the principle of *cuius regio, eius religio*. See, e.g., Wallace (2009) for historical illustrations of some of the steps that promoted the separation of politics and religion in European states during the period of the enlightenment.

pluralism is conditional on the fact that the members of the society reciprocally respect each other's right to religious self-determination.[185] Liberal societies, accordingly, ought to be allowed to demand respect for liberal principles, in order to promote a free-standing conception of politics and the public sphere, and the social preconditions for democratic forms of political government.[186]

The question whether liberal societies are required to demand such respect, is more difficult to answer. On the one hand, liberal societies are required to uphold the social preconditions that facilitate social pluralism and democratic forms of government. On the other hand, the further question, whether anti-democratic attitudes actually tend to undermine the social pre-conditions of democratic self-government, depends on the number of persons who hold such views. If the number is comparatively small, the problem might be irrelevant in practice. On the other hand, if the number of persons who hold anti-democratic view is significant, then the social preconditions for the acceptance of democratic legitimacy may have been undermined already. Although the practice of democratic self-government presupposes that citizens hold pro-democratic attitudes, personal attitudes cannot be coercively imposed on citizens.

If the maintenance and diachronic continuation of liberal-democratic institutions is indeed not merely a preference but a normative requirement of liberal political philosophy, it follows that liberal societies are under no obligation not to discriminate against religious beliefs that undermine liberal values, such as secularism and social pluralism, or publicly contradict principles of democratic government. Fundamentalist religious positions as defined above are incompatible with basic principles of liberal democracy, and I would maintain that liberal societies are quite generally not obliged to tolerate fundamentalist religious beliefs, i.e., neither among

---

185 Rawls (1993a) repeatedly states that it is an *intuitive* idea that in liberal societies individual members reciprocally recognize each other as free and equal citizens. The mere existence of non-liberal societies, however, reveals that this idea is not at all "intuitive". It articulates a "comprehensive" liberal idea and achievement of the philosophy of enlightenment. According to the practice account, comprehensive liberalism is indeed required for successful realization of democratic government, because the practice of democracy in fact presupposes a certain degree of comprehensively liberal-democratic attitudes on the part of citizens, professional politicians, and administrators; see Chwaszcza (2021).

186 As I will argue in chap. 9, liberal societies also ought to demand respect for basic human rights, such as equal legal status of women, protection of children, prohibition of forced marriage, etc., also in private life.

co-citizens nor with respect to potential immigrants. To the extent that the preservation of the basic liberal order of any society depends on the number of persons who hold fundamentalist religious views, however, liberal-democratic societies should be free to collectively decide to tolerate them, because the number of persons who hold them might be marginal. In principle, however, societies would be justified in deciding not to tolerate them.

From a transnational perspective it should be recalled once more that only a minority of states qualify as liberal-democratic. Quite a few societies publicly have endorsed Islam as a political doctrine or have implemented sharia law, and some of those societies actually absorb large numbers of guest workers and voluntary migrants, e.g., United Arab Emirates, Saudi Arabia, Oman, or Dubai. It thus cannot be argued that fundamentalists have no option to practice their religion not only as a private commitment, but as a principle for the organization of sociopolitical life and public spheres, unless they are granted political inclusion in liberal-democratic societies. As a matter of fact, it is not obvious that – or why – fundamentalist migrants might prefer liberal host societies to non-liberal societies, but for the sake of the argument, I will assume that they do so for other reasons, e.g., legal protection from exploitation, access to options of visa-free traveling, or other personal advantages.

Since a transnational account of migration has to take into account that non-ideal political reality is constituted by a plurality of heterogeneous societies and states that ought to be granted a right to collective self-determination, the considerations above apply exclusively to domestic affairs of liberal societies. They articulate justified reasons for the protection of the liberal constitution of (potential) host societies, and do not apply in the same way to inter-state relations between liberal and non-liberal societies. The reason is that recognition of the right to collective self-determination implies that liberal societies ought to respect other societies' right to collective self-determination, and ought to tolerate non-liberal societies – including societies whose citizens collectively subscribe to fundamentalist views (which is different from an authoritarian regime that forces the population to live in accordance with them).[187]

---

187 The difficulty with such a claim is the same as with Rawls's category of "decent non-liberal societies": it is difficult to identify real-world societies, to which those qualifications apply. In addition, recognition of a right to collective self-determination at the international level is conditional on mutual (reciprocal) acknowledgment, and on general compliance with it.

I thus conclude that liberal societies have the right to deny naturalization and democratic citizenship to individual immigrants who hold anti-liberal fundamentalist religious beliefs.

A last point: I would like to strongly emphasize once more that the moral permissibility of denying naturalization and democratic citizenship to individual immigrants who hold fundamentalist religious beliefs does not deny fundamentalists their individual right to freedom of religion. What is at stake is the question whether the fundamentalist's interest in naturalization, in itself or combined with democratic inclusion, ought to be respected if his or her sociopolitical aims are incompatible with liberalism's commitment to democracy, and thus conflict with the right of relevant host societies to collective democratic self-determination. Denial of naturalization deprives the relevant persons neither of their universal right to state citizenship, nor of their right to freedom of religion, nor of participation in the collective social practice in their country of origin. The morally relevant point is that liberalism's commitment to democracy as a collective sociopolitical practice outweighs an individual interest in democratic inclusion. Discounting the weight of such an interest is quite different a matter from a denial of the human right to freedom of religion.

(3) The Moral Difference between Citizens and Non-citizen Residents

From the perspective of political reality, a more serious challenge arises from either (i) second generation immigrants who subscribe to fundamentalist religious views *and* hold dual citizenship, or (ii) naturalized and birthright citizens with single citizenship who hold fundamentalist views.

Since no principle qualifies as absolute and unconditional, it appears fully permissible to demand that individuals, who are granted dual citizenship and who reside a in liberal-democratic society, respect basic principles of liberal democracy. Since the normative status of democratic citizenship – in contrast to state citizenship – is tied to principles of popular sovereignty and democratic self-government, assignment of that status should be tied to the acceptance of those principles too. Thus, the criteria for the assignment of state citizenship and democratic citizenship can fall apart. Denying democratic inclusion does not deprive citizens with dual citizenship of their full political status in their country of origin. It can, however, justify withdrawal of one of two or more citizenships if that is the only viable option for democratic exclusion.

As concerns citizens with single state citizenship the problem is more complicated, because withdrawing (single) citizenship conflicts with the universal right to (state) citizenship. In addition, from a liberal point of view, all citizens who are members of a liberal-democratic society ought to be granted equal political status. Since state citizenship in liberal societies implies democratic inclusion, denial of democratic inclusion produces a conflict of norms. An adequate response might be to impose some general restrictions on the exercise of democratic citizenship, e.g., prohibition of the pursuit of unconstitutional political aims. Such general restrictions would treat all citizens – i.e., birthright citizens and naturalized citizens – equally, and preserve other civil and political rights implied by citizenship status. The main question is whether such restrictions would be supported by democratically minded co-citizens, and whether they can be effectively implemented in practice.

7.2.2. Discrimination on the Basis of Political Beliefs

Obviously, not all normative convictions that collide with basic principles of philosophical liberalism are religious. Thus, the question arises whether it makes any difference whether the anti-liberal beliefs are based on a religious doctrine or on political ideals. I think that it makes at best a marginal difference, insofar as certain anti-liberal political ideologies, such as communism or other authoritarian doctrines, commonly agree with institutional conventionalism (unlike fascism, which also qualifies as anti-liberal), but reject the principles of ethical individualism and the right to individual normative self-determination. Institutional conventionalism, however, is an account of social ontology rather than a normative principle. The principle of ethical individualism and recognition of an individual right to normative self-determination presuppose a commitment to institutional conventionalism, but not *vice versa*.

To the extent that anti-liberal doctrines reject either the principle of popular sovereignty, or the right to individual normative self-determination, or social pluralism, those doctrines conflict no less with core principles of liberal political philosophy than do fundamentalist religious doctrines. Liberal societies, again, are under no obligation to tolerate them unconditionally.

The main objection to the argument concerning non-religious anti-liberal doctrines appears to be the following: according to the principles of philosophical liberalism, liberal-democratic societies are required to respect anti-liberal political views among co-citizens. This argument, accordingly, suggests that liberal societies cannot deny the very same rights and liberties to potential immigrants, because liberalism requires that all persons ought to be treated equally.

The antecedent of the objection, as suggested above, can be normatively challenged, but for the sake of argument I will accept it. Still, the consequent does not follow, because co-citizens differ in a normatively important respect from potential immigrants. The sociopolitical status of state citizenship in liberal-democratic societies includes a guarantee to equal civil and political rights, liberties, and powers, including the liberty to voice and propagate anti-liberal political ideologies within the general constraints set out by democratic institutions and constitutions. In substance, however, citizenship is a normative relation that holds among co-citizens. Political rights, in this sense, are *special* relations. They are tied to some degree of institutional membership, and do not hold equally across institutions. Democratic rights that are supposed to guarantee citizens equal political status and roughly equal political power are not general in the sense that they apply equally to all persons irrespectively of their institutional affiliation; they apply specifically to the members of a particular society.

Although it is true that liberal political philosophy conceives of democratic citizenship as a requirement of political justice, which ideally should be realized in all societies, the reciprocal recognition of the status is tied to institutional and societal membership. As mentioned before, it may be the case that the organization of political associations in distinct societies and states will be replaced by a cosmopolitan empire some time in the future. But as long as statehood prevails, democratic citizenship qualifies as a particularistic political institution and status. Unequal treatment of citizens and non-citizens, I therefore conclude, can indeed be justified by impartial reasons.

7.3. Discrimination from the Perspective of Different Groups of Potential Migrants

A liberty right to migration does not invest potential migrants with the power to unilaterally choose the society or state to which they belong. Liberal-democratic societies do not infringe upon the liberty right to migration of potential immigrants who hold anti-liberal political views, if those societies allow the morally substantive claim to collective self-determination to trump immigrants' interests in naturalization or democratic inclusion. Again, discriminatory treatment of potential immigrants in no way denies them the right to hold the political views they hold. It simply states that if morally substantive claims of potential host societies conflict with justified interests of potential migrants, the former weigh heavier than the latter, as far as the acquisition of dual citizenship, change of citizenship, and non-citizenship-based forms of democratic inclusion are concerned.

To complete the argument, however, it will be necessary to present the normative perspective of other groups of immigrants too.

Against the background of political reality and the increasing number of authoritarian regimes, democratic citizenship qualifies *de facto* as a *privilege* in Hohfeld's sense. An extension of democratic citizenship in practice, however, requires first and foremost the maintenance and diachronic continuity of liberal-democratic societies as long as they exist, and accordingly implies that liberal-democratic societies are justified in prioritizing immigrants who share liberal-democratic attitudes and values. Non-liberal societies, of course, have an equivalent right, but since they do not share liberal values, they might disregard the principle of non-discrimination for reasons of their own.

If the arguments above are sound, two corollaries follow.

First, liberal-democratic societies ought to be allowed to discriminate positively in favor of democratically minded immigrants as far as concerns democratic inclusion.

Second, and in light of the first corollary, it seems to me fully justifiable that potential host societies also ask potential residents and immigrants to declare their acceptance of the norms and principles that are required for reasons of sociopolitical stability and well-ordered social life. The problem of such "citizenship tests", as so often, is rather one of their implementation and content.

7.4. Citizenship Tests

Unfortunately, the discussion of requirements of integration or citizenship test is so closely tied to debates about multiculturalism and cultural identity that the present considerations must be supplemented by the criticism of multiculturalism in chapter 10. I therefore will here address only a few core issues.

As I have argued in chapters 3 and 4, the right of societies to collective self-determination should be restricted to their political constitutions – in the case of liberal societies these are the principle of democratic government and the social pre-conditions of democratic practice. I therefore agree with Mason, who argues that

> citizenship tests are most plausibly defended on the grounds that they promote conditions that are either required for a reasonably just society to be created or sustained, or which are conducive to the creation or maintenance of such a society.[188]

Host societies thus can demand that potential immigrants – temporary or permanent, naturalized or non-naturalized – respect the law of the land, as well as the social standards concerning manners and etiquette in public life. Liberal societies, of course, cannot require that immigrant-residents endorse the standards of manners and etiquette of host societies fully and wholeheartedly, or that they become ardent admirers of liberal-democratic institutions. But they can ask immigrant residents to adjust their conduct to those standards and institutions as long as they stay. Obviously, non-liberal societies can make equivalent requests.

If immigrants intend to stay for long-term periods or permanently, they can also be asked to acquire language skills that enable them to communicate with citizens as well as public administrators, at least to the degree that they can participate in social life and comprehend the contents of official bureaucratic and legal regulations.

Finally, if immigrant residents also apply for naturalization or democratic citizenship, it is a modest and reasonable demand of future citizens that they respect and support the political institutions of the relevant host society, and be to some degree familiar with its sociopolitical institutions, its history, and current holders of higher political offices.

A standard objection to requirements of integration is that it requires a form or degree of assimilation that is not demanded from non-immigrant citizens. I find the objection simply mistaken. Ordinary socialization in the family and educational training in public (and most private) schools, etc., are standard mechanisms for the integration of younger generations into society. Citizens, therefore, are no less required to integrate than immigrants. Fairness simply requires that citizenship tests for immigrants ought not demand better knowledge of the sociopolitical system and histo-

---

188 Mason (2014), p. 137.

ry of any host society, or more sophisticated linguistic competence, than educational curricula for children of citizens do.

Although I have argued so far that toleration is restricted to the preservation of the political system of host societies and its social preconditions, I should add a few words why I disregard considerations concerning the preservation of a society's culture, pending the outline of a broader picture to be given in chapter 10.

I think that the most important point in debates concerning the apparent contrast between multiculturalism vs. assimilation is that the contrast is false. Rules of conduct, manners, and etiquette are not rigidly fixed and unalterable, but are dynamic and fluid. They change constantly also within societies, e.g., from one generation to the next, or due to cognitive revolutions, technological, and social transformations. From the perspective of ethical individualism and institutional conventionalism, the essence of culture is its openness to change. It is obvious that social standards in liberal societies are fluid, and that the differences in attitudes between different generations of citizens, or between different social strata of citizens,[189] are often just as large as differences between citizens and immigrants. It is equally obvious that the cultural standards of liberal host societies have often been influenced by immigrants, especially when they form large groups, as has been the case with immigrants from former colonies or commonwealth-states. The important point of my conjectures is that change should follow the model of the melting pot rather than a clash of cultures. Chapter 10 will outline a pluriculturalist understanding of the unity of society that presents a liberal pluralistic alternative to requirements of multiculturalism, as well as to (monoculturalist requirements of) assimilation.

If non-citizen residents' intentions concerning naturalization change, then it seems fair that societies that demand such citizenship tests from foreign residents who apply for naturalization or democratic citizenship from abroad, should also require them from non-citizen residents who want to change their status and apply for naturalization or democratic inclusion. If citizenship tests are not required for temporary stays and short-term residence, then the fact that non-citizen residents have already resided in the host society for some time is not a sufficient reason to treat them differently from immigrants who apply from abroad for naturalization or democratic citizenship.

---

189 Think of, e.g., differences between residents of big cities and of rural areas.

7.5. A Short Remark on Group-discrimination on the Basis of Special Historical Relations

As mentioned before, political agency can also occur at the international level and generate particularistic requirements of justice that hold between societies. Such special normative relations can justify positive or negative discrimination of groups of potential immigrants with respect to their nationality. Rather straightforward cases of special relations obtain if a history of shared political institutions exists, which was broken up by de-colonisation or the disintegration of empires. Another case arises from special relations between countries, which derive from large-scale emigration from one country to the other. Similarly, a shared history of enmity or war can justify negative discrimination against groups of potential immigrants from relevant societies, and a history of defense or war alliances can justify positive discrimination due to particularistic requirements deriving from special relations.[190]

Since these cases do not matter much in the present context, I will not address them, apart from three general remarks.

First, decolonization and the breakdown of the USSR multiplied the number of states in the world, but left many issues concerning the drawing of borders and the composition of societies contested. As concerns justifiable discrimination, I think that it should be restricted to immigration, and cannot be easily extended to residents in the territory of the new states who held citizenship there before. The reason is that exclusion of those persons would leave them stateless, and thus violate the universal right to citizenship. There may be some hard cases where particular individuals might be denied state citizenship, e.g., due to their active role in past acts of massive injustice, but denial of citizenship should be an exception.

Second, the justificatory potential of historical relations derives from the fact that such relations can generate particularistic spheres of justice of intergenerational relevance. This relevance, however, is a matter of time. Unless special relations between different societies are continually reinforced, they lose their special quality after two or three generations. Positive discrimination of immigrants, e.g., from former colonies, or *ius*

---

190 Think of, e.g., local support of military troops in Vietnam or Afghanistan.

sanguinis-rules that apply to third or fourth generations of emigrant descendants,[191] can be unfair with respect to other groups of migrants.[192]

Second, supra-state organization such as the EU can establish positive discrimination through treaty-based agreements. Since free movement within the EU is often cited as an example of increasing liberalization of migration rules, I want to recall that freedom of movement is largely restricted to citizens of the states that are signatory to the Schengen Agreement. To date, legal liberalization for so-called third-country citizens who do not qualify as refugees cannot be observed.

---

191 Think, e.g., of Argentinian citizens with Italian ancestry who apply for Italian citizenship in order to live and work in Spain.

192 A similar claim of time-based limitations has been defended by Bauböck, whose stakeholder account of citizenship will be discussed in chap. 8. Bauböck, however, ties these limitations to the criterion of residence and the continuation of sociopolitical relations, rather than to considerations of fairness towards other groups of migrants.

Chapter 8. Residence and Democratic Inclusion

Quite a few normative theories argue directly or indirectly that residency ought to imply democratic inclusion. The idea has a long pedigree in the tradition of liberal and republican accounts of citizenship. As conceptions of the *demos* became more and more inclusive, the political-status term "the people" became more or less equivalent to "all persons subjected to the law of the land" or to "the entire population of the state territory above a certain age".[193] Both phrases imply that state citizenship, country of residence and democratic citizenship (ought to) coincide.

Transnational phenomena of migration do not fit the traditional assumption of citizenship debates, because state citizenship and country of residence have been separated. That raises the question whether country of residence and democratic citizenship should continue – or ought – to be tied together. The new challenge actually has two sides, because it concerns democratic inclusion of non-citizen residents as well as non-resident citizens. This chapter, however, will critically examine normative arguments for the democratic inclusion of resident non-citizens due to residence only.

To avoid a likely objection from the start, I want to recall, first, that voluntary migration often differs from the traditional paradigm of settler migration, insofar as migrants do not always intend to stay in host societies forever and to naturalize. Second, a rule-based conception of citizenship takes a highly favorable stance towards the democratic inclusion of long-term and permanent non-citizen residents *if* they are democratically minded. However, immigrants might not want to pursue such an option, and arguments for democratic inclusion can have (unintended) exclusionary

---

193 In 16th and 17th century it was more obvious that "the people" is a technical term, because it was mainly reserved for those members of the population who qualified as male and economically independent legal subjects, e.g., landowners. Obviously, historical developments of democratic – and social – inclusion in the United States of America and in Europe, where democratic government was the exception, differ widely, but the general tendency to democratic inclusion is clearly driven in all cases by the same normative logic of the principle of ethical individualism, which rules out all distinctions and discriminations in the moral and legal status of individual persons that are morally arbitrary and cannot be justified by impartial reasons.

consequences for immigrants who do not yet reside in the country. As argued before, all rules of inclusion can be over-inclusive or have unintended exclusive implications. If we conceive of access, naturalization, and democratic inclusions as consecutive steps, we should not tie access too tightly to democratic inclusion if an increasing number of migrants do not intend to become permanent members of their host society.

The first subsection will critically examine an argument to the effect that resident immigrants have a *duty* to naturalize. The main part of the chapter, however, will focus on arguments that defend a *right* of immigrants to democratic inclusion, on the basis of universal liberal principles or communitarian and republican ideals of the unity of society.

8.1. Do Immigrants Have a Duty to Naturalize?

In an essay which won the British Academy Brian Barry Prize, Helder De Schutter and Lea Ypi defend compulsory inclusion of long-term immigrants with the argument that the status of non-citizen residents as compared to that of citizens is unjust, because it allows immigrants to enjoy all the benefits of social membership, but spares them all the costs that citizens proper have to bear.[194]

The argument can be summarized in three steps. (1) The argument starts from the observation that citizenship – which here presumably means state citizenship – is rarely assigned by consent, i.e., *actual* consent. (2) For De Schutter and Ypi this obvious fact justifies the assumption that assignments of state citizenship qualify as involuntary or coercive. (3) Introducing an "all affecting" (sic!) principle as a standard of legitimacy, De Schutter and Ypi then claim that differences in treatment, or status, of long-term immigrants and citizens are unjust, because citizenship produces not only advantages but also obligations. Whereas immigrants reap the benefits of equal advantages, they – unlike citizens – do not have to bear any of the obligations.

From the perspective of a rule-based account of citizenship assignments, the first and the second step, which implicitly appeal to voluntaristic theories of justification, are unsound. For the sake of argument, however, I will accept steps (1) and (2), and raise a few objections to step (3), which proposes the all affecting principle for the assignment of *democratic* citizenship. The principle is stated as follows:

---

194 De Schutter/Ypi (2015).

> If agents affect one-another (for example, by making use of the pub-
> licly provided education system, by walking their dogs in the park
> or by organizing noisy parties), they should be willing to be part
> of a democratic process where they can explain their practices and
> discuss possible demands for compensation or change. Call this the
> 'all-affecting' [sic!] principle (AIF). The principle can be formulated as
> follows: all those who repeatedly (significantly [...]) affect others, have
> a duty to participate in a democratic process in which justifications for
> particular courses of action are advanced.[195]

As I have argued in chapter 5, appeals to any "all affected persons" principle (AAPP) outside the traditional context of domestic spheres of political
government and legislation suffer from the fact that it is utterly unclear
what "being affected" is supposed to mean. The same holds for "affecting".
De Schutter and Ypi illustrate their understanding of "affecting" in a
footnote to the passage cited above:

> Most defenders of the all-affected [sic!] principle affirm that not every
> type of being affected counts; one should in some way be relevantly
> or significantly affected [...]. We sideline this discussion here, and
> think we are justified in doing so, for it is clear that sharing the same
> welfare system, educational services, roads, parks, schools and theatres
> is going to meet the relevance or significance threshold. (This still
> does not require non-citizens to justify all their actions, only those
> that 'relevantly' or 'significantly' affect others. But we do not need to
> establish the precise cut-off point; what matters is that a democratic
> forum uniting all the inhabitants as citizens exists in different political
> communities and requires each member of it to participate.)[196]

Whereas it can reasonably be argued that long-term residents ought to be
offered the option of naturalization and democratic inclusion, the gist of
De Schutter and Ypi's argument is that long-term immigrants are *obliged* to
(naturalize and) participate in the practice of democracy.

It is not clear whether the argument is meant to contribute to citizenship debates or to elucidate an "antagonism" of liberal political philosophy, but I will assume the former, and start by examining more closely
the unequal balance of advantages and obligations attributed to long term
immigrants as opposed to citizens.

---

195 De Schutter/Ypi (2015), p. 242.
196 De Schutter/Ypi (2015), p. 242 fn.

From the quotation above, it is evident that the civic duties which De Schutter and Ypi invoke concern participation in democratic forums. Given that most liberal-democratic states have replaced compulsory conscription into military service by professional armies, and given that respect for the law, subjection to taxation, and compulsory contribution to social security schemes apply to non-citizen residents and citizens alike, we can assume that democratic participation is the sole difference as concerns burdens of citizenship. To the extent that democratic practice must be conceived of as a burden, it is not difficult to identify a normative rationale for compulsory inclusion, which can be stated straightforwardly: the willingness of citizens to participate in politics is an obvious social precondition for the sustainability of democracy.

To provide a charitable reading of De Schutter and Ypi's argument, I will agree that the normative value of democratic citizenship might indeed be undermined by the presence of large numbers of long-term non-citizen residents.[197]

The idea is not as absurd as it might sound. After all, in the real world foreign citizenship *is* frequently pursued as a mere commodity, because it frees the person who has it from visa requirements in other parts of the world, or gives them access to tax havens. Citizenship as a mere commodity would not be much different from a prolonged stay in a holiday resort or a fancy hotel – at least for those who can afford it. Quite a few states offer citizenship in exchange for either substantial amounts of money or domestic economic investments. As Ayelet Shachar warns:

> Unless confronted head-on, the prospering transactional approach may irrevocably and irreversibly re-write citizenship as we know it, crowding out its association with the political *demos*, paradoxically replacing it with government-sponsored market-oriented rationality and valuation in determining whom, among those not born as citizens, to lawfully admit as 'worthy' new members.[198]

Nevertheless, a duty of naturalization is too strong a demand for non-citizen residents, for three reasons.

The most important objection is that the practice of democracy can function well only if citizens endorse democratic attitudes. It therefore

---

197 If we consider municipalities or islands which attract large numbers of tourists or retirees rather than territorially extended nation states, the threat is not as far-fetched as it *prima facie* might seem.

198 Shachar (2017), p. 810.

makes no sense to demand that immigrants join in, unless they are democratically minded, in which case, I assume, they would ask for inclusion themselves. Most probably, enforced participation would practically be pointless, because democratic practice presupposes that participants share democratic attitudes and are at least minimally self-motivated to participate – both of which are subjective attitudes that cannot be compulsorily demanded. The idea of a duty to participate, therefore, is unconvincing from a practice point of view. In the worst case, enforced participation would be counterproductive and would destroy the legitimating potential of democratic procedures.

A second reason is that most modern democracies do not demand political activism from birthright citizens either. Only a few societies mandatorily require participation in elections.

Third and finally, better alternatives for the preservation of the practice of democracy are available, because it would be unacceptable to demand that societies ought to tolerate the permanent presence of non-citizen residents if that endangers their political system. If the composition of a society is such that the presence of large numbers of non-citizen permanent residents indeed creates a threat to the preservation of democratic self-government, then that society would be morally justified in withdrawing residency permits for those who refuse to naturalize after so-and-so many years, or in restricting the duration or the overall number of possible renewals of temporary residency permits.

Although I fully agree with those theorists who worry that the normative value of democratic citizenship will be undermined if (democratic) citizenship is reduced to a commodity, I seriously doubt that compulsory (naturalization and) democratic inclusion is a viable option that will contribute to the preservation of the normative value of democratic self-government.

Most arguments for democratic inclusion of non-citizens on the basis of their residency, in fact, require that long-term immigrants be granted a *right* to naturalize and to apply for democratic citizenship – and I agree for reasons similar to Shachar's. From the perspective of a transnational account of migration, however, the arguments that support the justification of such a right should be consistent with requirements of transnational justice. Unfortunately, this is not always the case, as I will argue by examining Michael Walzer's communitarian argument, Ruth Rubio-Marín's universal-rights-based argument, and Rainer Bauböck's republican stakeholder account of citizenship.

8.2. *Walzer on Social Integration, Community, and Citizenship*

The perhaps most quoted contribution by Walzer to migration debates is his criticism of European guest worker policies in *Spheres of Justice*. He argues that exploiting guest workers as labor force but denying them democratic citizenship, resembles the distinction between the members of the *demos* and the *metics* in classical Athens:

> Admission and exclusion are at the core of communal independence. They suggest the deepest meaning of self-determination. Without them, there could not be *communities of character*, historically stable, ongoing associations of men and women with some special commitment to one another and some special sense of their common life.

> But self-determination in the sphere of membership is not absolute. It is a right exercised, most often, by national clubs or families, but it is held in principle by territorial states. Hence it is subject both to internal decisions by the members themselves (*all* members, including those who hold membership simply by right of place) and to the external principle of mutual aid. Immigration, then, is both a matter of political choice and moral constraint. Naturalization, by contrast, is entirely constrained: every new immigrant, every refugee taken in, every resident and worker must be offered the opportunities of citizenship. (...) No community can be half-metic, half-citizen and claim that its admission policies are acts of self-determination or that its politics is democratic.[199]

A closer look at Walzer's argument reveals that his communitarian ideal of the unity of a democratic society is only *prima facie* inclusive. Given Walzer's understanding of the unity of society in terms of "communities of character", it is evident that democratic inclusion can only apply to resident immigrants who share a host society's historically grown self-image and communal values. His demand that all persons who have been granted access must also be offered the option of naturalization and democratic inclusion, has the implicit consequence that it allows societies to exclude potential immigrants, who do not meet such expectations, even from access to, and temporary residence in, host societies.[200] As it stands, Walz-

---

199 Walzer (1983), p. 62; emphasis in the original.
200 See Hardin (2005) for a more extensive criticism of the exclusionary effects of the communitarian focus on shared values.

er's argument actually justifies excessive restrictions on access, because he maintains that "admission and exclusion are at the core of communal independence" and are "a matter of political choice", restricted only by a requirement of assistance towards refugees, which, he says, constitutes a moral constraint.

Walzer's objection to the toleration of differences in the political status of democratic citizens and non-citizen residents upholds the traditional assumption that residence, social unity, and democratic citizenship ought to coincide. His argument has some plausibility against the background of traditional settler migration. But as far as concerns new forms of transnational migration, i.e., temporarily restricted economic migration, Walzer grants insufficient weight to the justified interests of potential migrants. If every non-citizen resident ought to be granted the option of naturalization and democratic inclusion, then individuals who do not fit the community's own image of its character should not be granted access in the first place. The community's right to control "admission and exclusion" thus becomes the crucial crossroad, and in light of Walzer's communitarian ideal of societies as "communities of character", exclusion from access is exclusively a matter of discretion of the relevant community (within the moral constraint of a moral duty of assistance towards refugees). The only normative requirement is that the choice qualifies as a collective choice, backed up by democratic procedures.

Potential individual immigrants are thus denied any moral status in their own right. Only after they have been graciously granted access to the community does the moral quality of communal life require that they also be acknowledged as bearers of a moral status *vis-à-vis* the community. In other words, the moral status of individual persons depends fully on what the particular community, in which they reside, collectively determines that status to be.

Walzer's communitarian argument is hard to square with the principle of ethical individualism. It also rejects requirements of transnational justice, and potentially collides with the recognition of an individual right to normative self-determination. This objection is not new, and has been raised against Walzer in debates concerning humanitarian intervention before.[201] The collective right to self-determination defended in chapter 3 does not grant societies unrestricted discretion as regards the selection of rules of inclusion and exclusion, because the relevant rules must be

---

201 See, e.g., Luban's objection to Walzer's anti-interventionist position in Luban (1980).

generally justifiable by impartial reasons. In addition, the right of societies to collective self-determination is not the only morally relevant consideration, because societies also must acknowledge that individual persons – citizens as well as foreigners – are "self-authenticating sources of valid normative claims" according to ethical individualism, and that potential migrants ought to be granted a *prima facie* liberty right to migration.

Walzer's communitarian conception of the unity of society is – and always has been – rather remote from the social reality of contemporary liberal-democratic societies. A pluralistic and liberal-democratic ideal of society, as outlined in chapters 3, 4 and 7, will restrict *liberal* societies' right to self-preservation primarily to the preservation of the practice of democracy and its social preconditions. It will make democratic inclusion conditional on a willingness to support democratic government and social pluralism. But it will not require that temporary or permanent immigrants conceive of host societies as "communities of character" to which they have to assimilate.[202]

The main conclusion I would like to draw from the foregoing examination of Walzer's argument is this: it is not necessarily a moral scandal if citizens and non-citizen residents have an unequal moral status as concerns their democratic inclusion. Quite the contrary, in light of new forms of transnational migration, status concepts for resident foreigners, denizens, citizens, etc. ought to be diversified. If social reality changes, we should not reinvoke traditional normative ideals but rather should be willing to rethink whether traditional philosophical concepts are still adequate.

I thus conclude that transnational phenomena of migration require further diversifications of citizenship concepts, and more nuanced assessments of the status of non-citizen-residents than Walzer foresees.

---

202 Chap. 10 will outline a liberal-pluralistic ideal of democratic society. Here, I would only like to mention that a liberal-pluralistic society is supposed to present an alternative to culturalist ideals, regardless of whether they are presented as communitarian, mono-culturalist (nationalist), or multiculturalist ideals. The social pre-conditions of the practice of democratic government support pluralism, but not the development of parallel societies in form of diaspora communities or ghettos. See Guiraudon (2014) for conditions of successful economic integration of immigrants; see Koopmans (2016) and Koopmans (2017) for conditions of successful sociopolitical integration.

8.3. Rubio-Marín on Immigration and Democratic Inclusion

Somewhat different from Walzer's argument is Rubio-Marín's claim that the very status of non-citizen residents poses a challenge to democracy, because it excludes an increasing numbers of residents from democratic participation.[203] The present *status quo* of democratic exclusion of non-citizen residents from political participation, according to Rubio-Marín, conflicts with liberal standards for democratic inclusion of all social groups into the electorate, which drove the historical development of civil rights movements in modern liberal democracies. The criticism, I take it, is that exclusion of non-citizen residents from the electorate is morally deficient because it is inconsistent with the recognition of a universal right to democratic inclusion.

While I fully agree with the idea that democratic societies should open legal paths to naturalization and democratic citizenship for resident immigrants, I disagree with Mario-Rubín's argument for reasons that should by now be familiar. Democratic inclusion with respect to intra-societal groups of persons who have been historically excluded is driven by a commitment to treat all members of society equally. But the status of non-citizen residents differs in normatively relevant respects from that of co-citizens, because they already have citizen status in another society (though not necessarily democratic citizenship). The question therefore concerns either temporary residence, or double citizenship, or changes of citizenship. The principle that similar cases ought to be treated equally is fully compatible with different treatment of different cases.

In addition, I want to emphasize that democratic exclusion of non-citizen residents does not conflict with the liberal commitment to a universal right of citizenship, because voluntary migrants are not stateless persons. As argued in chapter 2, we must distinguish conceptions of state citizenship and democratic citizenship. For analytical reasons, the universal right to citizenship is best identified with a universal right to state citizenship. My criticism of Rubio-Marín's argument deprives immigrants neither of their political status in their society of origin, nor of the possibility to apply for naturalization and democratic citizenship. For reasons indicated above, it certainly appears morally desirable that immigrants – especially those who intend to stay permanently – be offered the option of naturalization and democratic inclusion. However, recognition of a universal right to citizenship does not annihilate moral difference between the con-

---

203 See Rubio-Marín (2000).

cept and status of state citizenship (which is a universal right) and the concept and status of democratic citizenship (which is a particularistic requirement of sociopolitical justice in liberal-democratic societies).

Transnational migration no doubt changes the realities of social life as well as traditional ideals of citizenship. Attention to the differences between state citizenship and democratic citizenship and further diversifications of citizenship concepts, in my view, are a first step towards post-national citizenship concepts.

8.4. *Partial and Multiple-layered Citizenship: Bauböck's Stakeholder Argument for Democratic Inclusion*

Bauböck's stakeholder theory of citizenship recognizes and accepts the distinction between state citizenship and democratic citizenship.[204] The concept of stakeholder citizenship has primarily been developed for the discussion of multiple-layer citizenship. It was originally meant to articulate a republican account of citizenship, not a contribution to discussions of migration. Nevertheless, it is closely connected in substance to many of the problems discussed in present chapter.

The stakeholder account of democratic inclusion starts from republican premises. Skipping the details of the argument, the gist of it appears to be that according to republican conceptions of citizenship, long-term residents must be included in the democratic *demos*, because they are diachronically affected – or rather coerced – by the political decisions of the societies in which they reside. Bauböck explicitly distinguishes his stakeholder account from an "all affected persons" principle, as discussed in chapter 5: stakeholders are not merely contingently "affected" by the politics of where they live, but are diachronically subjected to political decisions and legal regulations of the host societies in which they reside. Bauböck appears originally to have thought about guest workers and other persons with temporary or permanent residency permits, whose status as stakeholders is due to the fact that they were invited. Whereas "affected persons", according to Bauböck, ought to be consulted and offered the option of voicing their interests, stakeholders ought to be democratically included and be granted the right to vote.

If we abstract from normative implications, the main difference between stakeholders and merely affected persons appears to be that the former, but

---

204 See Bauböck (2017) and Bauböck (2018).

not the latter, diachronically continuously *reside* in the host society, and are diachronically continuously subjected to the political decisions and laws of their society of residence.

According to Bauböck, however, there is no reason to assume that inclusion in democratic *demoi* requires naturalization, because there can be multi-level *demoi* (at least in federal political associations, be they states or supra-national entities, such as the EU). Thus, long term residents and permanent residents might be included in the *municipal demos* of the place where they live, while retaining their original state citizenship (or democratic citizenship) in their society of origin, if – and more precisely: *only if* – they continue to uphold social and political relations with their societies of origin. As mentioned before, the stakeholder account requires – if not residency, then – continuous sociopolitical relations, and thus takes a rather restrictive view of democratic inclusion of non-resident citizens.

Bauböck's republican argument for democratic inclusion of non-citizens appears to focus exclusively on the single aspect of subjection to the law of the country *qua* residence. The argument mentions no normative requirements for democratic inclusion concerning non-citizens' democratic attitudes. For reasons elaborated in the previous chapter, I consider this a weakness of the stakeholder account of citizenship. But I am not sure, whether Bauböck would reject further requirements such as pro-democratic political attitudes.

My main criticism of Bauböck's proposal is that it does not address issues related to transnational phenomena of migration. An early version of the stakeholder account of citizenship explicitly addresses the issue of "migrant transnationalism".[205] Migrant transnationalism in Bauböck's sense stands for the phenomenon that many migrants remain sociopolitically related to family members and political affairs in their society of origin, while they simultaneously also engage in sociopolitical activities in host societies. Their activities include remittances, but also contributions to political campaigns directed at societies of origin, or lobbying from abroad. Migrant transnationalism, however, is for Bauböck a one-generational phenomenon, whereas citizenship is an intergenerational one. If that assumption is unwarranted, then the stakeholdership must either be separated from residence and newly defined, or else the principle collapses.

Moving beyond Bauböck's own theoretical interests, a further objection to the stakeholder concept is that it might have unintended over-inclusive consequences, if we assume that different groups of migrants compete

---

205 See Bauböck (2003).

for access to society. The focus on residency tends to overlook legitimate claims of non-resident (potential) migrants.

If the objections above are correct, Bauböck's stakeholder concept of citizenship raises an objection similar to Walzer's argument for democratic inclusion. It remains within the traditional paradigm of domestic political theory. If transnational phenomena of migration increase, and if that has the effect that the number of non-citizen residents increases too, then the nexus between residence and citizenship must actually be revised in two ways, because transnational migration produces not only non-citizen residents, but also non-resident citizens.

8.5. Beyond Residence: Challenges to Transnational Citizenship

My plea for a revision of our theoretical concepts of democratic citizenship is not entirely new, but the topic is still underexplored at present, although an increasing number of scholars recognize the need to pursue it.[206] Detaching the analysis of citizenship concepts from the traditional context of the model of the nation-state is a first step. Recognition of the fact that the connection between residence and democratic inclusion is less tight if state citizenship and democratic citizenship do not coincide is a second step. Transnational phenomena of migration might require that we adjust our theories to the transformations of social reality rather than the other way around.

8.5.1. Dual or Multiple Citizenship

Since it is widely supposed to be morally desirable that permanent residents receive the citizenship of their host society, a further question arises about whether they should be permitted to retain the citizenship of their country of origin. As Peter Spiro observes, most arguments that favor dual or multiple citizenship are of a practical nature, and largely reflect *interests* of immigrants, e.g., economic, legal, familial interests;[207] or interests of societies of origin in upholding good relations to out-of-state diasporas; or

---

206 See, e.g., Rogers M. Smith (2017) for the present state of the debate.
207 Dual citizenship is often justified by arguments to the effect that emigrants who have given up the state citizenship of their country of origin lose civil rights, such as the right to own estate there, or other rights and entitlements in

interests of host societies in attracting preferred groups of immigrants.[208] Although it is not entirely clear whether dual citizenship is always an advantage for those who have it, because it subjects them to two legal systems and makes them legally liable in two states, I will assume that it is desirable.

Whereas societies might have an interest in accepting and conferring dual citizenship, it is not obvious to me that immigrants are entitled to dual citizenship, if host societies are reluctant to grant it (they may very often want to grant it in order to attract immigrants).

First, pragmatic considerations concerning the status of emigrants in their country of origin appear not to be decisive. As long as non-resident citizens continue to hold state citizenship in their country of origin, they could exert political pressure in their home countries in order to change the conditions there.

Second, dual citizenship tends to introduce inequalities of civil and political status: most citizens of both the host societies and the societies of origin will not have the economic and legal advantages of dual citizenship, such as access to tax havens, visa-free travel options, etc. Dual citizenship thus can generate unequal legal powers. It also generates unequal political powers. This point requires some explanation, because political power is often identified with the principle "one man one vote", i.e., the weight granted to each person's vote *relative* to that granted to the votes of co-participants in a collective decision. That principle is not violated by dual citizenship, because dual citizenship does not increase the weight of any person's vote relative to co-voters in either the country of origin or the country of residence.

The normative issue is rather that dual citizenship grants *the right* to vote in two political associations. It generates a special option for holders of dual citizenship, that grants them the option of avoiding the practical consequences of the collective vote, which is not available to holders of single citizenship. From a normative perspective, dual citizenship actually creates a new political right, because it separates democratic inclusion from subjection to the law of the land. Requirements of an egalitarian political status, accordingly, cannot be reduced to the weight of one's vote, but should be assessed in terms of a broader understanding of legal and political status of individual persons, and the accumulated benefits of citizenship in two

---

private law that accrue to citizens only. The situation is different in cases where societies of origin do not permit emigrants to give up their citizenship.

208 See Spiro (2017).

political associations. The inequality derives from the fact that holders of dual citizenship can reap advantages from society B that are not available for co-citizens in society A (or vice versa), and that they can participate in collective decisions in society A (or society B) without having to bear the consequences of those decisions. In other words: they can opt out of collective decisions in ways that are not open to their co-citizens with single citizenship. In this respect I agree with Bauböck: the exercise of democratic rights by citizens *in absentia* is hard to square with the concept of popular sovereignty, especially in cases of dual citizenship.

Third, and finally, granting dual citizenship for instrumental reasons devalues the status of citizenship, and will most likely contribute to conceptions of citizenship as a mere commodity. The next step, then, might as well be "Why should persons be treated differently from economic corporations that can choose the state for their headquarters rather freely?" – which is a step that some individuals have already taken, when they buy citizenship in tax havens. From a democratic point of view, the problem of dual (or multiple) citizenship is not so much the fact that it might generate conflicting or competing civic duties – although such conflicts are certainly possible –, but that the instrumental nature of the reasons for granting it tends to devalue the normative significance of citizenship as a civil and political status.

An alternative to dual citizenship is a legal status that grants long-term residents (denizens) the legal rights that are necessary for socioeconomic and social agency short of democratic inclusion, i.e., the right to own property, access to bank accounts, free access to and exit from the country, options of health insurance, unemployment benefits, etc.

8.5.2. Illegal Immigration and the Normative Weight of *de facto* Social Integration

As a matter of principle, liberal theory is committed to preferring the rule of law over anarchy and the exercise of brute force. Acceptance of illegal immigration, therefore, is diametrically opposed to the liberal ideals of the rule of law and sociopolitical order through law. Illegal migration, however, so evidently falls within the sphere of non-ideal theory that questions concerning the attribution of moral responsibility among the relevant participants must also be addressed.

To start with the principled point of view: illegal immigration evidently violates societies' right, or even the duty, to uphold and enforce the law.

It also evidently conflicts with requirements of fairness with respect to different groups of potential immigrants. Tolerance of illegal immigration, therefore, also violates requirements of transnational justice, especially if illegal immigration obstructs paths of legal immigration or deprives other groups of immigrants of the option to apply for immigration by legal ways. Finally, tolerance of illegal immigration constitutes a genuine moral evil if it stimulates human trafficking or the abuse, enslavement, or extortion of trafficked persons.[209] One need not endorse Thrasymachos' cynical thesis that *dikaiosyne* (which can be translated either as justice or the law) is an "invention of the weak in order to subdue the strong",[210] in order to recognize that the lack of willingness to *enforce* legal regulations hardly ever benefits the weak but sacrifices them. It empowers the ruthless and criminally minded.

From a practical point of view, however, three caveats need to be mentioned.

First, potential immigrants *ought* to be offered ways and means to apply legally for immigration. Illegal immigration ought not be the only path to migration for persons who fail to qualify as refugees, stateless persons, or asylum seekers. From the perspective of philosophical liberalism, it should be acknowledged that the recognition of a *prima facie* right to migration is a requirement of transnational justice.

Second, if – as is presently the case in the USA – illegal immigration has been tolerated by public authorities for a considerable time for economic or political reasons, then public authorities have cooperated in undermining the rule of law, and also in damaging the general idea of the rule of law. Although shared guilt does not nullify the illegal quality of illegal immigration, fairness demands that illegal immigrants not be the only persons that are to be held responsible for their illegal status. Since their presence has been tolerated, they should be given a chance to legalize their status within more or less the same constraints and limitations as any other groups of applicants.

The constraints mentioned above, I think, also hold for immigrants who have socially integrated themselves into the society of the host country. As mentioned in chapter 2, Joseph Carens maintains that the only legitimate

---

209 The moral issues at stake here is not whether those evils are intended or not, but that they are clearly foreseeable and avoidable.
210 See Plato's *Republic*, bk. I.

criterion for citizenship assignment is social integration.[211] Understood literally, Carens' thesis implies that questions concerning the legality or illegality of arrival are obsolete, once immigrants are socially integrated. It is not far-fetched to assume that this implication is not unintended.

Unfortunately, it is not the only implication. A probably unintended consequence of Carens' thesis is that it undermines a moral claim to migration because potential migrants appear to be socially integrated first and foremost in their country of origin. Being primarily concerned with birthright citizenship, i.e., state citizenship, Carens' thesis also has the probably unforeseen implication that it de-naturalizes long-term emigrants since they are no longer integrated. In a scenario of competition among different groups of immigrants, it could justify even rejection of immigrants who have not yet reached the shores of a host society. I think that it is evident that those implications contradict Carens' moral motivation, and can hardly be justified if we assume that different groups of migrants compete for access to comparatively few societies. If social integration were the *only* relevant consideration, the criterion would, so to speak, honor the effort of illegality by granting illegal residents a competitive advantage with respect to other groups of immigrants. These considerations do not speak against accepting social integration as one criterion among others, but they show why social integration cannot be the sole criterion.

A third caveat concerns victims of human trafficking and immigrants who were lured into migration by false promises and ended up being coerced into prostitution or slavery. Such persons are victims rather than perpetrators of illegal activities. They ought to be granted the full protection of the law, the right to pursue the prosecution of their exploiters, and also the option of legalizing their status if they intend to apply for temporary or permanent immigration. If legal regulations for immigration require a clean personal or criminal record, no charges grounded in activities into which they were coerced should be held against them.

Since a very common form of illegal immigration, especially in the USA, is an overstay of visas or work permits, a few words should be said about short-term immigration programs. Temporary work permits and visas for academic education or professional training are often part of inter-state programs or policies that are meant to promote economic development or to facilitate technological exchange between economically more and less advanced societies. They are undertaken for the benefit of the societies of

---

211 See Carens (2005) and Carens (2015). Unlike Walzer, Carens perceives of integration primarily in terms of social relations based on social interaction.

origin, and individual visa- or permit-holder are often expected to return home, because their acquired skills are needed in their home countries. Since the individual persons who benefit from such programs can justifiably be asked also to accept the duties that come with the benefits, the default rule should be that they should fulfill the obligations towards their country of origin that they voluntarily accepted.

This argument standardly faces the following objection. From a liberal perspective, the individual liberty to leave one's country cannot be compromised, unless normative considerations of equal or greater weight are at stake (e.g., criminal charges, military duties, etc.). Thus, even societies that suffer greatly from negative effects of emigration, such as brain drain and shortages in certain professions, cannot deny citizens the right to leave the country.

The moral situation, however, is different if it concerns participants in special programs who were granted the option of education or professional training abroad *on the condition* that they will practice their skills and professions at least for some period of time in their society of origin. In such cases, the right to leave one's country collides with a special obligation that persons, who want to benefit from such programs, have voluntarily accepted. Self-imposed obligations can restrict the right to leave one's country and can impose a duty to return to it – at least for some period of time.[212]

If no such obligations exist, visa- and permit-holders should be allowed to apply for long-term or permanent immigration like any other group. However, considerations of fairness from the perspective of other groups of potential immigrants who are not involved in such special programs might require that the time spent abroad due to such a special program should not count as time of residence for *ius soli* requirements.

---

212 MacKay (2016), however, argues – I think convincingly – that considerations of brain drain and brain waste ought to restrict the liberty of host societies actively to recruit immigrants with certain professional skills from countries which have invested scarce resources in their training. Since a discussion of the normative implications of brain drain and brain waste through migration is beyond the scope of the present book, I will not pursue the issue, but would like to illustrate its relevance. At the peak of the Ebola-crisis in Nigeria in 2015, where many persons lost their lives because they could not get timely access to medical care, it was observed that more Nigerian doctors and nurses practiced their profession in the USA than in Nigeria. This fact has even been exculpated by economists with the argument that doctors and nurses promote the common good more with their money transfers than they would if they practiced their profession in Nigeria. I wonder whether Nigerians in general agree with the economists' conception of the common good.

Chapter 9. Family Migration: A Transnational Perspective

Most societies recognize a legal right to family unification. In one respect, family migration resembles the traditional paradigm of settler migration, because most societies grant it to citizens and naturalized immigrants only. In two other respects, however, family migration is a genuinely transnational phenomenon. First, conceptions of the family as a social institution vary widely among societies. Family migration thus has a transnational dimension in a sociological or anthropological sense. Second, beneficiaries of family migration are family members abroad. As a consequence, family migration tends to contribute to the competition among different groups of potential migrants, where the relevant groups are migrants with family relations and migrants without it.

In this chapter, I would like to explore two rather special issues of family migration. The first is connected to the fact that the institution of the family is an essential element of the concept of society as an intergenerational entity. That raises the question "Who is authorized to define the concept of the family?", where the relevant options in contexts of migration are the following: individual family members conceived of as private individual persons, potential host societies, or societies of origin. The second issue reflects the common practice of transnational legal pluralism in family law. Recently, the question whether polygamy should be tolerated in immigration law has gained some attention among legal scholars in the USA, where polygamy is explicitly prohibited. As a matter of fact, the topic is not confined to the USA. As anthropologists have observed, recent dynamics of migration have triggered the spreading of the practice of polygamy among immigrant citizens also in European societies.[213] Transnational pluralism of family law also concerns issues, such as the prohibition of forced marriage and of child marriage, and rights of women and children, as enshrined in international human rights documents.

---

213 European countries rarely prohibit polygamy explicitly, but do prohibit bigamy.

9.1. Exposition of Two Problems

The family considered as a social institution is not a prominent object of study in current political and legal philosophy. Most contributions focus on the individual rights of family members, most importantly concerning the choice of spouses and the right to adopt children. It thus appears appropriate to start with a few words about the family as a social institution.

9.1.1. The Family as a Social Institution

Starting from an intra-societal perspective, the institution of the family is rightly considered a basic social institution, because the intergenerational continuity of societies is widely considered to be guaranteed by intergenerational familial continuity. It is therefore not surprising that in all societies the institution of the family is defined and protected by domestic *legal* regulations (sometimes a combination of legal regulations and traditional practices).

Family law includes (among other things) regulations concerning marriage, the status of spouses, relations of children to parents, inheritance, divorce, alimony and various responsibilities of financial support for family members. These regulations are in many societies strongly related to topics of the political agenda that are usually considered to fall within the sphere of domestic political agency, e.g., tax law, property law, demographic policies, and in societies with public institutions for the implementation of social security schemes, also social security entitlements. There are also several (international) human rights requirements that I will address shortly.

From the perspective of philosophical liberalism, the institution of the family is no less conventional than any other social institution. The legal and socially shared background rules that define it and regulate intra-family relations are deeply intertwined with other spheres of sociopolitical self-organization. Those regulations are not "private", i.e., a matter of individual or personal discretion, but are core components of *collective* social self-organization. A society can of course decide that family arrangements are a matter of private discretion, but such a decision must be backed up by socially shared sociopolitical practices and political legislation. In this sense, it is not a matter left to the discretion of any individual person. My characterization of the institution of the family as conventional, therefore, should not be misunderstood as implying that the relevant rules are socially or politically arbitrary. Quite to the contrary, they are intricately interlinked with a panoply of topics of the political agenda. The authority to determine conceptions of the family as a social institution, accordingly, ought to be attributed to societies or political associations considered as collective entities.

Given that political philosophers and legal theorists in the liberal tradition tend to think of the family primarily as a private sphere, and primarily in terms of individual rights of family members, I would like to recall that such a view articulates a genuinely liberal understanding of the family that is not transnationally shared.

As stated above, conceptions of the family and their legal regulation can differ widely from society to society. These differences include normative expectations as well as legal regulations attributed to interpersonal relations of family members, i.e., relations among spouses, parent-child relations, or more generally relations between male and female family members or among different generations. As far as social conceptions of marriage are concerned, they *may* emphasize emotional bonds – as most liberal and Western conceptions do – but they may also conceive of the family primarily in institutional terms, e.g., as inter-generational economic units, as a religious institution, etc. As a consequence, normative expectations concerning the status, social roles, and social standing of individual family members vary widely – not only between states but in some cases also at the domestic level. Quite a few societies constituted by social groups with heterogeneous social traditions practice a form of legal pluralism at the domestic level, in order to accommodate these heterogeneous traditions.

9.1.2. The Protection of the Family in International Human Rights Documents

Protection of the institution of the family has also been a traditional concern in international human rights treaties and regimes.[214] It has to be

---

214 See ICESCR, Art. 10:
The States Parties to the present Covenant recognize that:
1. The widest possible protection and assistance should be accorded to the family, which is the natural and fundamental group unit of society, particularly for its establishment and while it is responsible for the care and education of dependent children. Marriage must be entered into with the free consent of the intending spouses.

added, though, that the relevant human rights regulations are among the most contested issues of international human rights regimes.

The fact that requirements such as the prohibition of forced marriage and child marriage, requirements concerning the protection of women and children, and the acceptance of interconfessional marriage are enshrined in international treaties, has sometimes been celebrated by liberal theorists as evidence for an international conversion on universal human rights. Critics of liberalism, by contrast, tend to see it as evidence of legal imperialism by (liberal) Western societies, which use international law to impose their values on the rest of the world. But the verdict is premature in both cases. Quite a few societies have issued so-called reservations concerning the relevant regulations.[215] That means that certain states do not accept those articles as binding, and that the relevant articles have not been ratified, i.e., transformed into domestic law. The international legal *status quo*, accordingly, is not one of legal conversion, and does not rule out social practices which conflict with requirements inscribed in the international covenants.

From the perspective of philosophical liberalism, the requirements just mentioned articulate normative constraints for any acceptable conception of the family. Especially human rights requirements concerning the protection of children and the individual right to marry appear to have been widely employed by constitutional and supra-national courts in support of family migration. I will assume in the following that human rights requirements concerning the protection of the institution of the family are

---

2. Special protection should be accorded to mothers during a reasonable period before and after childbirth. During such period working mothers should be accorded paid leave or leave with adequate social security benefits.

3. Special measures of protection and assistance should be taken on behalf of all children and young persons without any discrimination for reasons of parentage or other conditions. Children and young persons should be protected from economic and social exploitation. Their employment in work harmful to their morals or health or dangerous to life or likely to hamper their normal development should be punishable by law. States should also set age limits below which the paid employment of child labour should be prohibited and punishable by law.

See also European Charter of Fundamental Rights, Art. 9:

The right to marry and the right to found a family shall be guaranteed in accordance with the national laws governing the exercise of these rights.

215 See Donders (2013) for an overview of state reservations concerning the prohibition of forced marriage, concerning respect for women's rights, and concerning inter-confessional marriage.

indispensable from a normatively liberal perspective, but I also recall that they are far from universally accepted in all societies.

9.1.3. Transnational Social Pluralism and Transnational Legal Pluralism

Besides the norms enshrined in international human rights documents, family law continues to be quite particularistic. From a transnational perspective, the heterogeneity of family law presents a challenge. In liberal societies, it is not uncommon to practice a form of transnational legal pluralism in family law, and to treat family-related issues of temporary foreign residents in accordance with the legal regulations in their country of origin.[216] Liberal-democratic societies in particular tend to attribute a high value to the private sphere, and to the liberty of individual persons to decide matters of lifestyle according to their own discretion (within legal constraints).

Transnational legal pluralism appears fully appropriate as an answer to family-law-pluralism, as long as it is reasonable to assume that foreigners will stay only temporarily and realign themselves with their societies of origin (I will add some normative qualifications below). The case, however, is less clear if naturalized citizens are concerned, not only because they can be assumed to reside permanently, but also because families are intergenerational units. They include second- and third generations of family members. That raises the question which legal framework should be applied to later generations. The issue accordingly is no longer one of transnational pluralism but of intra-societal pluralism, and – in most cases – concerns issues of collective self-determination. The sociopolitical relevance of family arrangements is the very reason why transnational particularism concerning the family is defended in the first place. Intra-societal legal pluralism raises normative questions concerning the liberal idea of legal equality. It is not *a priori* ruled out that intra-societal legal pluralism is justified, but whether it should be or not is a matter that belongs to the range of issues that fall into the sphere of collective self-determination – or so I will argue.

---

216 The application of transnational law is accepted to be constrained by *"ordre publique"* reservations. Those reservations, however, are often interpreted rather narrowly as concerning matters of constitutional stability only. It is highly unlikely that *ordre publique* reservations will be raised in cases concerning family law.

9.2. Who is Authorized to Define the Institution of the Family?

The promotion of international human rights, together with the recent focus on marriage, have the consequence that the social and political dimensions of conceptions of the family are increasingly replaced by individual-rights-oriented concerns. Progressive theorists nowadays overwhelmingly support the claim that individual persons ought to be granted the right to entertain forms of partnership, marriage, and family life according to their personal discretion. In current mainstream political philosophy and legal theory, the dynamics of LGBTQ movements and identity discourse have significantly transformed academic conceptions of gender, sex, childhood, parenthood, and marriage. Although in real world practice those transformations are not as unanimously endorsed as they are among academics, it seems justified to claim that most proponents of current mainstream political philosophy conceive of issues concerning the family through the lens of individual choice of spouses, and regard it as a matter of individual discretion and personal choice.[217] Such a normative perspective on conceptions of the family, however, is not widely shared outside liberal-democratic societies, and to some extent continues to be contested even within them. It represents a particular *liberal-progressive* approach to the matter.

In light of the recent focus on marriage it is hardly surprising that the topic of polygamy has resurfaced, and has been tied to normative assessments of the *status quo* of immigration law. As far as I can see, most of the relevant scholarly contributions are still published in the USA, due to the confluence of three rather diverse reasons: first, the explicit prohibition (and actual practice) of polygamy among Mormons is an established topic of relevant debates in USA;[218] second, in an influential article Kerry Abrams argues that political and legal discourse concerning Mormon polygamy and immigration law are historically connected;[219] and, third, constitutionalism in the USA supports the tendency to turn all socio-political controversies into legal issues. Greggary Lines, e.g., summarizes the gist of his article in the abstract as follows:

---

217 See, e.g., March (2011) for the defense of an individual right to polygamy, and the request that liberal states take a neutral stance towards conceptions of the family.

218 See Sigman (2006) for a reconstruction of historical legal debates.

219 See Abrams (2005). The historical link explores the correlation between the prohibition of polygamy in U.S. federal law and anti-immigration policies with respect to Chinese immigrants to California in the 19th century.

In recent years polygamy has taken center stage on prime-time television and in the nation's courts. After the Supreme Court's reexamination of marriage in Obergefell v. Hodges, polygamy was thought to be the next major issue the Court hears regarding the structure and purpose of marriage and family. The Sister Wives case, Brown v. Buhman, may have a broader effect on U.S. policies and laws than merely in the realm of marriage and cohabitation. In fact, it may be a gateway to offering other benefits, such as immigration benefits, to polygamist families.[220]

The practice of polygamy, however, is not confined to the USA. Polygamy is practiced in several societies that officially do not permit it, and in some of them it is even unofficially accepted by public authorities.[221] In addition, also in societies whose constitutions do not invest (domestic) constitutional courts with the legislative powers attributed to the Supreme Court in the USA, issues concerning conceptions of the family as well as immigration are increasingly referred to legal courts, be they domestic or supranational, especially in Europe. Such real-world developments raise general *normative* challenges very similar to those raised in U.S.-centered constitutionalism debates, especially if Alec Stone Sweet is correct that the deference to courts in political controversies can be increasingly observed also in Europe, especially within the European Union.[222]

Since liberal theorists are committed to defend the right to freely choose one's spouse or marriage partner, as guaranteed by the prohibition on forced marriage, there is a tendency to consider regulations concerning marriage exclusively as matters of personal choice, and to bypass considerations concerning the family as an intergenerational social institution. If we conceive of the institution of the family as conventional, it must be accepted that societies are free (within general normative constraints) to maintain conceptions of the family that they *collectively* decide to endorse and are reciprocally willing to accept. I therefore want to emphasize once more that the intergenerational institution of the family is a social institution, the regulations of which cannot be a matter of individual discretion – even though marriage – which traditionally is one of the central elements of the institution of the family – is rightly considered a matter of personal discretion (protected by human rights), not only in liberal societies.

---

220 Lines (2016), p. 477.
221 See Sona (2005), Zeitzen (2008), Charsley/Liversage (2013).
222 See Stone Sweet (2000).

That, however, does not transform marriage into an essentially private partnership or affair without any public consequences, like friendship as Luara Ferracioli suggests.[223] The problem is not that such a depoliticized account of the family is ruled out for normative reasons. The point is rather that such a position can be consistently defended only if it is accompanied by a general de-politicization of family relations. Libertarians, no doubt, have less trouble with such a position than theorists who emphasize individual social rights and redistributive ideals of social justice. However, if family membership determines interpersonal legal relations (e.g., parental duties), economic obligations (including divorce and inheritance), access to social and public security measures, then conceptions of the family are intrinsically political – not only from a feminist point of view, but from a social or sociological point of view as well.

To conceive of the family as a social institution does not rule out individual-rights-based regulations of marriage. It simply recalls the fact that the relevant legal regulations have been backed up by either collective political decisions or recourse to constitutional essentials, which are collectively accepted as constraining democratic choice.

9.3. Polygamy in Practice

I also want to add a few remarks concerning the practice of polygamy in reality, and the conditions that facilitate it in societies, where it is not legally recognized.

Polygamy is practiced almost exclusively as polygyny, which in the present context is meant to include concubinage.[224] For reasons of convenience, I will not differentiate between polygamy and polygyny in the following; all cases discussed below concern polygynic arrangements. Polygyny is not tied to any special religion or region of the world. It exists in many variations, and the status of women and children (of different wives) diverges widely among different variations.[225] In light of current migration dynamics, it appears worthwhile to emphasize, first, that the practice of

---

223 See Ferracioli (2016).

224 See Douglas White (1988) and Zeitzen (2008).

225 Many scholars complain that so many forms of polygamy with so many historical transformations have been documented that it is impossible to give an exact and general "definition" that fits all cases. In my view, this form of conceptual inexactness is hardly surprising given the conventional nature of family regulations, and their interrelatedness to historically and empirically contingent

polygamy is not unanimously accepted in all Muslim legal systems. Quite a few societies that endorse other principles of *sharia* law concerning the family, explicitly rule out polygyny. It is not even consensually accepted even in those regions and societies where it is officially permitted, especially among women and young bachelors.

According to Miriam Zeitzen, it appears to have been practiced in all continents – and appears to undergo a renaissance, increasingly in form of the reinvention of "local" or "ethnic" traditions; polygamy, accordingly, qualifies increasingly as a "politicized" issue.[226] In certain states it is practiced only by particular groups of the society. Even in societies that officially recognize it, not all persons who want to practice it can in fact afford to do so. As Zeitzen concludes: "Polygamy, as has been described throughout the book, was always the reality of few, but the ideal of many."[227]

Not all forms of polygamy are inspired by religious doctrines; in many cases it is supported by economic or demographic reasons and embedded in background systems of kinship or social hierarchies; in other cases, it is a matter of social prestige, e.g., a manifestation of wealth or social status. In some variations of polygyny, consent of the first wife is required for any further marriage, and also for the selection of any further wife; in some it is not. In some variations, the children of all wives are treated equally; in some they are not. The range of variability is considerable, and anthropologists seem to agree that even traditional practices of polygamy have undergone constant transformations, triggered by changes in the socio-economic or political environment or demographic transformations.

The theoretically most interesting aspect of the practice of polygamy in discussion of migration, accordingly, is the *fluidity* and *variability* of polygamous arrangements, and the transformations brought about by transnational lifestyles. Anthropologists have for quite some time studied the dynamical changes of family life that have been caused by the transnational biographies not only of permanent migrants, but also of seasonal workers or guest workers who leave their families behind.[228] Since anthropologists use mainly qualitative methods and conduct small-number case studies of particular groups in particular countries, their findings resist simple

---

circumstances of social self-organization. We should not expect a definition that fits all times and all places.

226 See Zeitzen (2008).
227 Zeitzen (2008), p. 181.
228 See, e.g., Carling (2008).

generalizations. Interestingly, however, anthropologists observe that the fact that polygamy is not recognized in many countries does not imply that polygamy is not practiced in those societies.[229]

Three legal conditions seem to facilitate "new" transnational forms of polygamy in societies where it is officially ruled out. First, it is possible for a man to marry one wife in accordance with civil law regulations of the society of residence, and then marry a second (or further) wife in the country of origin, in accordance with the legal regulations there. The second wife, although recognized as legal wife in the country of origin, does not qualify as a legal spouse in the country of residence, which has the consequence that charges of bigamy do not apply. First wives can be unaware of their husband's second marriage; even if they are not, they cannot raise legal charges of bigamy against him because the second marriage is not officially recognized. In light of one such case of geographically distant polygamy, Katharine Charlsey and Anika Liversage even suggest that such arrangements can resemble monogamy in its practical aspects[230] – although I assume that it is questionable whether the arrangement conforms to the legal practice of polygamy in the country of origin.

---

229 Naturally, it is very difficult to get reliable data about how widespread the unofficial practice of polygamy is. An assessment of the situation in the USA by Lines, which is probably outdated by now, might help to grasp the dimensions of the actual practice:

In 2007, half a million immigrants were granted legal permanent resident status ("LPR") from countries where polygamy is formally practiced. In 2010, the United States accepted 101,355 immigrants from Africa, where an estimated 20–50 % of marriages are polygamous. Additionally, many immigrants are arriving to the United States from the Middle East, South East Asia, and other areas where polygamous marriages are legal, traditionally practiced, and commonplace. Academics suggest that 50,000–100,000 Muslim immigrants from various countries secretly practice polygamy in the United States. Some speculate that polygamists entering the United States remain under the radar by bringing second and third wives to the United States as sisters or daughters. As civil wars and other conflicts rage on around the world, more polygamous families may immigrate to, or seek refuge in, the United States. (Lines 2016, p. 482).

230 The case concerns a woman with immigration background who married a UK citizen of Pakistani origin in the UK according to civil law. During a visit in Pakistan, the husband found out that his elderly parents needed support, and decided to take a second wife in Pakistan, who was charged with the task of supporting the elderly parents. When the UK wife found out about the second marriage, she reportedly felt ashamed and threatened her husband with divorce unless he divorced his second wife. See Charsley/Liversage (2013).

Second, some societies that do not recognize polygamy in civil law practice a form of legal pluralism by treating religious institutions as corporations invested with the power to regulate marriage and family affairs among their members in accordance with religious doctrines, without a duty to report their activities to civil law institutions. Most relevant from an empirical point of view in this case is the toleration of *sharia* law courts for Muslim communities in non-Islamic societies.[231] If the relevant religious authorities are not required to report religious marriages to the relevant administrative offices of the host societies, as seems to be the case, e.g., in Germany, then those marriages are never registered, never officially acknowledged, and accordingly legally inexistent.

Again, since accusations of bigamy cannot be raised, the practice of polygamy remains under the radar of legal regulations. Nevertheless, all wives are respected as legal wives among (the religious members of) the emigrant community. And again, the civil-law wife may not even be aware of the further marriages if the husband decides to settle his further wives in different homes. But even if the husband lives together with all of his wives in the same household, charges of bigamy do not apply, because the second and further wives do not officially qualify as wives. Home-sharing, unlike bigamy, is not legally forbidden.

Depending on the details of national social security system with respect to the protection of children, social security regulations can even provide incentives for new forms of polygamy. That can happen if "single mothers" qualify as "households" in their own right, and if subsidies for children are calculated by household. Under such conditions, unofficial marriage can be an economic advantage if second and further wives are officially recognized as "single mothers" (who claim not to know who the father of the child is), and thus qualify as a household in their own right.[232] Since *sharia* regulations make polygamous marriage arrangements

---

231 Toleration of *sharia* courts is often justified by the argument that it protects women in Muslim communities where men tend not to recognize civil law-based court rulings of their host society as valid, especially with respect to divorce. I find the logic of the argument odd, because the protection of women's rights might be promoted equally, if not better, by the requirement that their husbands ought to respect the civil law of the society of residence.

232 Eichenberger (2012) remarks that the aim of avoiding such economic incentives appears to be one of the reasons why the UK unofficially recognizes polygamous marriage arrangements in social law, because it allows the administration to adjust subsidies to the total number of children in one (polygamous) household.

conditional on the man's economic capacity to support all of his wives and children equally, state-paid subsidies can have the effect that they enable men who could not afford to practice polygamy in their country of origin to practice it abroad.

Third, legal professionals and administrators in liberal societies tend to conceive of family relations as a sphere of privacy, and to react to polygynic arrangements often by treating second and further wives as friends or additional family members (sisters of the wife or daughters of the husband).

9.4. Polygamy in Normative Debates concerning Immigration and Women's Rights

In light of the real-world practice of polygamy, several scholars have argued that polygamy should be recognized in U.S.-immigration law, for reasons of the protection and promotion of women's rights. The argument is actually an instrumental one that criticizes the unequal distribution of legal powers between the men as bearers, and women as potential beneficiaries, of family immigration. Since polygamy is prohibited in the USA, family-based immigration of spouses is generally restricted to one spouse, but it applies to all children who are officially recognized as children by the naturalized husband. Claire Smearman argues that the prohibition of polygamy has the effect that it transfers (legal) powers to resident husbands who (i) can select the wife whose immigration is facilitated (who need not be the first wife as long as she officially qualifies as "wife"), and who (ii) can alienate mothers from their children because male residents can apply for the immigration of all of the children they officially recognize as theirs.[233]

A different argument has been proposed by Sarah Eichenberger, who is primarily concerned with the legal status of (immigrant) women in polygamous marriage arrangements in the USA, where polygamy qualifies as a "crime of moral turpitude" according to Eichenberger. This constitutes a legal reason for the denial of immigration, and has implications for the legal status of second (or further) wives who have succeeded in entering the USA but, e.g., want to separate from their husband for reasons of abuse. They are denied the legal status and social support otherwise offered

---

233 See Smearman (2009).

to women in similar circumstances. Eichenberger therefore proposes that polygamy be eliminated from the list of crimes of moral turpitude.[234]

9.5. *Immigration and Transnational Legal Pluralism: Some Principled Objections*

From the perspective of migration as a transnational phenomenon, Eichenberger's argument appears reasonable and justified. Unless polygamy also qualifies as a crime in the women's country of origin, second (and further) wives should not be treated as criminals in host societies into which they immigrated after their marriage. I disagree with Smearman, however, for three reasons.

First, when we talk about rights of access of immigrants to host societies, we consider a one-generational phenomenon that concerns concrete individuals at a specific point in their life; when we talk about legal recognition of polygamy as a conception of the family, we consider an intergenerational institution. To the extent that family-based immigration is granted to naturalized citizens – not to temporary residents – it should be expected that naturalized immigrants intend to join the host society and stay there permanently. Which family law, then, should apply to *second* and *third* generations of immigrant citizens? The question concerns not only the legal status of children, but also questions concerning the social status of women in polygynic marriages in a sociocultural environment where polygyny is not accepted. If Smearman's proposal is indeed intended to promote women's rights, a better option, it seems to me, would be to offer women options of immigration *in their own right*.

---

234 See Eichenberger (2012). She also argues that official recognition of polygamy exclusively for immigrant families, as practiced in multi-culturalist Canada, protects the rights of women and children because it presents an apt legal measure for the regulation of inheritance, alimony, divorce, etc., for those families in accordance with the laws of the country of origin. I find it evident that the question whether women's rights are promoted by transnational legalism depends on the very content of the relevant legal regulations *and* the consequences of their *general* application. It cannot be excluded that recourse to transnational legal pluralism in cases where it would benefit women and children promotes its general application also to non-polygamy-related cases, where the legal regulations of the country of residence would protect the rights of women and children much better than the regulations of the society of origin or their parents' origin. It is no secret that women and girls in many societies are legally disadvantaged in family law.

Second, if a society decides that polygamy should be tolerated, then it should be legalized and generally recognized for all citizens, including non-immigrant citizens. I find it highly problematic from a liberal point of view to promote status-equality by treating immigrant families legally differently from non-naturalized citizens, *ceteris paribus*.[235] Liberalism is profoundly committed to the view that the law should be the same for all persons who are similar in relevant respects, and the relevant respect in the present case is the status of citizenship. I simply fail to see any normative difference between the case of immigrants on the one hand and non-immigrant Mormons, or any other persons who, e.g., want to legalize their *ménage à trois*.

If liberalism is committed to a conventional ontology of social institutions, including the family – and this is obviously an implicit premise of the arguments above –, then not only birthright citizens, but also immigrant citizens can be asked to revise their traditional practices.

Third, I find it hard to understand why the unequal distribution of legal powers is attributed to immigration law of host societies rather than the regulations of the polygamous family arrangement in the country of origin. If husbands in such arrangements have the power to alienate mothers from their children, and if this is morally undesirable, then the primary moral responsibility for providing a remedy lies with the country of origin. Either the regulations concerning parenthood and the status of women in polygamous family arrangements should be changed, or else special regulations concerning migration should be added. It can be assumed that in most cases polygamy, where it is legal, is regulated by sets of rules that define the status of children of second and further wives with respect to their mothers and fathers, inheritance, responsibilities of alimony, etc. If migration of parts of the family is not regulated by the traditional rules, then the primary moral responsibility for adjusting those rules to non-traditional practices, such as migration, lies with the relevant societies of origin. As indicated above, descriptive research shows that family arrangements in general – including the various practices of polygamy – are fluid

---

235 The normative situation is more complicated when humanitarian reasons play a role as in the case of refugees, or when particularistic requirements of justice are relevant as in the famous case of (traditionally polygamous) Hmong families, who were granted U.S. citizenship because they had supported U.S. troops in Vietnam, but have been denied official recognition of polygamous marriage. As always, morally complex cases can require exceptions, but they had better not be used as a precedent for new general norms. As the old saying goes, "Hard cases make bad law".

and constantly adjusted to structural transformations of socioeconomic and political spheres and demographic dynamics. Transnational migration changes the social life of emigrants as well as of societies of origin in many respects – so why not with respect to family law?

Generally, it appears to me that the normatively consistent response to the challenges raised by transnational differences concerning the institution of the family are two. (1) We can either combine the preservation of previously local legal regulations with geographical mobility, and promote transnational legal pluralism *intergenerationally* in *all* societies. That means that we give up on the liberal principle of equality before the law. (2) Alternatively, we can preserve the liberal ideal of the law as a system of general rules that apply to all citizens equally, and require that naturalized citizens respect the law of their society of residence.

Personally, I find the second option more convincing. In my view, the liberal ideal of equality before the law weighs very heavily against the acceptance of special legal arrangements for naturalized immigrant families. If a society were to collectively decide to accept the option of polygamy (the consent of intending spouses presupposed), then that should be accepted generally as an option for all citizens equally.

Equality before the law, however, is not the only normative principle that is at stake. If we conceive of the family as an institution, then we have to attend to the fact that family membership, like citizenship, is constituted by rules of inclusion and exclusion. Those rules and the relevant criteria, however, need not coincide with the rules for citizenship assignment of the host society. If host societies were required to acknowledge the family conceptions of all immigrant families, it would have the effect that the authority to specify immigration laws would be transferred from the legislative branch of political government of host societies to naturalized immigrants, i.e., individual persons. Family-based immigration therefore potentially conflicts not only with social regulations in (potential) host societies, but also with the right to collective self-determination. Host societies accordingly should be granted the right either to determine the conceptions of family that they accept, or at least the persons whom they acknowledge as family members in immigration law. Note that such a right does not ignore the interests and normative opinions of immigrant citizens, because family-based migration applies only to naturalized immigrants and birthright citizens, who – in democratic societies – are usually included in the democratic *demos*.

9.6. *A Brief Remark concerning the Normative Weight of Personal Preferences*

Is it really reasonable to assume that recognition of polygamy in immigration law will promote or protect the rights of women and children, if we assess the issue in light of family regulations as an intergenerational social institution?

I seriously doubt that the toleration and perpetuation of polygamous family arrangements are apt instruments for the promotion of the rights of women and children. The question cannot be answered conclusively *a priori*, because it is partly an empirical one. Nevertheless, *a priori* reasoning might at least clarify what kind of evidence would be required for answering the question.

Several versions of polygamy are straightforwardly patriarchal. Their intergenerational continuation will certainly not contribute to the promotion of women's rights. There is also evidence that, in practice, the percentage of child brides is relatively high as compared to monogamous marriages.[236] It is certainly true that *in practice* monogamous marriage arrangements are not always ideal protections of the rights of women and children either. There also exist patriarchal relations among spouses, and various forms of child abuse in the actual practice of monogamous marriages. But the spread and social implementation of liberal ideals in family law has had a strong impact on the recognition, promotion, and protection of the rights of women and children, because liberalism is committed to ethical individualism and to moral, as well as legal, equality. Traditional versions of polygamy, by contrast, seem overwhelmingly to be embedded in sociocultural practices that are significantly less individualistic and appear to value moral and legal equality less than do liberal societies. For this reason, I am inclined to expect that recognition of polygamy in immigration law will either reproduce non-liberal ideals in immigrant families, or it will reinforce feelings of alienation on the side of immigrant women in their new social environments.

---

236 See also Zeitzen (2008). In 2018, the Turkish Directorate for Religious Affairs, Diyanet, adopted on its official website an opinion, which appears to be widely held among literalist Muslims, that an adequate minimum-age requirement for brides is nine years. Diyanet had to withdraw the announcement after a wave of protest. The official, legal minimum-age requirement for brides in Turkey is currently 18 years, in special cases 16 years. It remains unknown, however, what the effects of Diyanet's withdrawal are among Turkish citizens who accept the religious authority of Diyanet.

Empirical assessments, unfortunately, are complicated, because at least some women report that they voluntarily have chosen polygamy and find it personally beneficial.[237] In light of the principle of ethical individualism, voluntary choices must be respected, unless they conflict with or violate the principle of social compatibility and equal respect for an equal liberty of other citizens. Philosophical liberalism also respects choices of a life of hardship, personal neglect, or religious devotion, if it qualifies as voluntary. The self-perception of those women therefore cannot be simply dismissed as irrelevant. It raises, however, a follow-up question, "When is consent voluntary?". That question cannot always be conclusively settled by a statement of personal preferences, because individual self-perceptions might express what economists call "adapted" preferences.[238] Personal preferences are not a matter of purely personal choice, but regularly reflect expectations of the agent's social environment, the options that are open to her, and the chances of success in realizing any one of these options. Due to the nature of their social environment, agents often devaluate certain preferences because the chances of their satisfaction appear small. A serious question within the context of (permanent) migration, accordingly, is whether the preferences that women developed in one social environment will remain the same when they move to a socially quite different environment. Migration appears to transform individual self-perception and personal preferences in many respects.

Finally, as remarked above, polygyny is far from uncontested especially among women, even in societies where it is officially allowed. If polygamy were accepted in immigration law, it might even have unintended effects that are counter-productive for the promotion of women's rights abroad, because its acceptance might counteract local opposition to its practice in societies of origin.

9.7. Beyond Access: Liberal Limits of Transnational Legal Pluralism with Respect to Foreign Residents

Transnational legal pluralism is not restricted to matters concerning family migration but extends to matters concerning temporary residence. It raises the general question to what extent host societies ought to tolerate social

---

237 See Ryan White (2009) for detailed references.
238 See also Elster (1985) on "sour grapes".

practices of family life that conflict with legal regulations considered as binding on citizens.

From a liberal point of view, the protection of the rights of women and children articulates a universal human rights requirement. Unlike other rights tied to citizenship-status, human rights protect not only citizens but also temporary and permanent residents. As mentioned in section 9.2.1, in the reality of statism quite a few societies do not comply with those requirements, and several have even officially made reservations, i.e., have not ratified the relevant articles of international human rights treaties. Even if transnational legal pluralism is defensible in the case of temporary residence, it has in my opinion a definite limit. It should not recognize regulations that violate international human rights, such as the prohibition of forced marriage and child marriage, the guarantee of an equal legal status for women, and the recognition of inter-confessional marriage. I suggest that we call these limitations the *Principle of Reciprocal Legal Recognition* (PRLR). It means that liberal societies should accept legal regulations of other societies only if those regulations meet human rights requirements concerning the status of women and children.[239]

Actually, promotion of transnational legal pluralism appears often to be supported by the assumption that pluralism will be mutually accepted, and that it will be practiced not only by liberal, but also by non-liberal societies, and that all societies respect the basic human rights requirements mentioned above. Such assumptions are not warranted when we look at political reality.

From a normative point of view, I think that liberal societies ought to respect the right to collective self-determination of all societies, including non-liberal ones, within the territory of the relevant society. But liberal societies should tolerate non-liberal conceptions of the family in the territory of their own society only to the extent that those conceptions respect the basic human rights mentioned above. The official or unofficial practice of conceptions of family life that collide with the prohibition of forced marriage, the prohibition of child marriage, and requirements for the protection of women and children is in my view incompatible with the most basic principles of philosophical liberalism, and therefore cannot be

---

239 PRLR is meant to operate at the level of bi- or multilateral inter-state agreements. In this respect it differs from theories of international constitutionalism, such as, e.g., Tomuschat (1999), that aspire to an integration of all states and societies under a single (liberal) international legal framework that functions as an international constitution.

justified on such a basis. Multiculturalist arguments to the effect that the social and cultural practices of all societies must be considered as being equally valuable, derive from metaethical relativism or cultural essentialism. Neither theoretical framework is compatible with recognition of the principle of ethical individualism or the idea of universal human rights.

Finally, transnational legal pluralism – like any other principle of mutual accommodation – cannot be unidirectional, but must be practiced reciprocally. PRLR, accordingly, requires not only that all societies whose regulations are tolerated must conform with basic human rights requirements, but also that they respect regulations of liberal states, as concerns residents and immigrants from liberal societies.

Obviously, the promotion of liberal conceptions of the family is not always served best by *legal* tools. Non-legal forms of social and political discourse and practice are often more successful. But legal tolerance of non-liberal legal frameworks is certainly *not* a promising way to promote liberal values.

9.8. Family-based Immigration and Requirements of Fairness among Different Groups of Immigrants

Last but not least, family migration must also be assessed from the perspective of competing groups of immigrants. Most societies appear to limit the overall number of family members that can benefit from family migration, and many restrict it to core members, i.e., (single) spouses, children, and in special cases also parents. Special regulations concerning family members in this narrow sense are, as far as I can see, largely uncontested in liberal societies,[240] whereas regulations concerning further family members, or the overall number of family members that qualify for family-based immigration are contested. The normative perspectives of family members and

---

240 Family-based immigration of parents is currently contested with respect to one special regulation in the USA, which otherwise has a rather generous scheme of family-based migration: that is the rule that all persons who were born in U.S.-territory receive U.S.-citizenship independently of any other condition. The main cause of contestation is the political controversy concerning so-called anchor babies. I will not pursue that issue, however, because the U.S.-regulation appears to be rather special. Generally, issues concerning abuse are different from questions concerning normative justifiability. All rules can be abused, and if abuse is frequent, the rule should be modified or supplemented by control mechanisms that prevent abuse.

(potential) host societies, however, are not exhaustive. Justified interests of other groups of (potential) immigrants also have to be taken into account.

9.8.1. Access

If the assumption is correct that different groups of immigrants compete for access to host societies, then restrictions of family-based migration in terms of either rules of inclusion or numbers of eligible family members can be a requirement of fairness with respect to groups of immigrants who apply for non-family-based immigration. For once we consider family relations beyond spouses and children, the difference between distant relatives and non-relatives begins to shrink, considered from a moral point of view that includes the perspectives of *all* groups of potential immigrants.

If the justified interests of all groups of potential immigrants ought to be equally respected, then justified interests and morally substantive claims of potential immigrants without naturalized relatives must not be discounted. In fact, justified interests of potential immigrants without family relations often are combined with morally substantive claims, and then might even weigh more heavily than those of remote family members. Since the problem concerns primarily the ratio of family-based immigration to non-family-based immigration, which cannot be assessed without empirical data,[241] a more detailed discussion is beyond the scope of this book. Nevertheless, restrictions on family-based immigration should not be ruled out *in principle* or be considered morally blameworthy. Any rule can become over-inclusive or over-exclusive under certain conditions. The normatively relevant point is that assessments of the prevailing conditions should take account of the effects that family-based immigration has on other groups of immigrants.

---

241 At the time of this writing, it seems that the percentage of family-based immigration (of non-European citizens) is highest in European societies, where family-based immigration is in some places the only practically relevant path to citizenship besides *ius sanguinis* or EU-citizenship; it is also comparatively high in the USA, but comparatively low in Canada and Australia, which regulate immigration according to a point system.

9.8.2. Naturalization and Democratic Inclusion

From the perspective of those groups of potential immigrants that cannot benefit from family-based immigration, it appears to be a requirement of fairness that beneficiaries of family-based migration should not be exempted from requirements concerning language capacities, familiarity with sociopolitical institutions, etc., if host societies require these from other immigrants. The reasons that justify such requirements apply equally to all groups of immigrants.

I also do not find it obvious that children should automatically be granted state citizenship and democratic citizenship when they reach the age of adulthood. The problem has two sides. On the one hand, they should be given the option of choosing between the state citizenship of their country of residence and the country of their parent's origin. On the other hand, if those children hold dual citizenship, it appears to be a matter of fairness with respect to other groups of long-term residents that residency not be *per se* considered sufficient for democratic inclusion. As argued in chapters 7 and 8, the relevant background institutions for the assignment of state citizenship and democratic citizenship are different. They should therefore not be automatically combined or identified. If this reservation holds for other groups of immigrants, then it should also hold for second-generation family members who entered the host society as children, for reasons of fairness with respect to different groups of immigrants.

9.9. A (Very) Preliminary Conclusion

There undoubtedly are many issues concerning family migration that have not been addressed here. The important point, in my view, is that rules concerning family migration – like any other rule of inclusion or exclusion – can be over-inclusive, and thus unfairly exclusive. From the perspective of a transnational moral point of view, family migration should not be the main, or even the sole, rule to which potential immigrants can appeal.

If we conceive of the family as an intergenerational social institution, then the final authority to define the family should be assigned to host societies, because it concerns core aspects of collective self-organization. That implies that prior philosophical arguments cannot settle many of the relevant questions. Nevertheless, from the perspective of philosophical liberalism, at least three arguments can be proposed for further discussion. First, legal regulations concerning the institution of the family should reflect the conception of the family as an intergenerational social institution, and should aim at intergenerational stability of legal regulations for *naturalized* immigrant families. That also means that questions concerning the institution of the family should not be reduced to issues concerning marriage, but must reflect all of the multiple aspects of family relations and their impact on other areas of legal regulation. Second, the principle of equality before the law can hardly be squared with the practice of transnational legal pluralism with respect to *naturalized* immigrant families. If social pluralism in family law is accepted, it should be accepted for *all* citizens alike, not only for naturalized immigrant families. Third, from the perspective of philosophical liberalism as well as from the perspective of international human rights documents, the protection of the rights of women and children, the prohibition of child marriage and forced marriage, and the acceptance of inter-confessional marriage all articulate normative constraints for the practice of transnational legal pluralism also with respect to *non-naturalized* foreign residents in liberal-democratic societies.

Chapter 10. Society and Culture: A Plea for Pluriculturalism

Finally, I would like to propose a liberal ideal of the unity of society, which I will call *pluriculturalism*. Pluriculturalism articulates a genuinely pluralistic alternative to multiculturalism and to monoculturalism, including communitarianism and liberal nationalism.

The name is not ideal, because pluriculturalism is explicitly intended to provide an alternative to *culturalism*. Culturalism, as I understand the term, is a group-focused ideal of collective social self-organization. It builds on the assumption that belonging to a particular cultural group provides group members with values and sociocultural orientations that are necessary for the pursuit of meaningful life plans. This assumption is the basis of most culturalist ideals of collective social self-organization – be it by emphasizing the need to support the preservation of *all* cultural groups of a society as groups, i.e., multiculturalism, or by emphasizing the need to support the preservation of the dominant or majoritarian cultural group, i.e., monoculturalism. From the perspective of a practice account, participation in rule-based social practices is the human form of life, and I would find it hard to deny that social practices are the core element of what is commonly understood by the term *culture*. Pluriculturalism, however, rejects the idea that belonging to a *particular* culture is essential, and that cultural belonging is an irreplaceable source of meaning in human life. Pluriculturalism emphasizes the right to *individual* normative self-determination, and defends a political ideal of collective social self-organization that supports social pluralism by protecting the moral status – not of cultural groups – but of individual persons.

Unavoidably, normative ideals build on normative premises that are contested, and not all contestations can be settled. Normative premises, however, are not the sole ingredient of ideals of the unity of society. Such ideals also standardly build on philosophical theories concerning human agency and theories of conceptual and explanatory analysis of social micro- and macro-phenomena, or to particular traditions in the methodology of the social sciences.[242] Cultural theorists often claim to address a *desideratum* of liberal political philosophy, by shifting the focus from abstract

---

242 See, e.g., Taylor (1985), Taylor (1989), and the critical examination of Taylor's position in Gutman (1994).

concepts of statehood and the basic structure to the normative value of the cultural dimensions of social life. Often, their theoretical motivations are combined with a defense of hermeneutics against either the imposition on social sciences of scientific ideals of natural sciences, or versions of constructivism that maintain that social phenomena are mere constructions.

My criticism of culturalism will focus on its methodological foundations and its general approach to the concept – or idea – of *culture*.[243] Whereas pluriculturalism maintains that the essence of culture is its openness to change, moral criticism, and dynamic transformations, proponents of culturalism conceive of culture mainly in terms of group-belonging, shared values, and historical traditions. They tend to endorse cultural essentialism,[244] and proponents of multiculturalism often endorse metaethical relativism, but the main brand mark of culturalism, as I understand the term, is its focus on group-identity and the claim that group-identity is constitutive of personal identity.

I will start with a few criticisms of culturalist styles of theorizing, before I sketch out the ideal of pluriculturalism. My criticisms are not new[245] and therefore can be short. The same holds for the outline of the pluriculturalist alternative.

10.1. *"Multiculturalism": Conceptual Sense and Nonsense*

Multiculturalism is not a well-defined concept. The theoretical motivations that promote it can vary from theorist to theorist.[246] Worse, multicul-

---

243 The concept 'culture' is strongly contested, and quite a few theorists avoid it because they find it borderline meaningless. As a matter of conceptual analysis, I agree. I will therefore not even try to provide a definition. Nevertheless, there are culturalist theories, and also a plurality of identifiable cultural practices in the real-world, which have to be addressed in some form. The situation, I think, is not too different from that concerning other contested concepts, which are heavily loaded with methodological implications, such as 'ethnicity', which likewise cannot easily be eliminated from social theory, as Wimmer (2013) argues.

244 Not all culturalist theorists endorse cultural essentialism; see Kymlicka (2015) for an overview of the relevant objections and replies.

245 See Barry (2001) and Sen (2006) for more detailed criticisms of various strands of culturalism.

246 Taylor (1989) is strongly influenced by Hegel, and focuses on topics concerning the politics of recognition. Kymlicka (1989) and Kymlicka (1995), by contrast, is mainly concerned with issues of social justice and a requirement of equal

turalism has increasingly become a political agenda promoted by various theorists and by various activist groups for various reasons. The political agendas of those groups are not always mutually coherent, and not all qualify as liberal. Three assumptions, in my view, articulate what might be called the "culturalist" core of methodological culturalism. They underlie monoculturalist theories, as well as multiculturalist theories, as well as several versions of identity politics.

The three assumptions are the following:

(1) The value of cultural belonging. Cultural belonging is supposed to be *intrinsically* valuable to persons due to its importance either for the pursuit of personal life plans or as an important dimension of one's personal identity. It is standardly (at least implicitly) assumed that cultural belonging is either universally valued by everybody, or that it is an irreplaceable source of "thick evaluations", which make life meaningful and shape personal identity of agents.[247]

(2) The distinctiveness of cultures. Multiculturalists implicitly or explicitly assume that there are clear cultural divides that make any particular culture distinct and unique, and that allow us to separate in-group persons from out-group persons. Multiculturalist theorists who focus on issues of justice often emphasize the claim that *all* cultural groups ought be recognized as *equally valuable.* Such a claim still presumes, at least implicitly, that cultural groups can be identified as distinct and unique units.[248] The differentiation of groups can invoke quasi-naturalistic criteria such as race or ethnicity (especially in the case of

---

respect for minority cultures. Parekh (2006) emphasizes the constitutive function of group belonging for personal identity. Meer/Modood (2012) and Modood (2014) defend a variation of culturalism which they call interculturalism. Miller's liberal nationalism can be interpreted as a version of culturalism, but Miller would not accept the three assumptions mentioned below, because he defends a liberal account of sociopolitical justice.

It appears fair to say that most cultural theorists explicitly take an "anti-individualistic" stance, either as concerns the methodology of the social sciences (following up on structuralism in sociology), or as concerns the constitution of moral consciousness (following Hegel's criticism of Kant), or as concerns requirements of normative justification (as, e.g., communitarians who defend the analytical or normative priority of shared and common values over individual rights). The practice-account-based analysis of social institutions in chap. 3, sects. 4 and 5, provides an alternative to "culturalist" approaches.

247 See, e.g., Parekh (2009).

248 Requests for equal recognition can be, but do not need to be, accompanied by a focus on in-group recognition; see, e.g., Parekh's observation that the

"indigenous cultures"), but is mostly tied to practices, e.g., to a common language,[249] a particular religion, a shared stigma, shared rituals or festivity traditions, or a particular form of social organization.[250]

(3) *Cultural groups are worth preserving for their own sake.* If (1) and (2) hold, so a common argument goes, then the intrinsic value of cultural belonging can only be maintained if particular cultures are preserved at the group level. The preservation assumption is sometimes presented as an ontological assumption, insofar as it maintains that cultural practices cannot be reduced to attitudes and orientations of individual beings, because individual attitudes and orientations have always already been shaped by their cultural environment. Preservation of a cultural group thus is understood to be valuable, or morally desirable, independently from the value that individual group members attribute to group practices from their subjective points of view.[251] Individual group members might personally opt out, but they have no right to demand a change of cultural practices. In combination with the claim that each culture ought to be considered to be as valuable as any other, culturalism promotes the preservation of all cultural groups. If cultural belonging is intrinsically valuable, and if cultures can only "exist" and be preserved at a group level, then individual group members ought not to be permitted to undermine the distinctiveness and particularity of any culture or let it go "extinct".

---

distinctiveness of any particular cultural group is partly constituted by how the group is perceived by outsiders (Parekh 2009).

249 Since quite a few languages are spoken in several countries, it should be added that multiculturalists usually focus on intra-social linguistic minority groups, e.g., the French-speaking Quebecois in Canada, the German-speaking community in Hungary, etc.

250 The latter point is often raised in contexts concerning the status of so-called indigenous peoples.

251 From an empirical point of view it is obvious that the assumption of homogeneity is an idealization. It articulates a normative ideal, not an empirical state of affairs. Most modern societies are pluralistic and pervaded by normative disagreement. But the rediscovery and renaissance of cultural practices is often promoted as a matter of respect for and protection of minority cultures, indigenous peoples, marginalized groups, or as a remedy for historic injustice.

10.2. Culturalism as a Normative Social Ideal

Multiculturalism, as characterized by these three assumptions, is at best a matter of scale, at worst an incoherent concept.[252] The concept can be applied to groups of persons settled in a bounded territory, or to groups of persons spread out across territorial boundaries if they share some cultural orientations. Cultural groups can inhabit specific areas of villages or towns as well as entire regions within or across states; they can be mobile, or dispersed in multiple diasporas. In principle, multiculturalism is fully compatible with the claim that societies ought to be granted the right to preserve their *national* culture, i.e., monoculturalism. If the preservation of national culture requires the deterrence of immigrants, then the preservation of national culture justifies it. Multiculturalism is even compatible with restriction of intra-societal migration if the national society is constituted of different peoples that inhabit different regions.

As mentioned above, multiculturalism is increasingly endorsed not as a theory, but as a political agenda. Will Kymlicka, e.g., openly defends multiculturalism as an instrumental measure for the improvement of the status of socially disadvantaged persons who are members of cultural minorities as compared to members of the majority culture for reasons of social justice. He assumes that their social disadvantaged status is caused by a lack of equal respect for minority cultures, and that that disadvantage can best be overcome by granting the same amount of financial support to the maintenance of minority cultures as is given to majoritarian cultural institutions.[253] At the beginning, at least, multiculturalism presented itself as a plea for the recognition of *minority* cultural groups *within* political associations.

In recent decades, promotion of cultural minorities is no longer considered merely a requirement of domestic political justice, but has been adopted in the agendas of many supra- and international organizations and INGO's. This development has generated a rather heterogeneous range of inter- and supranational regimes for the protection of minority rights, cultural human rights, and cultural heritages.[254] The interpretative openness

---

252 For critical assessments see, e.g., Eriksen/ Stjernfelt (2012); for analytic distinctions see also Triandafyllidou et.al. (2012), and Modood (2013).

253 See Kymlicka (1995) and Kymlicka (2015). Unfortunately, Kymlicka provides little evidence for his thesis.

254 See, e.g., Harrison (2013) for a cultural theory perspective; see Vrdoljak (2013) for an international law perspective.

of the term, in combination with the diversity and heterogeneity of the many different aims and projects that have been promoted in the name of multiculturalism, have made the concept even more incoherent. It also produced increasingly incoherent policies and legal regimes.[255]

Insisting on the preservation of cultural differences, multiculturalist theorists and activists, however, appear to continue to conceive of cultural groups (i) as internally homogeneous and diachronically stable groups, and (ii) essentially as *groups*.

It is evident that the culturalist focus on the moral status of groups is difficult to reconcile with the three principles of philosophical liberalism.

10.3. *Culturalism as a Descriptive Analysis of Individual and Social Identity*

10.3.1. A Criticism of Cultural Identity Concepts

Culturalist theorists often present their positions as a matter of conceptual analysis or as explanatory hypotheses rather than a normative ideal. From the perspective of a practice account, these claims are even less convincing than the normative defense of culturalism.

A notorious objection to assumption (1) – the intrinsic value of cultural belonging – has been raised by Amartya Sen, who complains that multiculturalism actually undermines the sense and concept of personal identity, because it tends to appeal to (one-dimensional) cultural stereotypes as group-criteria.[256] Objections similar to Sen's are increasingly voiced also among cultural anthropologists.[257] The idea that personal identity is primarily constituted by one-dimensional criteria, e.g., cultural upbringing or religious affiliations, is obviously an over-simplification. Not even all culturalist theorists share it.[258] Sen's alternative account of personal identity, which emphasizes the processual character of the formation of

---

255 See, e.g., Langfield et.al. (2010), part III.
256 To illustrate his point Sen recalls that conceiving of British citizens of the Muslim religion, e.g., citizens with Egyptian, Pakistani, Bangladeshi or Afghan background, as a quasi-unified cultural group of "British Muslims", ignores not only huge cultural differences, but distorts their self-understanding greatly. See Sen (2006) and Sen (2009).
257 See, e.g., Vertovec (2007); see also Modood (2015a). See also Modood (2015b) for the difference between conceptions of super-diversity, inter- and multi-culturalism.
258 See, e.g., Parekh (2009).

personal identities through learning, experience, and reflection is in my view more convincing. Such an account does not rule out that holding group-based cultural and normative orientations can play a role in the formation of personal identities, but it rightly maintains that subjective experience, rationality, reflection, and socioeconomic circumstances can transform cultural orientations.

No doubt, Sen's account of personal identity is to some extent an idealization that might not hold for all persons, in all societies, at all times.[259] But it certainly appears adequate and fitting for the circumstances that most persons face in modern liberal-democratic societies.

A standard objection to assumption (2) maintains that appeals for recognition of the differences among cultural groups is not politically innocent, but is often driven by strategic interests and power struggles.[260] Given the amorphous concept of cultural differences, the homogeneity of any group can *in principle* be challenged by any group of dissenters who recognize themselves as a cultural subgroup in their own right, or by any other minority sub-group within the larger group. Instead of preserving social cohesion through equal respect, policies of multiculturalism contribute to a dynamic that promotes group fragmentation at the societal level, and is more likely to trigger dynamics of social fragmentation and inter-group conflicts rather than egalitarian justice. Especially when the recognition of group status is rewarded by financial support, it can create a political or legal leverage against requests of inter-group accommodation. It is no accident that culturalism tends to discover ever more suppressed minorities and sub-minorities.

The strongest objection from a normative point of view concerns culturalist conceptions of group rights – an issue which is actually contested among multiculturalists. Two standards accounts of group rights can be distinguished. The first construes groups rights as genuinely holistic rights that can be held only by groups conceived of as collective entities, whose

---

259 The current "counter movement", i.e., the claim that everyone can "choose" his or her identity, expresses a similar discontent, but articulates an opposite extreme which is similarly unconvincing. Personal identity is not exclusively a matter of choice, because the range of possible options is unavoidably to some extent constrained by upbringing, pragmatic options, social circumstances, and luck.

260 See Sen (2006); Wimmer (2013) makes a similar point with respect to appeals for recognition of ethnic differences.

status is independent from that of the individual members of the group.[261] The second account proposes a distributive view. It conceives of group rights as ordinary individual claim rights that can be exercised only collectively.[262]

Defenders of the holistic analysis of group rights claim that if collective cultural regulations conflict with liberal values concerning, e.g., the social status of women or children, then cultural regulations must be respected as decisive, even if individual members of the group disagree with them. Individuals who object to the practice must be free to exit the group. But quite a few theorists and activists maintain that individual members of a group have no moral standing that allows them to demand changes of certain practices.

10.3.2. The Difference between Culturalism and a Practice Account

It is evident that holistic accounts of group rights are incompatible with ethical individualism. I therefore would like to point out the way in which my defense of a holistic analysis of moral status of societies and political associations, as outlined in chapter 3, differs from culturalist positions.

The claim that public sociopolitical and legal institutions are commonly assigned a normative status that includes responsibilities, competences, and powers that *for functional reasons* cannot be reduced to the rights and duties of the individual persons who constitute them, does not contradict the principle of ethical individualism. Investing those institutions with the responsibilities, competences and powers must be justifiable to the individuals who participate in those institutions. The direction of justification, so to speak, is bottom-up, not top-down. Far from denying those participants a moral status of their own, ethical individualism conceives of persons as self-authenticating sources of valid normative claims (to use Rawls's phrase).

Evidently, cultural groups are *not* institutions, and are not *established* for special purposes. It is therefore not possible from a functional point of view to assign irreducible normative responsibilities and competences to them, similar to the ones that I have claimed should be assigned to states

---

261 Standard examples of holistic group rights are rights of indigenous peoples to territory and its use.
262 A standard example of distributive group rights is the right to education in minority languages.

and societies conceived of as institutions within the system of statehood. I therefore think that the distributive view of cultural groups rights is the only one that is defensible from the perspective of philosophical liberalism.[263]

Fairness requires one to concede that the holistic account of group rights is contested even among proponents of multiculturalism, because it diametrically opposes normative premises of social-justice based arguments for the support of minority cultures.

Once the holistic concept of group rights is abandoned, however, the argument for the preservation of cultures at the group level collapses. A distributive account of group rights is hard to square with the idea that cultures are *intrinsically* valuable, and deserve to be preserved forever as they traditionally have been. These normative incompatibilities create a dilemma for theorists of multiculturalism. They either have to sacrifice basic liberal commitments – at which point it is no longer clear what normative support they have for requiring that all cultures *ought* to be considered equally valuable. Or they have to give up the idea of genuine group rights and with it a normative claim that supports the request that cultures ought to be preserved ("as they are", according to the relevant spokespersons). This dilemma is another reason for doubting that multiculturalism articulates a coherent concept.

From a liberal point of view, indeed, many cultural traditions do not deserve to be preserved. They reproduce power hierarchies, e.g., between men and women, elites and commoners, and social practices, such as nepotism or tribalism, that qualify as unfair if not outright unjust according to liberal standards of non-discrimination. A consistent liberal position would actually recommend, or even demand, a revision of such practices and values. Whereas it is not necessarily the primary task of liberal societies to *impose* their liberal views on the members of non-liberal societies at the international level, I find it simply incoherent to request that non-liberal views be protected and preserved within liberal-democratic societies. From the perspective of philosophical liberalism, therefore, multiculturalism – as characterized by the three assumptions above – is not only conceptually, but also normatively problematic.

---

263 Distributive accounts of group rights can allow for the abdication of an independent moral status of participants in social practice, but only if and to the extent that individuals have voluntarily abdicated their individual rights to the group (as, e.g., a monk abdicates certain individual rights when joining a cloister).

10.3.3. The Methodological Background of Early Culturalism Debates

Originally conceptions of culture and cultural belonging have overwhelmingly been promoted in political philosophy for theoretical reasons that point out the need to supplement abstract considerations concerning statehood by a more agency- and practice-oriented account of society and social life. In many respects, those theoretical motivations are not entirely different from the ones that underlie a practice account. It is no accident that several culturalist theorists draw on ordinary language philosophy, but often interpret its point quite differently from the outline given here in chapter 1. I would therefore like to address some of the methodological considerations that originally formed the philosophical background of culturalist positions – or at least originally formed it before the culture and identity discourses became heavily politicized and dominated by considerations of political correctness (which is not a *methodological* position, but a political *agenda*). I will briefly address two conceptual objections, and one methodological objection.

First, it is obvious that social practices or cultural values are very fluid. If only historical and traditional cultural practices were to qualify as culture, then quite a few cultural phenomena (such as, e.g., the transformations of sexual morality, food culture, and all the phenomena related to the spread of new social media) would not qualify as "cultural". Disciplines that belong to what used to be called "cultural sciences", such as cultural anthropology, archeology, or history, have long moved on to a much broader understanding of culture than historical traditions.[264] To the extent that they still use the term "culture" at all, they also apply it to studies of contemporary societal and dynamical transformations of socially shared practices, and emergent new social phenomena.

Second, it is equally obvious that it would be arbitrary to accept only those phenomena as "cultural practices" that one considers valuable and worthy of preservation, and to exclude all others, as if it were meaningless to speak of a "culture of political corruption", or "a culture of racism", or the "culture of *omertà* in organized crime".

Third, if one wants to understand the attractiveness of culturalism in political philosophy and some branches of the social sciences, one has to consider the methodological background against which those theories were developed. A primary motive for culturalist theorizing derives from

---

264 See, e.g., Harrison (2013).

the long-standing dispute about whether social sciences and humanities should follow the same methodology as the natural sciences, or not.

In 20th century treatments of the methodology of the social sciences and the humanities, that debate included assessments of the merits and faults of *methodological* (or *explanatory*) *individualism* versus *methodological* (or *explanatory*) *holism*. Methodological individualism (MI) maintains that social phenomena are adequately analyzed and explained only if they can be fully reduced to dispositions and actions of the individuals involved in their constitution or emergence. MI was strongly reinforced by the expectation that rational choice theory would provide scientific tools for the analysis of all kinds of social phenomena,[265] but there is no necessary connection between the two.[266] Methodological holists (MH), by contrast, argue that subjective dispositions and actions of individual persons are largely determined by social structures and socially shared values, orientations, etc.[267] The direction of explanation and analysis, so to speak, is directly opposite to what MI proposes.

Whereas MI-theorists raised the charge against MH that it provides no adequate explanation for the genesis – and more important – for dynamical transformations of social structures, because it undervalues the role of practical rationality in human agency, MH-theorists insisted that individualists' conceptions of rationality undervalue the social quality of human rationality and the role of socially shared norm- and value-orientations in human agency and practical reasoning.

10.3.4. The Practice Account as a Methodological Alternative to Culturalism

The two positions have for the most time been understood not only as mutually opposed to each other, but also as exhausting the range of possible options. But as so often, *tertium datur*. It appears fair to say that both ac-

---

265 See, e.g., Coleman (1990).

266 The failure of game-theoretic analysis of problems of cooperation and coordination, as modelled by the so-called *Prisoner's Dilemma* and *The Stag Hunt*, has definitely discredited rational-choice-based individualism. More recent developments of evolutionary game theory, although still "reductionist" no longer appeal to "choice" as rational guidance of human agency, but rather explore the evolutionary advantages of different strategies in different environments; see, e.g., Hargreaves-Heap/Varoufakis (1995).

267 See, e.g., Taylor (1985), or Sandel (1982).

counts have been discredited, because both suffer from severe methodological shortcomings. The general idea that the constitution and dynamics of the social world work either wholly bottom-up from subjective disposition and individual action to structure, or *vice versa* wholly top-down from structures to individual orientation ontology is unconvincing as a methodological starting point – as I have argued at length in chapter 3. Their main deficit is the assumption that explanation works in a uni-directional way. This assumption is an inadequate simplification. For individual and social practices are constantly objects of reflection and normative criticism.

A practice account of analysis, as outlined in chapter 1, offers a fruitful methodological alternative to methodological individualism, as well as to methodological holism, because it elucidates the complexity of social practices by distinguishing different sets of rules according to their different functions.[268] It also emphasizes the potential for dynamic transformation of rule-guided practices, and can explicate how human reasoning and deliberation (through reflection and social and moral criticism) contribute to those dynamical changes and transformations. A practice-account-based analysis reveals how social and individual aspects of human agency are integrated, and how both the normative logic of moral criticism and unintended mechanisms drive the dynamics of social transformation.

10.4. A Reassessment of the Value of Cultural Belonging

Where does that leave us with respect to the plausibility of what I called the first core assumption of culturalism, i.e., the claimed intrinsic value of cultural belonging? I seriously doubt the plausibility of the assumption. It cannot be generally observed that all persons attribute intrinsic value to cultural membership or turn out to be unable to escape it.

To avoid a likely misunderstanding: cultural participation is essential for human beings, because culture – as opposed to instincts or natural determination – is the human form of life. Culture requires social relations and practices, and enables humans to develop them. The issue of disagreement is the idea that membership in a *particular* cultural group – or the particular group to which the individual is assigned to – is intrinsically valuable.

As a descriptive statement about what persons value, assumption (1) is empirically implausible. It is obvious that most persons in the mod-

---

268 See chap. 1, sect. 2.

ern world participate in a heterogeneous variety of societal and cultural practices. Most persons are multiply affiliated, e.g., familially, professionally, politically, academically, or by membership in sports teams, churches, political movements, etc. There is little evidence that the overwhelming majority of most persons world-wide, and outside of university seminars, believes that one affiliation is fundamental for their identity.

As soon as one realizes that relations between individuals and groups are diversified and heterogeneous, the assumption that belonging to *one particular* cultural group is especially valuable also becomes normatively unattractive as an ideal, for three reasons.

The first is that such an ideal does not further social attitudes that are necessary preconditions for the proper functioning of liberal democratic government, such as civic trust, tolerance of cultural and normative pluralism, mutual respect for diverging interests and normative opinions, and impartial respect for the interests and normative orientations of persons not affiliated with oneself.

The second reason is that such an ideal is most likely incompatible with the historical dynamics not only of migration, but also of social mobility. If cultural belonging indeed were of such great importance for the possibility of leading a meaningful life, or for personal identity, then it seems that people would be best off if they stayed in the cultural environment in which they grew up. Moving to a foreign society, moving from rural areas to cities, or even moving from blue-collar parents to a white-collar job, can be very unsettling. But it does not deprive those persons who undergo it of an intrinsic value or their personal identity. In addition, I am convinced that the experience of migration is much less unsettling when one's new societal environment is culturally open and pluralistic, and when foreign residents and immigrants (or socially mobile co-citizens) are not immediately confronted with cultural stereotypes. Culturalist accounts of cultural belonging, unfortunately, tend to promote cultural seclusion rather than cultural openness.

There is no doubt that human beings strive for meaning, and that participation in cultural practices and exchange is considered meaningful by most persons. But meaningfulness does not require cultural homogeneity. There is no lack of culture in pluralistic societies, and it cannot be claimed that members of pluralistic cultures suffer generally from a lack of personal identity or of meaning in their lives.

My third and last objection to culturalist understandings of culture is that the thesis that preservation of cultural traditions is intrinsically valuable is rarely supported by evidence. Even though it is true that *some* people care a lot about cultural traditions, many do not. They care about personal achievements, economic success, and the well-being of their family and friends. Others care about progressive and innovative approaches towards global justice, animal rights, or the protection of the environment. I do not think that orientations of the second or the third sort are less valuable for those who hold them than is cultural belonging. As a matter of fact, I assume that most (potential) migrants pursue the option of migration because they care about economic success and the well-being of their families, but are dissatisfied with the social or cultural environment in their country of origin. It is, I think, objectionable to underestimate the degree to which voluntary migrants are open to new and different social and cultural orientations.

The ideal of pluriculturalism, as I conceive it, rejects the assumption that belonging to a particular culture is intrinsically valuable. However, it neither denies that participation in social practices is the essential form of human life, nor does it exclude the possibility that some individuals do attribute intrinsic value to group membership, including cultural membership. It grants individual persons the *liberty* to pursue the cultural orientations that they subjectively endorse (within the usual normative constraints).

10.5. Pluriculturalism: A Liberal-democratic Proposal

Pluriculturalism starts from the assumption that the essence of culture is change.[269] It criticizes culturalism in all its variations. Accordingly, pluriculturalism also opposes demands for assimilation. It is a plea for cultural pluralism and mutual respect for diverging cultural orientations of *persons considered as individuals.*

There is one restriction, because pluriculturalism is not a normative anything-goes position, but is explicitly committed to the recognition of the right of individual normative self-determination. Respect for cultural orientations accordingly should be limited to orientations that are compatible with the acceptance of a secular understanding of political government, a conventional understanding of political institutions, and an acceptance of a free-standing sphere of politics as defended in previous chapters. Pluriculturalism thus presupposes that we can draw some line of

---

269 For a vivid illustration of how economic transformations and intra-societal migration transform social life in a village in the Vaucluse see Wylie (1964).

demarcation between cultural orientations that guide individual life plans, on the one hand, and political attitudes or expectations about how to organize political associations given the conditions of social pluralism, on the other hand. Pluriculturalism also presupposes that we can draw some line of demarcation between the private and the political.

I am fully aware that the separation of the private from the political is notoriously contested. But this is not a new development triggered by transnational phenomena of migration – it has been contested for a long time for various reasons, some philosophical and some political. It also becomes more and more evident that the increasing politicization and legalization of semi-private and private spheres by legal regulations, protocols, and manuals of best practices concerning conduct and speech, seriously undermines the very effort to draw such a divide between the private and the political. The more legal measures regulate private spheres the less individual liberty remains. The increasing legalization of social agency does not help in maintaining the right to normative individual self-determination and social pluralism.

Many recent measures are motivated by a concern for the protection of the rights and emotional status of individuals. But concerns for individual rights and the pluralistic openness of social spaces have to be balanced against each other. Although the dynamics that drive the so-called "culture wars" have less to do with culture and more with power politics, they increasingly tend to annihilate – or rather demand the annihilation of – all differences among cultural and societal orientations. It cannot be doubted that the legal institution of individual claim rights is an irreplaceable instrument for the protection of the liberty of individual persons. But the maximal expansion of the substantive contents of claim rights is not. If we conceive of individual claim rights as legally empowering individuals with the authority to constrain the liberty of other persons who are the addressees of those claim rights, then it is obvious that acknowledgment of more and more encompassing individual rights restricts the liberty of everybody. This is not a matter of political ideology, but a matter of the logic of how individual claim rights work. In philosophy and the law, as in any other sphere of life, no one gets anything for free: even moral goods produce moral costs. The tendency to protect more and more personal orientations or lifestyle decisions, by turning them into individual claim rights, tends in the end to reduce liberty rather than to support it. The problem is obviously one of degree, and of finding the right balance.[270] Nobody who really appreciates cultural values, mutual respect, and rationality would aim at a uniform, conformist, cultural world, nor – what would be even worse – at a world in which each individual defines her own cultural values and is granted the (claim) *right* to impose her values and views on everybody else.

To sum up. Cultural orientations are not cast in stone; they never have been. Cultural exchange and appropriation of cultural techniques have benefitted mankind since its very beginnings. With the possible exception of some tribes or societies that have never encountered any other tribe or society, there is very little that is "authentic" to any culture. It is sometimes said that Bela Bartok's search for the authentic Hungarian elements in Hungarian folk music led him to discover that what he considered to be typically Hungarian had been highly influenced by musical traditions shared with Turks and Roma. Whether this is true or not, it is certainly correct that ideals of cultural authenticity, as they were celebrated, e.g., during the Romantic age, are overwhelmingly chimerical. As is well-known, 19th century nationalism had to impose uniform language and cultural education on the population of the then-new institution of the nation-state (and was very much helped to do so by the spread of compulsory schooling for children of all social classes).

The ideal of pluriculturalism derives from a dynamical and inclusivist understanding of societies as spaces for interpersonal exchange and cooperation, as well as collective political agency. It focuses not on the substantive contents of cultural practices and values, but on interpersonal civic attitudes, respect for the rights and liberties of other citizens, and the standards for their normative (and critical) evaluation.[271]

Critical normative discourse can reinforce prevailing standards, but can also challenge, modify, and transform them. But standards *qua* standards apply generally to all reasons and arguments that are considered relevant.

---

270 It does, however, speak against proposals, such as Joppke's, that group-conceptions of culture should be replaced by concerns for the protection of individual cultural rights; see Joppke (2017).

271 The dynamics of cultural transformations, of course, are not exclusively driven by reflection and discourse. They are often unintended consequences of other projects and activities, or simply happen due to transformation or changes of the overall conditions of social and economic life. One might think of industrialization, or of the transformation of economic landscapes and property rights through technological progress or war, or of the development of social media, etc.

They are neutral to who the person is who appeals to them. And they cannot be changed unilaterally whenever doing so is favorable for one's own position.

Culture is the human way of coping with challenges and changes that arise not only in the natural, but – even more important – in social environments. But culture is not a special, or separate, sphere of human values that is disconnected from the economic sphere, the political sphere, education, or the arts, etc., but rather manifests itself in the practices of all those spheres.

Pluriculturalism articulates a societal ideal as well as an individual one. As a societal ideal it requires mutual respect and tolerance for different cultural orientations, within the limits of conditions necessary for the practice of democratic government. Pluriculturalism protects the individual liberty to engage in different cultural practices, as well as changing or abandoning or transforming them through critical discourse and open contestation with others *interactively*. The ideal of pluriculturalism is one of merging cultures, i.e., of cultural exchange and mutual adjustments, not an ideal of the uncritical preservation of cultural traditions.

As an individual ideal, pluriculturalism aims at the development of competences and capacities that enable persons to engage with people from different social backgrounds. Multilingualism is definitely one such capacity, and it is *de facto* quite widespread in many countries. Whereas multiculturalist theorists request that cultural minorities be offered education in their native language, pluriculturalism suggests the teaching of multiple languages to both minority groups and the majority. Although culture cannot be *identified* with traditional practices, it is always reasonable to study their historical emergence and compare them with alternative paths of development. One can neither understand the dynamics of cultural transformations, nor take a critically reflective stance towards one's own cultural orientations and standards of evaluation, if one never asks what they are and where they came from, from a historical point of view. Personally, I am convinced that historical awareness will often reveal the empirically contingent nature of cultural orientations, and their dynamical fluidity. In my opinion, there is no return to the "habits of the heart"[272], and no socially promising path to homogeneity of cultural groups – not only due to migration, but for many reasons.

Since pluriculturalism requires respect for cultural differences, it also values the competence to adjust to different cultural environments and

---

272 See Bellah et.al. (1985).

to merge with different cultural or social groups. But it requires neither assimilation nor the "trading" of one particular culture for another (although that sometimes happens).

As a guide to the integration of temporary and permanent migrants, pluriculturalism advises integration and intermingling rather than separation in diasporas and ghettos. As a social ideal, pluriculturalism is neither arcane nor utopian, as long as citizens accept social pluralism and resist the temptation to turn every disagreement into a moral or legal crusade, and as long as *common sense* is not surrendered to ideological purism.

Pluriculturalism preserves the normative priority of individuals *vis-à-vis* groups, and accentuates the reflective and dynamical nature of cultural orientations. It demands respect for the individual autonomy of normative self-determination, not least in form of the liberty to practice and pursue one's cultural orientations, as long as doing so is compatible with an equal liberty of everybody else and the maintenance of social pluralism.

10.6. A Final Thought

Society hardly ever has been what it used to be. New phenomena of transnational migration are just one source of social transformation among many others. From a practical point of view, pursuit of the ideal of pluriculturalism is not unrealistic, but its realization requires some revisions of the increasingly moralistic and dogmatic style of current sociopolitical discourse. Given the transformations of social life, to which transnational migration contributes, some degree of re-thinking of traditional concepts of social membership appears unavoidable. But that does not mean that we have to give up on the idea of democratic citizenship as a special relation or to eliminate politics from conceptions of post-national political justice. The normative ideals and practical challenges, to which the idea of democratic citizenship responds, are far from obsolete in present-day societies. For that reason, neither the return to national ideals of citizenship nor the appeal to de-politicized ideals of progressive cosmopolitanism is convincing. What is required, rather, is a reevaluation of the function and political purpose of political association and citizenship from a transnational perspective.

Personally, I prefer such a reevaluation to be guided by a rational, politically and morally informed social discourse, rather than by technocratic social engineering or the agendas of special interest groups. Taking a reflective stance towards various conceptions of citizenship seems to me to provide a rational framework for debates about migration. Democratic societies should be well-suited for contributing the other ingredients.

It might be objected that democracy is itself an outdated liberal ideal, which has been replaced by output-oriented technocratic forms of global governance. From the perspective of philosophical liberalism, the main question is, "Can such new forms of government replace democratic legitimacy?" – I doubt it.

Bibliography

Abrams, Kerry (2005): "Polygamy, Prostitution, and the Federalization of Immigration Law", *Columbia Law Review* 105/3 (2005) 641–716.

Angelos, James (2015): *The Full Catastrophe. Travels among the New Greek Ruins*, New York: Broadway Books.

Anscombe, G.E.M. (1957/2000): *Intention*, Cambridge, Mass./London: Harvard University Press 2000.

— (1985): "Review: Wittgenstein on Rules and Private Language", *Ethics* 95/2 (1985) 342–352.

Austin, J.L. (1979a): "Performative Utterances", in: id: *Philosophical Papers*, ed. by J.O. Urmson/G.J. Warnock, Oxford: Oxford University Press, ³1979, 232–252.

— (1979b): "A Plea for Excuses", in: id: *Philosophical Papers*, ed. by J.O. Urmson/G.J. Warnock, Oxford: Oxford University Press, ³1979, 175–204.

— (1979c): "Other Minds", in: id: *Philosophical Papers*, ed. by J.O. Urmson/G.J. Warnock, Oxford: Oxford University Press, ³1979, 76–116.

Baier, Kurt (1965): *The Moral Point of View. A Rational Basis of Ethics*, 2nd. abr. ed., New York: Random House.

— (1978): "The Social Source of Reasons", *Proceedings and Addresses of the American Philosophical Association* 51/6 (1978) 707–733.

Barry, Brian (1995): *Justice as Impartiality*, Oxford: Oxford University Press.

— (2001): *Culture and Equality*, Cambridge, Mass.: Harvard University Press.

Bauböck, Rainer (2003): "Towards a Political Theory of Migrant Transnationalism", *International Migration Review* 37/3 (2003) 700–723.

— (2017): "Political Membership and Democratic Boundaries", in: Shachar et.al. (2017), 60–82.

— (2018): "Democratic Inclusion: A Pluralist Theory of Citizenship", in: *Democratic Inclusion. Rainer Bauböck in Dialogue*, Manchester: Manchester University Press, 3–102.

Beitz, Charles (1979): "Bounded Morality: Justice and the State in World Politics", *International Organization* 33/3 (1979) 405–434.

— (1979/99): *Political Theory and International Relations*, Princeton, 2ⁿᵈ. ed., NJ: Princeton University Press.

— (2009a): "The Moral Standing of States Revisited", *Ethics and International Affairs* 23/4 (2009) 325–347.

— (2009b): *The Idea of Human Rights*, Oxford: Oxford University Press.

Bellah, Robert N./Richard Madson/William M. Sulivan/Ann Swindler/Steven M. Tipton (1985): *Habits of the Heart*, Berkeley et.al.: University of California Press.

Benhabib, Seyla (2001): *Transformations of Citizenship. Dilemmas of the Nation State*, Assen: Koniklijke Van Gorcum BV.

Biccheri, Cristina (2017): *Norms in the Wild*, Oxford: Oxford University Press.

Blake, Michael (2001): "Distributive Justice, State Coercion, and Autonomy", *Philosophy and Public Affairs* 30/3 (2001) 257–296.

— (2017): "Jurisdiction and Exclusion: A Response to Sarah Song", in: *Immigration, Emigration, and Migration* (Nomos LVII) ed. by Jack Knight, New York: New York University Press 2017, 69–78.

Boeri, Tito/Herbert Brückner/Frédéric Docquier/Hillel Rapoport (2012): *Brain Drain and Brain Gain. The Global Competition to Attract High-skilled Migrants* (A Report for the Fondazione Rodolfo Debenedetti), Oxford: Oxford University Press.

Bourdieu, Pierre (1998): *Practical Reason*, Stanford, CA: Stanford University Press.

Boghossian, Paul (2006): *Fear of Knowledge. Against Relativism and Constructivism*, Oxford: Oxford University Press.

Bosniak, Linda (2008): *The Citizen and the Alien. Dilemmas of Contemporary Membership*, Princeton, NJ: Princeton University Press.

Brock, Gillian (2016): "Justice for Irregular Migrants, Refugees and Temporary Workers: Some Issues for Carens", *Journal of Applied Philosophy* 33/4 (2016) 435–442.

—/Michael Blake (2015): *Debating Brain Drain. May Governments Restrict Emigration?*, Oxford: Oxford University Press.

Carens, Joseph H. (1987): "Aliens and Citizens: The Case for Open Borders", *Review of Politics* 49/2 (1987) 251–273.

— (2005): "The Integration of Immigrants", *Journal of Moral Philosophy* 2/1 (2005) 29–46.

— (2015): *The Ethics of Immigration*, Oxford: Oxford University Press.

Carling, Jørgen (2008): "The Human Dynamics of Migrant Transnationalism", *Ethnic and Racial Studies* 31/8 (2008) 1452–1477.

Charsley, Katharine/Anika Liversage (2013): "Transforming Polygamy: Migration, Transnationalism, and Multiple Marriages among Muslim Minorities", *Global Networks* 13/1 (2013) 60–78.

Christiano, Thomas (1996): *The Rule of the Many. Fundamental Issues in Democratic Theory*, Boulder, Colorado: Westview Press.

— (2008a): "Immigration, Political Community, and Cosmopolitanism", *San Diego Law Review* 45 (2008) 933–961.

— (2008b): *The Constitution of Equality: Democratic Authority and Its Limits*, Oxford: Oxford University Press 2008.

— (2017): "Democracy, Migration, and International Institutions", in: *Immigration, Emigration, and Migration* (Nomos LVII) ed. by Jack Knight, New York: New York University Press 2017, 239–276.

Chwaszcza, Christine (2008): "The Theory and Practice of Multicultural Theorizing", *Ethnicities* 8/2 (2008) 261–265.

— (2009): "The Unity of the People, and Immigration in Liberal Theory", *Citizenship Studies* 13/5 (2009) 451–474.

— (2010): "The Concept of Rights in Contemporary Human Rights Discourse", *Ratio Juris* 33/3 (2019) 333–364.

— (2011a): *Moral Responsibility and Global Justice. A Human Rights Approach*, 2nd rev. ed., Baden-Baden: Nomos Verlag.

— (2011b): "Kollektive Autonomie. Volkssouveränität und individuelle Rechte in der liberalen Demokratie", *Deutsche Zeitschrift für Philosophie* 59/6 (2011) 917–935.

— (2012): "The Practical Conditions of Sovereignty of the People: The Status of Citizens in Multilevel Political Organizations", in: *Territories of Citizenship* ed. by Ludvig Beckman/Eva Erman, Houndsmill, Basingstoke: Palgrave McMillan 2012, 81–99.

— (2017): *Social Agency and Practical Reasons. A Practice Account*, New York: Peter Lang.

— (2021): "Democracy as a Social Practice", *metodo. International Studies in Phenomenology and Philosophy* 8/1 (2021) 25–50.

Coleman, James S. (1990): *The Foundations of Social Theory*, Cambridge, Mass.: Harvard University Press.

Cox, Adam B. (2017): "Three Mistakes in Open Borders Debates", in: *Immigration, Emigration, and Migration* (Nomos LVII) ed. by Jack Knight, New York: New York University Press 2017, 51–68.

Daniels, Norman (1980): "On Some Methods of Ethics and Linguistics", *Philosophical Studies* 37/1 (1980) 21–36.

Dauvergne, Catherine (2016): *The New Politics of Immigration and the End of Settler Societies*, Cambridge: Cambridge University Press.

Descartes, René (1647): "Meditations on First Philosophy", in: *The Philosophical Writings of Descartes*, vol. II, transl. by John Cottingham/Robert Stoothoff/ Dugald Murdoch, Cambridge: Cambridge University Press 1984, 1–65.

De Schutter, Helder/Lea Ypi (2015): "The British Academy Brian Barry Prize Essay: Mandatory Citizenship for Immigrants", *British Journal of Political Science* 45/2 (2015) 235–251.

Donders, Yvonne (2013): "Cultural Pluralism in International Human Rights Law. The Role of Reservations", in: *The Cultural Dimension of Human Rights*, ed. by Ana Vrdoljak, Oxford: Oxford University Press, 205–239.

Dryzek, John S. (2006): *Deliberative Global Politics: Discourse and Democracy in a Divided World*, Cambridge: Polity Press.

Dworkin, Ronald (1977): *Taking Rights Seriously*, Cambridge, Mass.: Harvard University Press.

— (1987): *Law's Empire*, Cambridge, Mass.: Harvard University Press.

Eichenberger, Sarah L. (2012): "When Better is for Worse: Immigration Law's Gendered Impact on Foreign Polygamous Marriage", *Duke Law Journal* 61 (2012) 1067–1110.

Elster, Jon (1985): "Sour Grapes", in: id.: *Sour Grapes. Studies in the Subversion of Rationality*, Cambridge: Cambridge University Press.

Eriksen, Jens-Martin/Frederik Stjernfelt (2012): *The Democratic Contradictions of Multiculturalism*, New York: Telos Press Publishing.

Estlund, David M. (2008): *Democratic Authority*, Princeton: Princeton University Press.

Feinberg, Joel (1970): "The Nature and Value of Rights", *Journal of Value Inquiry* 4/4 (1970) 243–257.

Ferracioli, Luara (2016): "Family Migration Schemes and Liberal Neutrality. A Dilemma", *Journal of Moral Philosophy* 13/5 (2016) 553–575.

Goldberg, Bruce (1971): "The Linguistic Expression of Feeling", *American Philosophical Quarterly* 8/1 (1971) 86–92.

Goodin, Robert E. (1988): "What is So Special about Our Fellow Countrymen?", *Ethics* 98/4 (1988) 663–686.

— (2003): *Reflective Democracy*, Oxford: Oxford University Press.

—/Kai Spiekermann (2018): *An Epistemic Theory of Democracy*, Oxford: Oxford University Press.

Griffin, James (2008): *On Human Rights*, Oxford: Oxford University Press.

Grimmel, Andreas/Gunther Hellmann (2019): "Theory Must Not Go on Holiday. Wittgenstein, the Pragmatists, and the Idea of Social Science", *International Political Sociology* 13/2 (2019) 198–214.

Guiraudon, Virginie (2014): "Economic Crisis and Institutional Resilience: The Political Economy of Migrant Incorporation", *West European Politics* 37/6 (2014) 1297–1313.

Gutman, Amy (ed.) (1994): *Multiculturalism. Examining the Politics of Recognition*, Princeton, NJ: Princeton University Press.

Habermas, Jürgen (1983): "Diskursethik: Notizen zu einem Begründungsprogramm", in: id.: *Moralbewußtsein und kommunikatives Handeln*, Frankfurt a.M.: Suhrkamp Verlag 1983, 53–126.

— (1987): *Theorie des kommunikativen Handelns*, 4th ed., Frankfurt a.M.: Suhrkamp Verlag.

— (1991): "Erläuterungen zur Diskursethik", in: id.: *Erläuterungen zur Diskursethik*, Frankfurt a.M.: Suhrkamp Verlag 1991, 119–226.

— (1995): "Reconciliation Through the Public Use of Reason. Remarks on John Rawls's 'Political Liberalism'", *Journal of Philosophy* 92/3 (1995) 109–131.

Hafner, Gerhard (2004): "Pros and Cons Ensuing from Fragmentation of International Law", *Michigan Journal of International Law* 25/4 (2004) 849–863.

Hanfling, Oswald (1989): *Wittgenstein's Later Philosophy*, Albany, N.Y.: SUNY Press 1989.

— (2000): *Philosophy and Ordinary Language*, London/New York: Routledge.

Hardin, Russel (2005): "Migration and Community", *Journal of Social Philosophy* 36/2 (2005) 273–287.

Hargreaves-Heap, Shaun/Yanis Varoufakis (1995): *Game Theory. A Critical Text*, London: Routledge.

Harrison, Rodney (2013): *Heritage. Critical Approaches*, London/New York: Routledge.

Hart, H.L.A. (1955): "Are There Any Natural Rights?", *Philosophical Review* 64 (1955) 175–191.

— (1961/1997): *The Concept of Law*. Rev. 2nd ed., ed. by Penelope Bulloch/Joseph Raz, Oxford: Oxford University Press.

Held, David (2006): *Models of Democracy*, Cambridge, Polity Press.

—/Daniele Archibugi (1995): *Cosmopolitan Democracy: An Agenda for a New World Order*, Cambridge: Polity Press.

Hobbes, Thomas (1651): *Leviathan, or the Matter, Forme, & Power of a Commonwealth Ecclesiasticall and Civill*, ed. by Richard Tuck, Cambridge: Cambridge University Press 1991.

Huemer, Michael (2010): "Is There a Right to Immigrate?", *Social Theory and Practice* 36/3 (2010) 429–461.

Hume, David (1739/1740): *A Treatise of Human Nature*, ed. L.A. Selby-Bigge/P.H. Nidditch, Oxford: Clarendon Press, 2nd ed., 1978.

— (1777): "Enquiry concerning the Principles of Morals", in: id.: *Enquiries concerning Human Understanding and concerning the Principles of Morals*, ed. by L.A. Selby-Bigge, Oxford: Clarendon Press.

Joppke, Christian (1999): *Immigration and the Nation-state. The United States, Germany, and Great Britain*, Oxford: Oxford University Press.

— (2005): "Exclusion in the Liberal State. The Case of Immigration and Citizenship Policy", *European Journal of Social Theory* 8/1 (2005) 43–61.

— (2010): *Citizenship and Immigration*, Cambridge: Polity Press.

— (2011): *Citizenship and Integration*, Cambridge: Polity Press.

— (2014): "Europe and Islam: Alarmists, Victimists, and Integration by Law", *West European Politics* 36/6 (2014) 1314–1335.

— (2015): *The Secular State under Siege. Religion and Politics in Europe and America*, Cambridge: Polity Press.

— (2017): *Is Multiculturalism Dead?*, Cambridge et.al.: Polity Press.

Kant, Immanuel (1793): "On the common saying: That may be correct in theory, but it is of no use in practice", in: id.: *Practical Philosophy*, transl. & ed. by Mary J. Gregor, Cambridge: Cambridge University Press 1999, 273–310.

Koller, Peter (2017): "Die Geltung sozialer Normen", in: *Souveränität, Transstaatlichkeit und Weltverfassung* ed. by Jochen Bung/Armin Engländer, Stuttgart: Franz Steiner Verlag, 109–132.

Kolodny, Niko (2014): "Rule Over None", *Philosophy and Public Affairs* 42/4 (2014) 287–336.

Koopmans, Ruud (2015): "Does Assimilation Work? Sociocultural Determinants of Labour Market Participation of European Muslims", *Journal of Ethnic and Migration Studies* 42/2 (2015) 197–216.

— (2016): "Statistical and Perceived Diversity and Their Impacts on Neighborhood Social Cohesion in Germany, France and the Netherlands", *Social Indicators Research* 125/3 (2016) 853–883.

— (2017): *Assimilation oder Multikulturalismus. Bedingungen gelungener Integration*, Berlin: Lit Verlag.

—/Ines Michalowski (2017): "Why Do States Extend Rights to Immigrants? Institutional Settings and Historical Legacies Across 44 Countries Worldwide", *Comparative Political Studies* 50/1 (2017) 41–74.

Koskenniemi, Martti (Study Group of the International Law Commission) (2006): *Fragmentation of International Law: Difficulties Arising from the Diversification and Expansion of International Law*, United Nations, General Assembly A/CN.4/L682, International Law Commission, 15th session at Geneva 2006.

—/Päivi Leino (2002): "Fragmentation of International Law? Postmodern Anxieties", *Leiden Journal of International Law* 15 (2002) 553–579.

Kratochwil, Friedrich (2018): *Praxis. On Acting and Knowing*, Cambridge: Cambridge University Press.

Krisch, Nico (2010): *Beyond Constitutionalism. The Pluralistic Structure of Postnational Law*, Oxford: Oxford University Press.

— (2011): "Who Is Afraid of Radical Pluralism? Legal Order and Political Stability in the Postnational Space", *Ratio Juris* 24/4 (2011) 386–412.

Kymlicka, Will (1989): *Liberalism, Community and Culture*, Oxford: Oxford University Press.

— (1995): *Multicultural Citizenship: A Liberal Theory of Minority Rights*, Oxford: Oxford University Press.

— (2015): "The Essentialist Criticism of Multiculturalism: Theories, Policies, Ethos", in: in: Uberoi Varun/Tariq Modood (eds.): *Multiculturalism Rethought*, Edinburgh: Edinburgh University Press (2015) 209–249.

Lagerspetz, Eerik (2010): "Wisdom and Numbers", *Social Science Information* 49/1 (2010) 29–59.

Langfield, Michele/William Logan/Máiréad Nic Craith (eds.) (2010): *Cultural Diversity, Heritage and Human Rights. Intersections in Theory and Practice*, London/New York: Routledge.

Langford, Peter/Ian Bryan (2012): "Hans Kelsen's Theory of Legal Monism. A Critical Engagement with the Emerging Legal Order of the 1920s", Journal of the History of International Law/Revue d'histoire du droit international, 14/1 (2012) 51–86.

—/— (2019): "From Wolff to Kelsen: The Transformation of the Notion of Civitas Maxima", in: Peter Langford/Ian Bryan/J. McGarry (eds.): *Hans Kelsen and the Natural Law Tradition*, Leiden/Boston: Brill, 161–187.

La Torre, Massimo (2005): "Global Citizenship? Political Rights under Imperial Conditions", *Ratio Juris* 18/2 (2005) 236–257.

— (2012): "Citoyennité", in: *Traitè international de droit constitutionelle, vol. III*, ed. by Michel Troper/Dominique Chagnollaud/Dalloz-Sirey 2012, 358–387.

Lindahl, Hans (2018): *Authority and the Globalisation of Inclusion and Exclusion*, Oxford: Oxford University Press.

Lines, Greggary E. (2016): "Polymigration: Immigration Implications and Possibilities Post *Brown v. Buhman*", *Arizona Law Review* 58/2 (2016) 477–510.

List, Christian/Robert E. Goodin (2001): "Epistemic Democracy: Generalizing the Condorcet Jury Theorem", *Political Philosophy* 9/3 (2001) 277–306.

Locke, John (1689): *An Essay concerning Human Understanding*, ed. by P.H. Nidditch, Oxford: Clarendon Press 1975.

— (1690): *Second Treatise on Government*, ed. by C.B. Macpherson, Indianapolis: Hackett 1980.

Luban, David (1980): "The Romance of the Nation-State", *Philosophy and Public Affairs* 9/4 (1980) 392–397.

MacKay, Douglas (2016): "Are Skill-selective Immigration Policies Just?", *Social Theory and Practice* 42/1 (2016) 123–154.

March, Andrew F. (2011): "Is There a Right to Polygamy? Marriage, Equality and Subsidizing Families in Liberal Public Justification", *Journal of Moral Philosophy* 8 (2011) 246–272.

Marshall, T.H. (1950/1992): *Citizenship and Social Class*, ed. by Tom Bottomore, London: Pluto Press.

Mason, Andrew (2014): "Citizenship Tests: Can They Be a Just Compromise?", *Journal of Social Philosophy* 45/2 (2014) 137–161.

McIntyre, Alasdair (1995): "Is Patriotism a Virtue?", in: Ronald Beiner (ed.): *Theorizing Citizenship*, Albany, N.Y.: SUNY Press, 209–228.

Meer, Nasar/Tariq Modood (2012): "How Does Interculturalism Contrast with Multiculturalism?", *Journal of Intercultural Studies* 33/2 (2012) 175–196.

Miller, David (1995): *On Nationality*, Oxford: Oxford University Press.

— (2007): *National Responsibility and Global Justice*, Oxford: Oxford University Press.

— (2008): "Immigrants, Nations, and Citizenship", *The Journal of Political Philosophy* 16/4 (2008) 371–390.

— (2016): *Strangers in Our Midst. The Political Philosophy of Migration*, Cambridge, Mass.: Harvard University Press.

Modood, Tariq (2013): *Multiculturalism*, Cambridge et. al.: Polity Press, 2nd edition.

— (2014): "Multiculturalism, Interculturalism and the Majority" (Kohlberg Memorial Lecture), *Journal of Moral Education* 43/3 (2014) 302–315.

— (2015a): *Post-immigration 'Difference' and Integration*, London: British Academy Policy Centre 2015.

— (2015b): "Rethinking Multiculturalism, Interculturalisms and the Majority", in: Uberoi Varun/Tariq Modood (eds.): *Multiculturalism Rethought*, Edinburgh: Edinburgh University Press (2015) 348–368.

Nasström, Sofia (2007): "The Legitimacy of the People", *Political Theory* 35/5 (2007) 624–665.

Offe, Claus (2011): "From Migration in Geographic Space to Migration in Biographic Time: Views from Europe", *The Journal of Political Philosophy* 19/3 (2011) 333–373.

Owen, David (2011): "National Membership and the Democratic State: Modes of Membership and Voting Rights", *Critical Review of Social and International Philosophy* 14/5 (2011) 641–663.

— (2018): "Populus, demos, and Self-rule", in: *Democratic Inclusion. Rainer Bauböck in Dialogue*, Manchester: Manchester University Press, 183–203.

Özdem, Caglar/Maurice Schiff (2006) (eds.): *International Migration, Remittances & the Brain Drain*, Washington: The International Bank for Reconstruction and Development/The World Bank; Houndsmill et.al.: Palgrave Macmillan.

Parekh, Bikhu (2006): *Rethinking Multiculturalism*, London: Red Globe Press, 2nd ed.

— (2009): "The Logic of Identity", *Politics, Philosophy and Economics* 8/3 (2009) 267–284.

Plato: *Republic*, ed. by G.M.A. Grube, Indianapolis: Hackett 1992.

Pogge, Thomas W. (1989): *Realizing Rawls*, Cornell: Cornell University Press.

— (2002): *World Poverty and Human Rights*, Cambridge et.al.: Polity Press.

Quine, Willard Van Orman (1973): *The Roots of Reference (Paul Carus Lectures)*, La Salle, Ill.: Open Court Publ.

Rawls, John (1955): "Two Concepts of Rules", *Philosophical Review* 64/1 (1955) 3–32.

— (1958): "Justice as Fairness", *Philosophical Review* 67/2 (1958) 164–194.

— (1971): *A Theory of Justice*, Cambridge, Mass.: Harvard University Press.

— (1980): "Kantian Constructivism in Moral Theory: The Dewey Lectures", *Journal of Philosophy* 77/9 (1980) 515–572.

— (1993a): *Political Liberalism*, New York: Columbia University Press.

— (1993b): "The Law of Peoples", in: *On Human Rights. Oxford Amnesty Lectures on Human Rights 1993*, New York: Basic Books, 41–83.

— (1999): *The Law of Peoples*, Cambridge, Mass. et.al.: Harvard University Press.

— (2001): *Justice as Fairness. A Restatement*, ed. by Erin Kelly, Cambridge, Mass: Harvard University Press.

Reiner, Hans (1948): "Die 'Goldene' Regel", Zeitschrift für Philosophische Forschung 3/1 (1948) 74–105.

Rousseau, Jean-Jacques (1762): "On the Social Contract", in: Jean-Jacques Rousseau: *The Basic Political Writings* ed. by Peter Gay, transl. by Donald A. Cress, Indianapolis, Cambridge: Hackett 1987, 141–227.

Rubio-Marín, Ruth (2000): *Immigration as a Democratic Challenge. Citizenship and Inclusion in Germany and the United States*, Cambridge: Cambridge University Press.

— (2014): *Human Rights and Immigration*, Oxford: Oxford University Press.

Sandel, Michael J. (1982): *Liberalism and the Limits of Justice*, Cambridge: Cambridge University Press.

Schatzki, Theodore E./Karin Knorr Cetina/Eike von Savigny (eds.) (2001): *The Practice Turn in Contemporary Theory*, Oxon: Routledge.

Schmitt, Carl (1932/2015): *Der Begriff des Politischen*, 9th corr. ed., Berlin: Duncker & Humblodt.

Searle, John R. (1995): *The Construction of Social Reality*, New York: The Free Press.

— (2001): *Rationality in Action*, Cambridge, Mass.: MIT Press.

— (2010): *Making the Social World. The Structure of Human Civilization*, Oxford: Oxford University Press.

Sen, Amartya (2006): *Identity and Violence. The Illusion of Destiny*, London: Penguin Books.

— (2009): "The Fog of Identity", *Politics, Philosophy and Economics* 8/3 (2009) 285–288.

Shachar, Ayelet (1998): "Group Identity and Women's Rights in Family Law: The Perils of Multicultural Accommodation", *Journal of Political Philosophy* 6/3 (1998) 285–305.

— (2009): *The Birthright Lottery. Citizenship and Global Inequality*, Cambridge, Mass.: Harvard University Press.

— (2017): "Citizenship for Sale?", in: Shachar et.al (2017) 789–816.

—/Ian Hirschl (2014): "On Citizenship, States, and Markets", *Journal of Political Philosophy* 22/2 (2014) 231–257.

—/Rainer Bauböck/Irene Bloemraad/Marten Vink (eds.) (2017): *The Oxford Handbook of Citizenship*, Oxford: Oxford University Press.

Sigman, Shayna (2006): "Everything Lawyers Know about Polygamy is Wrong", *Cornell Journal of Law and Public Policy* 16/1 (2006) 102–185.

Smearman, Claire A. (2009): "Second Wives' Club: Mapping the Impact of Polygamy in U.S. Immigration Law", *Berkeley Journal of International Law* 27/2 (2009) 382–447.

Smith, Michael (1987): "The Humean Theory of Motivation", *Mind* 96 (1987) 36–61.

Smith, Rogers M. (2017): "Citizenship and Membership Duties Towards Quasi-citizens", in: Shachar et.al. (2017) 817–837.

Somek, Alexander (1998): "National Solidarity, Global Impartiality, and the Performance of Philosophical Theory: The Example of Migration Policy", *Ratio Juris* 11/2 (1998) 103–125.

Sona, Federica (2005): "Polygamy in Britain", *osservatorio delle libertà ed istituzioni religiosi*, www.olir.it/areetematiche/104/documents/Sona_Polygamy_in_Britain.pdf.

Song, Sarah (2017): "Why Does the State Have the Right to Control Immigration", in: *Immigration, Emigration, and Migration* (Nomos LVII) ed. by Jack Knight, New York: New York University Press 2017, 3–50.

Soysal, Yasemin Nohoglu (1994): *The Limits of Citizenship. Migrants and Postnational Membership in Europe*, Chicago: University of Chicago Press.

Spiro, Peter J. (2017): "Multiple Citizenship", in: Shachar et.al. (2017) 621–643.

— (2018): "Stakeholder Theory Won't Save Citizenship", in: *Democratic Inclusion. Rainer Bauböck in Dialogue*, Manchester: Manchester University Press, 204–224.

Steiner, Hillel (1992): "Libertarianism and the Transnational Migration of People", in: *Free Movement: Ethical Issues in the Transnational Migration of People and Money* ed. by Brian Barry/Robert E. Goodin, University Park, PA: Pennsylvania State University Press 1992, 87–94.

Stone Sweet, Alec (2000): *Governing with Judges. Constitutional Politics in Europe*, Oxford: Oxford University Press.

Taylor, Charles (1985): *Human Agency and Language. Philosophical Papers 1*, Cambridge: Cambridge University Press.

— (1989): *Sources of the Self. The Making of Modern Identity*, Cambridge, Mass.: Harvard University Press.

Tesón, Fernando R. (2008): "Brain Drain", *San Diego Law Review* 45 (2008) 899–932.

Tomuschat, Christian (1999): "International Law: Ensuring the Survival of Mankind on the Eve of a New Century. General Course on Public International Law", in: 281 *Recueil des Cours* 10/25 (1999), 9–438.

Triandafyllidou, Anna/Tariq Modood/Nasar Meer (eds.) (2012): *European Multiculturalisms. Cultural, Religious and Ethnic Challenges*, Edinburgh: Edinburgh University Press.

Vertovec, Steven (2007): "Super-diversity and Its Implications", *Ethnic and Racial Studies* 30/6 (2007) 1024–1054.

Viehoff, Daniel (2017): "The Truth in Political Instrumentalism", *Proceedings of the Aristotelian Society* CXVII/3 (2017) 273–295.

Vrdoljak, Ana Filipa (ed.) (2013): *The Cultural Dimension of Human Rights*, Oxford: Oxford University Press.

Waldron, Jeremy (1999): *Law and Disagreement*, Oxford: Oxford University Press.

Wallace, James D. (2009): *Norms and Practices*, Ithaca/London: Cornell University Press.

Walzer, Michael (1977): *Just and Unjust Wars. A Moral Argument with Historical Illustrations*, New York: Basic Books.

— (1994): *Thick and Thin. Moral Argument at Home and Abroad*, Notre Dame, Ind.: Notre Dame University Press.

— (1980): "The Moral Standing of States: A Response to Four Critics", *Philosophy and Public Affairs* 9/3 (1980) 209–229.

— (1983): *Spheres of Justice. A Defense of Pluralism & Equality*, Oxford: Basil Blackwell.

Wellman, Christopher/Phillip Cole (2011): *Debating the Ethics of Migration: Is There a Right to Exclude?*, New York: Oxford University Press.

White, Douglas R. (1988): "Rethinking Polygyny. Co-Wives, Codes, and Cultural Systems", *Current Anthropology* 19/4 (1988) 529–572.

White Ryan (2009): "Two Sides of Polygamy", *Journal of Law & Family Studies* 447 (2009) 447–454.

Wilder, Colin F. (2012): "Teaching Old Dogs New Tricks: Four Motives of Legal Change from Early Modern Europe", *History and Theory* 51 (2012) 18–41.

Will, Frederick L. (1997): *Pragmatism and Realism*, London et.al.: Rowman & Littlefield.

Williams, Bernard (1981): "Internal and External Reasons", in: id.: *Moral Luck. Philosophical Papers 1973–1980*, Cambridge: Cambridge University Press, 101–113.

Winch, Peter (1958): *The Idea of a Social Science and Its Relation to Philosophy*, London: Routledge & Kegan Paul.

Wimmer, Andreas (2013): *Ethnic Boundary Making. Institutions, Power, Networks*, Oxford: Oxford University Press.

—/Nina Glick Schiller (2003): "Methodological Nationalism, the Social Sciences, and the Study of Migration: An Essay in Historical Epistemology", *The International Migration Review* 37/3 (2003) 576–610.

Wittgenstein, Ludwig (1958): "Philosophical Investigations", trans. by G.E.M. Anscombe, Oxford: Basil Blackwell, 2nd ed.

Wylie, Laurence (1964): *Village in the Vaucluse. An Account of Life in a French Village*, New York: Harper & Row, 2nd edition.

Zeitzen, Miriam Koktvedgaard (2008): *Polygamy. A Cross-cultural Analysis*, London: Bloomsbury.

Name Index

Abrams, Kerry 176
Angelos, James 88
Archibugi, Daniele 104
Anscombe, G.E.M. 23f.
Austin, J.L. 14, 22-24

Baier, Kurt 14, 22, 26, 67, 116, 120, 123
Barry, Brian 79, 194
Bartok, Bela 208
Bauböck, Rainer 105, 117, 153, 158, 163-165, 167
Beitz, Charles 22, 57f., 70, 74, 127
Bellah, Robert 209
Benhabib, Seyla 47, 104
Bicchieri, Cristina 88
Blake, Michael 16, 68, 86, 94, 100-102, 116
Boeri, Tito 61
Boghossian, Paul 32
Bosniak, Linda 43
Bourdieu, Pierre 22
Brock, Gillian 68, 116
Bryan, Ian 71

Carens, Joseph H. 12, 15, 40-43, 45, 52, 54f., 57, 59, 62, 80, 89, 94, 124f., 129, 168f.
Carling, Jørgen 179
Charlsely, Katherine 177, 180
Christiano, Thomas 82, 108, 113
Chwaszcza, Christine 47, 72, 74, 76, 108, 110f., 120, 144
Cole, Phillip 48, 63
Coleman, James 203
Cox, Adam B. 94

Daniels, Norman 28
Dauvergne, Catherine 11, 116, 138
Descartes, René 23
De Schutter, Helder 155-157
Donders, Yvonne 174
Dryzek, John S. 104
Dworkin, Ronald 83, 108

Eichenberger, Sarah L. 181-183
Elster, Jon 187
Eriksen, Jens-Martin 197
Estlund, David 82

Feinberg, Joel 23, 71
Ferracioli, Luara 178

Glick Schiller, Nina 61
Goldberg, Bruce 23
Goodin, Robert E. 57, 60, 78-81, 83f., 86, 89
Griffin, James 74
Grimmel, Andreas 22
Guiraudon, Virginie 161
Gutman, Amy 193

Habermas, Jürgen 103f., 114
Hafner, Gerhard 92
Hanfling, Oswald 23f.
Hardin, Russel 159
Hargreaves-Heap, Shaun 203
Harrison, Rodney 197, 202
Hart, H.L.A. 14, 22-24, 26, 30f., 71f., 76f., 123
Hegel, G.W.F. 194f.
Held, David 104
Hellmann, Gunther 22
Hirschl, Ian 117
Hobbes, Thomas 30, 47
Hofeld, Wesley N. 67, 149
Huemer, Michael 63
Hume, David 23, 60f.

Joppke, Christian 48, 117, 136-138, 208

Kant, Immanuel 49, 135, 195
Kelsen, Hans 26, 71
Koller, Peter 26
Kolodny, Niko 76
Koopmans, Ruud 138, 140, 161
Koskenniemi, Martti 92
Kratochwil, Friedrich 22
Krisch, Nico 92
Kymlicka, Will 194, 197

Langford, Peter 71
La Torre, Massimo 20, 112
Lagerspetz, Eerik 110
Langfield, Michele 198
Leino, Päivi 92
Lindahl, Hans 117
Lines, Greggary 176f., 180

List, Christian 80
Liversage, Anika 177, 180
Locke, John 23, 30, 47, 72
Luban, David 70, 160

MacKay, Douglas 170
March, Andrew F. 176
Marshall, T.H. 97
Mason, Andrew 150
McIntyre, Alasdair 27
Meer, Nasar 195
Michalowski, Ines 138
Miller, David 12, 16, 62, 74, 79, 86, 94-100, 102, 124, 128-130, 195
Modood, Tariq 195, 198

Nasström, Sofia 46

Offe, Claus 68
Owen, David 47, 105
Özdem, Caglar 61

Parekh, Bikhu 195f., 198
Plato 36,168
Pogge, Thomas W. 58, 70, 74

Quine, Willard Van Orman 23

Rawls, John 14, 22, 25, 30f., 37, 50, 53f., 56, 58, 61, 72, 76f., 79, 82f., 95, 101, 104, 106f., 109, 123-126, 142-145
Reiner, Hans 29
Rousseau, Jean-Jacques 30, 47f., 109f.
Rubio-Marín, Ruth 137, 158, 162

Sandel, Michael J. 203
Schatzki, Theodore E. 22
Schiff, Maurice 61
Schmitt, Carl 94
Searle, John R. 32
Sen, Amartya 139, 194, 198f.
Shachar, Ayelet 117, 125, 137, 157
Sigman, Shayna 176

Smearman, Claire A. 182f.
Smith, Michael 120
Smith, Rogers M. 165
Somek, Alexander 66-68, 97
Sona, Federica 177
Song, Sarah 94
Soysal, Yasemin Nohoglu 137
Spiekermann, Kai 80
Spiro, Peter J. 43, 165f.
Steiner, Hillel 49
Stjernfelt, Frederik 197
Stone Sweet, Alec 92, 177

Taylor, Charles 193f., 203
Tesón, Fernando R. 116f.
Thrasymachos 168
Tomuschat, Christian 188
Triandafyllidou, Anna 197

Varoufakis, Yanis 203
Vertovec, Steven 139, 198
Viehoff, Daniel 76
Vrdoljak, Ana 197

Waldron, Jeremy 83, 108
Wallace, James D. 24, 27, 143
Walzer, Michael 27, 37, 70, 158-162, 165, 169
Wellman, Christopher 48, 63
White, Douglas R. 178
White, Ryan 187
Wilder, Colin F. 92
Will, Frederick L. 21
Williams, Bernard 120
Wimmer, Andreas 61, 194, 199
Winch, Peter 28
Wittgenstein, Ludwig 14, 22, 24, 27
Wylie, Laurence 206

Ypi, Lea 155-157

Zeitzen, Miriam Koktvegard 177-179, 186

Weitere Bände in der Reihe
STUDIEN ZUR THEORIE UND EMPIRIE DER DEMOKRATIE

Das Prinzip der Republik
Die Entstehung des Politischen im Modus der Rechtsfindungspraxis
von Martin Stellmacher,
2018, 322 S., broschiert, 69,– €, ISBN 978-3-8487-5233-1

Nation und Repräsentation
Theorie, Geschichte und Gegenwart eines umstrittenen Verhältnisses
von Michel Dormal,
2017, 298 S., broschiert, 59,– €, ISBN 978-3-8487-4036-9

Nation und Repräsentation
Theorie, Geschichte und Gegenwart eines umstrittenen Verhältnisses
von Dr. Michel Dormal,
2017, 298 S., geb., 59,– €, ISBN 978-3-8487-4036-9

Einschluss und Ausschluss durch Repräsentation
Theorie und Empirie am Beispiel der deutschen Integrationspolitik
hrsg. von PD Dr. Markus Linden,
2014, 437 S., broschiert, 39,– €, ISBN 978-3-8487-1789-7

Ungleichheit und politische Repräsentation
hrsg. von Dr. Markus Linden, Prof. Dr. Winfried Thaa,
2014, 272 S., broschiert, 29,– €, ISBN 978-3-8487-1298-4

Politisches Handeln
Demokratietheoretische Überlegungen im Anschluss an Hannah Arendt
hrsg. von Prof. Dr. Winfried Thaa,
2011, 187 S., broschiert, 19,90 €, ISBN 978-3-8329-6678-2

Krise und Reform politischer Repräsentation
hrsg. von Dr. Markus Linden, Prof. Dr. Winfried Thaa,
2011, 327 S., broschiert, 29,– €,ISBN 978-3-8329-6685-0

Die politische Repräsentation von Fremden und Armen
hrsg. von Dr. Markus Linden, Prof. Dr. Winfried Thaa,
2009, 261 S., broschiert, 24,– €, ISBN 978-3-8329-4439-1

Inklusion durch Repräsentation
hrsg. von Prof. Dr. Winfried Thaa, Universität Trier,
2008, 212 S., broschiert, 29,– €, ISBN 978-3-8329-3065-3

Politische Integration im vereinten Deutschland
hrsg. von Markus Linden,
2006, 324 S., broschiert, 39,– €, ISBN 978-3-8329-2206-1

 nomos-elibrary.de

Bestellen Sie im Buchhandel oder
versandkostenfrei online unter nomos-shop.de
Bestell-Hotline +49 7221 2104-37
E-Mail bestellung@nomos.de | Fax +49 7221 2104-43
Alle Preise inkl. Mehrwertsteuer